"Linda Goudsmit connects all the dots of political ideology, human psychology, and social engineering in her stunning, prescient, and personal warning to the American electorate. *The Book of Humanitarian Hoaxes: Killing America with 'Kindness'* is a must-read in advance of the crucial 2020 American presidential election. If you really want to understand the motives underlying the outrageous shenanigans in the world of politics, then you HAVE to read Ms. Goudsmit's brilliant book. *Humanitarian Hoaxes* is a twenty-first-century affirmation of Abraham Lincoln's nineteenth-century Gettysburg defense of liberty and hope that 'government of the people, by the people, for the people, shall not perish from the earth.'"
—**Steve Emerson**, counterterrorist investigator, author of thousands of articles and six books, producer of two documentaries, *Jihad in America* and *Grand Deception*, and Executive Director of Investigative Project on Terrorism · InvestigativeProject.org

"Trenchant and incisive, Linda Goudsmit has a penetrating style all her own. She doesn't mince words and never shies away from spotlighting stark reality. Goudsmit has a uniquely disciplined, hard-punching way of teaching while at the same time providing singularly unusual insights into each topic that she approaches. Reading Linda Goudsmit's new release, *The Book of Humanitarian Hoaxes: Killing America with 'Kindness'*, is commensurate with attending high-level college classes in political science, psychology, history, current events, and classic philosophy all at once. For those of us who remember professors who caused us to 'sit up and take notice,' we can relate those experiences to Linda Goudsmit's writings. She is a 'born teacher' and all of her work reflects her native talent and depth of knowledge. *The Book of Humanitarian Hoaxes: Killing America with 'Kindness'* offers intriguing, thought-provoking new ways to think about current events and critical issues of our era that threaten America's unique culture. Each chapter reinforces Goudsmit's consistent theme of hoaxes masquerading as benevolent systems of governance designed to collapse America from within. It is an essential read before the critical 2020 U.S. presidential election. I enthusiastically endorse Linda Goudsmit's outstanding new release, *The Book of Humanitarian Hoaxes: Killing America with 'Kindness'*."
—**Charlotte Baker**, well-known Internet editor, commentator, aggregator, and distributor

"Like a skilled surgeon with a scalpel, Linda Goudsmit has excised the virulent humanitarian hoaxes inflicted on Americans for the last fifty years. Think global warming, zero population growth, open borders, or the New World Order have any legitimacy? Think again! Goudsmit explains the twisted rationales, invasive techniques, and devious methods used in leftist attempts to transform America into a socialist 'paradise' on earth. Totally riveting . . . every page!"
—**Joan Swirsky**, New York–based journalist and author

"Linda Goudsmit is a frequent and popular guest on my CRN digital talk radio show, *Talkback with Chuck Wilder*. Her sensational new release, *The Book of Humanitarian Hoaxes: Killing America with 'Kindness'*, exposes the sinister underbelly of the Leftist/Islamist/Globalist axis attacking America, American democracy, and America-first President Donald J. Trump. Written in her signature conversational style, each hoax chapter unmasks a distinct and destructive axis policy deceitfully presented to an unsuspecting public as humanitarian. Americans do not like being duped. Linda Goudsmit is the consummate truth-teller in an era of profound political deceit. *The Book of Humanitarian Hoaxes: Killing America with 'Kindness'* should be compulsory reading in advance of the crucial 2020 U.S. presidential election."
—**Chuck Wilder**, CRN host

"Linda Goudsmit's extraordinary Humanitarian Hoax series of articles is now a sensational book. Goudsmit has a rare ability to identify the core of conflicts. She knows that whenever something does not produce the results it logically should, something else is going on. Her new release, *The Book of Humanitarian Hoaxes: Killing America with 'Kindness'*, is a powerful exposé of the sinister policies and practices of the Leftist/Islamist/Globalist axis attempting to destroy America from within. Goudsmit's unique talent is deciphering the many political hoaxes being played on us by those who present themselves as our advocates but who are, in fact, America's enemies. This remarkable book tells us the many ways in which we've been had—but don't know it. It is a rare author who entertains while educating readers. Linda is such an author."
—**Marilyn MacGruder Barnewall**, International Banking Consultant (Ret.), "Guru" of North American Private Banking, started first private bank in the United States, is listed in *Who's Who in America*, *Who's Who of American Women*, *Who's Who in Finance and Business*, *Who's Who in the World*

—— THE ——
BOOK OF
HUMANITARIAN
HOAXES

KILLING AMERICA WITH 'KINDNESS'

— THE —

BOOK OF

HUMANITARIAN

HOAXES

KILLING AMERICA WITH 'KINDNESS'

LINDA GOUDSMIT

CONTRAPOINT PUBLISHING
ST. PETE BEACH, FL

Cover and Interior Design by The Book Cover Whisperer:
ProfessionalBookCoverDesign.com

978-0-9835425-5-1 Hardcover
978-0-9835425-2-0 Paperback
978-0-9835425-4-4 eBook

Library of Congress Control Number: 2020904148

Printed in the United States of America

FIRST EDITION

To my beloved husband, Rob, for a lifetime of love, loyalty, and for making all of my dreams come true.

To my dear friend Joan Swirsky, with profound gratitude for encouraging me to sing my song.

CONTENTS

ACKNOWLEDGMENTS

To Rita Samols, whose extraordinary editing skills are rivaled only by her exccptional gentleness, courtesy, and patience.

PREFACE

EAR America,

The ancient Chinese philosopher Lao Tzu, founder of Taoism, famously said, "Give a man a fish and you feed him for a day. Teach him how to fish and you feed him for a lifetime."

Lao Tzu's wisdom transcends time and space. In two simple sentences he expresses the fundamentals of dependence and independence. His 2600-year-old maxim is key to understanding not only family life and politics, but also the overarching twenty-first-century battle between nationalism and globalism.

Families and entire countries can be taught to become independent or taught to remain dependent. America's founding ethos, which prevailed for over two hundred years, was one of fierce independence, where the trinity of American life—God, family, and government—cooperated in common cause to produce proud, independent, autonomous citizens.

Americans were known worldwide for their swagger and the self-confidence that derives from competence and self-sufficiency. In the 1990s, however, I began to notice a disturbing trend in society toward dependence and away from maturity.

I wrote down my observations, analyzed why chronological adults were behaving like narcissistic young children, and developed a theory of behavior to explain the dynamic. In 2011, I published the theory in my philosophy book, *Dear America: Who's Driving the Bus?*

My editor casually remarked that the book was very political. Political? I was stunned. I had written *Dear America* to help people understand why they behave the way they do and to offer a useful paradigm that would help them lead more productive adult lives. I did not understand then that the pervasive pressure for regression on individuals and families in society was deliberate and intensely political.

I began to question the situation. What was the motive for giving people fish instead of teaching them to fish? What could possibly explain deliberate societal pressures toward dependence and infantile narcissism in adults? I remembered a helpful tip on parenting: "If you want to know the motive, look at the result." I began to consider who would benefit from an infantilized America.

I thought about how our extraordinary individual freedoms and ordered liberty require a citizenry of emotional adults. That was when I realized that a nation of children is easily controlled, and that the enemies of the United States were deliberately infantilizing Americans! It was a kaleidoscope moment—the patterns and elements of my worldview rearranged forever.

Of course *Dear America* is political! Freedom is an adult enterprise. Regression has the sinister political purpose of infantilizing America in order to collapse it from within. It is difficult for the civilized mind to process such intentional destruction, but doing so is essential to understanding humanitarian hoaxes and how menacing they are to freedom.

The Book of Humanitarian Hoaxes is based on my independent, stand-alone articles written during a two-year period, from July 2017 to October 2019. The articles were originally posted and archived on my web page, http://goudsmit.pundicity.com, and then published in the United States, Canada, Israel, and New Zealand.

Each article was written in response to a current event that infuriated me because the leftist political hucksters were deliberately presenting their crippling, dependency-producing policies as altruistic and humanitarian. Their deceitfulness and hypocrisy were staggering. Radical leftist politicians, in league with the globalist elite, are attempting to destroy America by offering her citizens eternal childhood—giving us free fish!

The Book of Humanitarian Hoaxes: Killing America with 'Kindness' is my 2020 political sequel to *Dear America: Who's Driving the Bus?* The hoaxes reveal how the behavior model introduced in *Dear America* has been exploited by the globalist enemies of national sovereignty in a coordinated effort to destroy America.

I realized that there is an alliance of leftists, Islamists, and globalist elite collaborating to shatter the U.S. Constitution and remove President Donald Trump from office. The leftists believe they will ultimately prevail and replace the Constitution with socialism. The Islamists believe they will ultimately prevail and replace the Constitution with Islamic Sharia law. But the globalist elite are the puppeteers pulling the political strings of their leftist/Islamist allies.

Here is the dirty little secret of the globalist humanitarian hucksters. Socialism and social chaos are prerequisites for imposing the New World Order of a supranational one-world government. Leftists and Islamists are too arrogant to realize that they are being manipulated to prepare America for rule by the globalist elite.

In October 2019, when I began preparing my online articles for *The Book of Humanitarian Hoaxes*, I was shocked to discover that so many hyperlinked source documents and videos had been deleted from the Internet. One of the tactics of the Leftist/Islamist/Globalist alliance—the information war and its ability to censor content, restrict free speech, and manipulate public opinion—had become acutely personal.

The malicious, coordinated, systematic effort to remove duly elected America-first President Donald Trump, is pervasive and deranged. The globalist elite are desperate to replace him with an operative sympathetic to the imposition of a one-world government. One-world government is a return to medieval feudalism, where the globalist elite will rule the world under the auspices of the corrupt United Nations.

I never intended to become a political analyst or to write another book, but I feel compelled to warn my fellow Americans that our freedom and national sovereignty are at great risk. The lawless anti-American coup attempts, including the ongoing politicized, weaponized impeachment proceedings against President Trump, have made it imperative for me to publish this book in advance of the pivotal 2020 election. Ignorance is not bliss—it is national suicide.

The choice between globalism and national sovereignty is the essence of Lao Tzu's wisdom. Globalism promises to give us fish and keep us dependent upon a permanent ruling class. President Trump is teaching Americans how to fish again, how to be independent, sovereign, and free—a government of the people, by the people, and for the people.

I choose fishing and freedom.

Most sincerely,
Linda Goudsmit
USA 2020

Leftism/Islamism/Globalism
v. President Donald J. Trump

HOAX 1

The Humanitarian Hoax of Transgender Training in the Military

July 15, 2017

THE humanitarian hoax is the deliberate and deceitful tactic of presenting a destructive policy as altruistic. The humanitarian huckster presents himself as a compassionate advocate when in fact he is the disguised enemy.

Barack Obama, humanitarian huckster-in-chief, weakened the U.S. military for eight years, presenting his crippling policies as altruistic when in fact they were designed for destruction. His legacy, the leftist Democrat party and its "resistance" movement, is the party of the humanitarian hoax, attempting to destroy American representative democracy and replace it with socialism.

In a stunning reversal of military protocols and procedures, Obama perpetrated the Humanitarian Hoax of Transgender Training in the Military. Scheduled to take effect July 1, 2017, Obama's "Tier Three Transgender Training" materials, PowerPoint, and accompanying lesson plan were presented as compassionate and deeply respectful of the minuscule population of transgender soldiers. In fact, these protocols and procedures were designed to weaken the military by making the feelings of a few soldiers more important than combat readiness, and by placing the needs of individuals over the well-being of their units. Obama's policies were not misguided; they were deliberate.

The mission of the military is unequivocally national defense—the protection of America and her people. The military is one of only a few appropriate collectives in a democracy. It is a unique culture with unique rules, where collective units, not individuals, are essential and where the mission supersedes the men and women who serve. Police departments are another form of appropriate collective in a democracy, serving the same mission of defense, only at local and state levels. Obama and his leftist Democrat party are deliberately trying to weaken and undermine American police departments as well.

Obama's long-term plan for socialism and its cradle-to-grave government control is a political power grab that steals individual rights and replaces them with national-government "rights." Like other predators, the Democrat party focuses its prey on the short game and disguises its long-term objective. Sexual predators do not lure children with vegetables; they offer candy. Political predators do not lure voters with hard work; they offer them free college, free health care, free food, free housing, free phones, free everything—and then the windows close, the doors lock, and the prey is captured and exploited.

Socialism is political candy for Americans, who have been indoctrinated to believe that it will provide social justice and income equality. There are no individual rights in socialism—all rights belong to the national government. There are no property rights in socialism—all property belongs to the national government. Social justice and income equality under socialism mean that everyone is equally poor and equally exploited.

The leftist Democrat party is attempting to invert American life by democratizing the military and socializing the society. It presents itself as America's advocate while it is in fact America's enemy.

The irony of the entire leftist humanitarian hoax designed to destroy American democracy and replace it with socialism is that the leftists are too arrogant to understand that they are just useful idiots in the larger and more sinister plan of the globalist elite. Socialism is a means, not an end, for the globalists.

Socialism, with its complete government control, is the prerequisite social structure for the globalist elite to internationalize the socialist countries and impose a one-world government.

One-world government is the New World Order that the globalist elite themselves intend to rule. It is unapologetically described in chilling detail in Lord Bertrand Russell's 1952 book, *The Impact of Science on Society*. One-world government is a binary sociopolitical system of masters and slaves. There is no social justice in a one-world government, no income equality, no leftists or political agitators of any kind—only a docile, compliant population of slaves ruled by the globalist elite.

One-world government is the goal and the underlying motive of the campaign to destroy America from within. American democracy, with President Donald Trump as its leader, is the single greatest existential threat to a one-world government. If the globalist elite are successful in their efforts to weaken the U.S. military, overthrow the U.S. government of President Donald Trump, and transform America into a socialist country, the next step is global conquest and imposition of a one-world government.

After 241 years of American freedom, the world will be returned to the dystopian existence of masters and slaves because a willfully blind American public was seduced by political candy and followed the leftist predators into the awaiting socialist sedan—the windows close, the doors lock, and the prey is captured and enslaved. Game over.

HOAX 2

The Humanitarian Hoax of Open Borders

July 16, 2017

THE humanitarian hoax is the deliberate and deceitful tactic of presenting a destructive policy as altruistic. The humanitarian huckster presents himself as a compassionate advocate when in fact he is the disguised enemy.

Barack Obama, humanitarian huckster-in-chief, weakened U.S. borders for eight years, presenting his crippling homeland "security" policies as altruistic when in fact they were designed for destruction.

Open borders for "suffering" refugees is the prime humanitarian hoax of the twenty-first century being perpetrated by both leftist and Islamist hucksters. The leftist humanitarian hucksters and their colluding mainstream media present sympathetic images of displaced refugees seeking shelter in order to seduce the American public into believing that their open-border policy is humanitarian and the epitome of human kindness. Even Elmo gets a prime-time interview on CNN to encourage parents to reinforce *Sesame Street*'s message that refugee children are just like them—another generation of indoctrinated youth.

Open borders have a twin purpose for the leftist humanitarian hucksters. First, open borders are designed to flood America with illegal immigrants, many of whom will vote illegally for their Democrat party benefactors. Second, opening America's borders to masses of immigrants from Islamic countries with cultural norms hostile to America will facilitate the social chaos necessary for the destruction of American democracy—the overarching goal of the leftist Democrat party and its humanitarian hucksters.

The Islamist humanitarian hucksters are trying to convince the Western world that open borders are a humanitarian effort that will benefit the

West because their peaceful religion will provide cheap labor, cultural enrichment, and cultural diversity.

Europe is the harbinger of cultural suicide. Leftist leaders in Europe have already opened their borders and demanded that native European populations adapt to the hostile cultural norms of Muslim immigrants. Rape, murder, terrorism, beheadings, every imaginable form of savagery has followed. Immigrants with hostile cultural norms have no intention of working or assimilating. To the contrary, their mass immigration is a political tactic of demographic jihad that will conquer host countries through population growth and then transform them into Islamic states ruled by Islamic Sharia law.

Sharia law is a comprehensive system of religious principles regulating every aspect of Muslim life. Sharia is derived from the religious and moral precepts in the Koran, the holy book of Islam, and the sacred text the Hadith, a record of the words and deeds of Muhammad.

The Leftist/Islamist axis has the initial shared goal of destroying American democracy, but the ultimate goals of the axis members are diametrically opposed to one another. Leftists want to impose socialism because they believe it will provide social justice and income equality. Islamists want to impose Sharia law because they believe the world will be at peace only when every country in the world has been conquered and converted to Islam.

The conflicting end goals of the leftists and Islamists present no problem for the globalist elite who fund leftist and Islamist humanitarian hucksters. The elite are using both groups as useful idiots to facilitate the great Humanitarian Hoax of Open Borders worldwide. Global open borders will create the overwhelming social chaos necessary to internationalize the police force and impose the elite's totalitarian brand of a New World Order.

The leftists and Islamists are too arrogant to understand that they are simply pawns in the elite's own end game.

If the globalist elite are successful in their efforts to weaken Homeland Security, create social chaos through open borders and illegal immigration, overthrow the U.S. government of President Donald Trump, and transform America into a socialist country, the next step is global conquest and imposition of a one-world government.

After 241 years of American freedom, the world will be returned to the dystopian existence of masters and slaves because a willfully blind American public was seduced by leftist and Islamist humanitarian hucksters into believing that surrendering their sovereign borders and freedoms was compassionate and "kind." The Humanitarian Hoax of Open Borders will have succeeded in killing America with "kindness."

HOAX 3

The Humanitarian Hoax of Raising the Minimum Wage

July 17, 2017

THE humanitarian hoax is the deliberate and deceitful tactic of presenting a destructive policy as altruistic. The humanitarian huckster presents himself as a compassionate advocate when in fact he is the disguised enemy.

Barack Obama, humanitarian huckster-in-chief, weakened the U.S. economy for eight years, presenting his crippling economic policies as altruistic when in fact they were designed for destruction.

Raising the minimum wage has been an anthem for the leftist Democrat party. Democrats rail against "heartless" Republicans for not caring or having loving kindness for the "little people." Leftists insist the 99 percent are being victimized by the ruthless 1 percent. Let's examine the subjective reality, where feelings replace facts, of the leftist fiction being propagated by these humanitarian hucksters.

Raising the minimum wage to $13 or $15, a demand repeated incessantly by the colluding mainstream media, is a great sound bite for the hucksters. The objective reality, however, is that raising the minimum wage to $13 or $15 has resulted in devastating consequences for the poorest working Americans. A report published by the University of Washington found that when wages increased to $13 an hour companies often responded by cutting low-wage workers' hours. Instead of continuing to work a full-time, forty-hour workweek, workers found their hours reduced to a part-time, twenty-hour workweek, with benefits reduced accordingly.

The humanitarian hucksters are not stupid—just deceitful. They knew the outcome, because there are many educated economists among them and they know that businesses that cannot sustain the wage increase will reduce hours in order to keep their businesses open. So, why would the leftist humanitarian hucksters deliberately make such a destructive demand?

The answer is that the goal of the leftist Democrat party is to destroy American democracy and replace it with socialism. Leftists already know that unsustainable wage increases that result in reduced hours also result in increased welfare rolls that will overwhelm the system and devastate the economy.

Obama's mentor, radical socialist Saul Alinsky, hoped to transform American democracy into socialism through "community organizing" in the 1960s. Fellow radicals, Columbia University professors Richard Cloward and Frances Piven, devised an economic strategy to deliberately overload the U.S. welfare system in order to precipitate a crisis that would lead to a replacement of the welfare system with a socialist system of national guaranteed minimum income (GMI).

The Cloward-Piven strategy was first outlined in their article "The Weight of the Poor: A Strategy to End Poverty," published in the May 2, 1966, edition of *The Nation*.

The problem is that the guaranteed annual income is guaranteed to collapse the economy and increase poverty. As former British Prime Minister Margaret Thatcher so succinctly put it, "Socialism cannot work—eventually you run out of other people's money." Demanding an unsustainable raise in the minimum wage is a humanitarian hoax.

What is essential to understand is that socialism may be the end game for the leftist lemmings determined to overthrow American democracy—but it was never the end game of the globalist elite, who actually have the power and intend to rule the world with their own New World Order of a one-world government.

The leftist Democrat party and its leaders are useful idiots being used by the globalist elite (monarchs, aristocrats, royalty, world bankers, and industrialists) to transform America into a socialist country. The leftist Democrats are too arrogant to understand that they are participating in their own destruction. They have been indoctrinated to believe that they are fighting for "social justice and income equality" when in fact they are helping to establish the dystopian nightmare of one-world government, where there is no middle class, no upward mobility, no national sovereignty, and no individual freedoms. There are only the ruling globalist elite and the enslaved population that serves them. American socialism is the required stepping-stone.

American representative democracy is the single greatest existential threat to a one-world government, and President Donald Trump is unapologetically committed to preserving it. If the globalist elite are successful in their efforts to weaken the U.S. military, create social chaos through open borders and illegal immigration, collapse the economy through an unsustainable minimum wage, overthrow the U.S. government of President Donald Trump, and transform America into a socialist country, the next step is global conquest and imposition of a one-world government.

After 241 years of American freedom, the world will be returned to the dystopian existence of masters and slaves because a willfully blind American public was seduced by leftist humanitarian hucksters promising social justice and compassionate income equality. By demanding unsustainable economic benefits without commensurate work, the Humanitarian Hoax of Raising the Minimum Wage will have succeeded in killing America with "kindness."

HOAX 4

The Humanitarian Hoax of Climate Change

July 21, 2017

THE humanitarian hoax is the deliberate and deceitful tactic of presenting a destructive policy as altruistic. The humanitarian huckster presents himself as a compassionate advocate when in fact he is the disguised enemy.

Barack Obama, humanitarian huckster-in-chief, weakened and politicized the U.S. Environmental Protection Agency for eight years, presenting his crippling policies as altruistic when in fact they were designed for destruction.

The Environmental Protection Agency (EPA) was established by President Richard Nixon on December 2, 1970, by executive order and then ratified by committee hearings in the House and Senate. The primary mission of the EPA was the protection of human health and the environment through writing and enforcing regulations based on laws passed by the U.S. Congress. At that time the growing public awareness of environmental issues stimulated the creation of non-governmental environmental protection agencies as well. The most famous was Greenpeace, created by environmental activists from Canada and the United States.

Founding Greenpeace member Patrick Moore is now a vociferous critic of Greenpeace and its support for the unscientific, politically motivated insistence upon *manmade* climate change. An extraordinary six-minute video shows Dr. Moore's testimony in front of the U.S. Senate Committee on Environment and Public Works, Subcommittee on Oversight, on February 25, 2014.

The video chronicles Moore's environmental activism as a young man and a member of Greenpeace, from 1971 to 1986, to his current unequivocal rejection of the pseudoscience being used to support the unsupportable claims of manmade global warming and climate change.

The <u>transcript</u> of his testimony and the chapter on climate change in his book, *Confessions of a Greenpeace Dropout: The Making of a Sensible Environmentalist*, are part of the public record.

To understand why huckster-in-chief Obama insisted and continues to insist that climate change is manmade and the greatest threat to America, it is necessary to understand the huckster and the hoax.

The Huckster

Barack Obama was groomed by the globalist elite to bring "hope and change" to America, but it was neither the hope nor the change that most Americans understood those words to mean. Obama is a globalist and a radical socialist tutored in Saul Alinsky's 1971 book, *Rules for Radicals*. *Rules* is a manual for social revolution, a how-to for transforming a representative democratic America into a socialist state. Socialism, with its cradle-to-grave government control, is the necessary political structure for imposing the globalist elite's end game of a one-world government. Barack Obama is a malignant narcissist whose self-aggrandizing personality made him the perfect puppet for the globalist elite and the most lawless president in U.S. history. His stunning executive overreach was rivaled only by his greater crime of corrupting the impartiality of the U.S. government by politicizing its agencies and using them to advance his personal political goals in order to weaken and destroy America. Barack Obama is a pawn of the globalist elite—the perfect con man.

The Hoax

The Humanitarian Hoax of Climate Change is the whopper of the twenty-first century. It is a deliberate political scheme to transfer the wealth of industrialized, productive nations (particularly the United States) to non-industrialized, non-productive nations. It is globalized socialism.

The hoax has two parts. First, it is necessary to focus attention on the fabricated specter of catastrophic climate occurrences that will devastate the planet in order to deflect attention away from the actual threats to America from a nuclear Iran, the spread of Islamic terrorism, and the economic instability of an unsustainable trade deficit.

Second, Obama's long-term plan of an internationalized, globalized world requires the de-industrialization of America. His crippling energy restrictions were designed to weaken America's defenses by destroying

America's energy industry, making us more dependent on foreign energy and increasing our trade deficit to unsustainable levels. On September 3, 2016, <u>Obama signed</u> the punitive, anti-American Paris Agreement, deceitfully presented as the premier humanitarian effort to save the planet from catastrophic climate change. Obama disguised his crippling rules and regulations that would destroy U.S. energy as altruism and a humanitarian concern for the planet.

In a laughable outburst, former Vice President Al Gore, the quintessence of the big footprint, accused President Donald Trump of "tearing down America's standing in the world" by withdrawing from the Paris Agreement. Only in the eyes of a deceitful globalist can withdrawing from an anti-American agreement be considered destructive. Gore actually said with a straight face on NBC's *Today* show, "The climate crisis is by far the most serious challenge we face." Al Gore's 2006 Academy Award–winning documentary, *An Inconvenient Truth*, is in fact a very "convenient lie."

One-world government is the goal and the underlying motive of the campaign to destroy America from within. American democracy, with President Donald Trump as America's leader, is the single greatest existential threat to a one-world government. The globalist elite are desperate to stop Trump, because if Obama is exposed as a con man it leaves them without their prime-time huckster to continue marching America toward anarchy and social chaos with his seditious "resistance" movement. The globalist elite who fund the leftist humanitarian hucksters are using them as useful idiots to facilitate the great Humanitarian Hoax of Climate Change worldwide that will create the overwhelming social chaos necessary to internationalize the police force and impose their own totalitarian brand of a New World Order.

Obama and his leftist lemmings are too arrogant to understand that they are being used as puppets in the globalists' end game. If the globalist elite are successful in their efforts to weaken America with the lie of man-made climate change, collapse the economy through an unsustainable trade deficit, overthrow the U.S. government of President Donald Trump, and transform America into a socialist country, the next step is global conquest and imposition of a one-world government.

After 241 years of American freedom, the world will be returned to the dystopian existence of masters and slaves because a willfully blind

American public was seduced by the Humanitarian Hoax of Climate Change—the sinister "convenient lie" peddled by leftist humanitarian hucksters promising to save the planet.

HOAX 5

The Humanitarian Hoax of Bullying Prevention

July 24, 2017

THE humanitarian hoax is the deliberate and deceitful tactic of presenting a destructive policy as altruistic. The humanitarian huckster presents himself as a compassionate advocate when in fact he is the disguised enemy.

Barack Obama, humanitarian huckster-in-chief, weakened the United States by bullying America for eight years into accepting his crippling, politically correct policies as altruistic when in fact they were designed for destruction.

The leftist Democrat party under Obama embraced a hypocritical anti-bullying campaign with religious fervor. Presenting himself as the agent of change to make schools safe from bullying, Obama launched his anti-bullying campaign at the White House Conference on Bullying Prevention in 2011, saying:

> If there's one goal of this conference, it's to dispel the myth that bullying is just a harmless rite of passage or an inevitable part of growing up. It's not. Bullying can have destructive consequences for our young people. And it's not something we have to accept. As parents and students, teachers and communities, we can take steps that will help prevent bullying and create a climate in our schools in which all of our children can feel safe.

Sounds great—an anti-bullying campaign designed to make schools a safe space for students. Who could object?

Obama's popular anti-bullying campaign of kindness was expanded to engage the public and private sectors to combat bullying together. Private, non-profit, and federal commitments were made and millions of dollars were spent on the effort to stop bullying. The Humanitarian Hoax of Bullying Prevention was launched.

Instead of providing safety and protection for all students, however, the bullying prevention campaign was the ideal vehicle for leftist indoctrination in the schools that promoted the leftist intersectional agenda, which focuses on race, class, and gender as interconnected systems of discrimination. Feelings were prioritized over facts, and curricula were overhauled to adhere to the leftist tenets of political correctness, moral relativism, and historical revisionism.

The Left insisted that its members had been victimized and marginalized by white privilege and therefore required protections from bullying. The so-called victimized Left needed Obama's anti-bullying campaign to keep them safe from opposing ideas. What is the net effect of leftist bullying prevention? More bullying! Leftist bullying through censorship, leftist bullying through intimidation, and leftist bullying through violence have all increased. Let's review.

Bullying through Censorship

The Left marches, self-righteously holding anti-bullying signs while destroying freedom of speech on campuses by bullying campus administrators into canceling opposition speakers. In a particularly absurd example, white women on campus at Pitzer College in Los Angeles were told by jeans-clad hypocrites that they could not wear hoop earrings because they are a cultural appropriation of African and Hispanic fashion. The hypocritical cultural fashion police are not bothered by their own cultural appropriation of wearing American blue jeans invented by white American Levi Strauss in 1871.

Bullying through Intimidation

The leftist Democrat party is an orthodoxy that does not permit dissent. Their politically correct vision of what America should be like and look like is most evident in television programming. Beyond the fake news and liberal bias in the mainstream media, the casting and plot summaries of programs adhere strictly to the leftist narrative. The globalist mega-corporations and media moguls who own the stations support only programming and programmers that reflect their globalist perspective. The Hollywood glitterati fawn over *Hamilton*, a vulgar play dramatizing the murder of President Trump, and they laugh when a comedian holds up the mock severed head of President Trump. These hypocrites would need safe spaces and Play-Doh if conservatives assassinated Obama on stage or laughed at his beheaded image. Hypocritical bullying through intimidation is a leftist specialty.

Bullying through Violence

The anti-bullying protesters fomenting violence against President Trump, Trump supporters, and the police are a contradiction in terms. Their violence is bullying of the most egregious and lawless kind. Students at Washington's Evergreen College wielding bats to patrol housing and campus have already assaulted white students who supported white biology professor Bret Weinstein. Professor Weinstein refused to leave campus when black and Latino students tried to force whites off campus on a self-declared "Day of Absence." In another egregious occurrence of leftist hypocritical bullying, Jewish LGBTQ marchers in Chicago were told to leave because the Star of David on their flags was offensive to pro-Palestinian marchers. An anti-bullying campaign designed to protect students of color and a marginalized gay community resulted in reverse racist bullying of white students and anti-Semitic dismissal of Jewish marchers. The hypocrisy is stunning. The intersectional Left demands bullying protection while it bullies anyone who is not an intersectional leftist.

What is the purpose of Obama's Humanitarian Hoax of Bullying Prevention?

Each form of bullying is designed to break down American cultural norms and create social chaos. The Humanitarian Hoax of Bullying Prevention is designed to present leftist bullying as kindness and any opposition to the Left as bullying. It is a deliberate effort to impose conformity to leftist groupthink through reverse bullying and to weaken America toward collectivism and socialism.

One-world government is the goal and the underlying motive of the campaign to destroy America from within. The globalist elite who fund the leftist humanitarian hucksters are using them as useful idiots to facilitate the Humanitarian Hoax of Bullying Prevention in order to create the overwhelming social chaos necessary to internationalize the police force and impose their own totalitarian New World Order.

Obama and his leftist lemmings are too arrogant to understand that they are being used as puppets by the globalist elite, who have an end game of their own. If the globalist elite are successful in their efforts to weaken America and collapse freedom of speech through their deceitful anti-bullying campaign, overthrow the U.S. government of President Donald Trump, and transform America into a socialist country, the next step is global conquest and imposition of a one-world government.

There is no social justice in a one-world government, no income equality, no leftists, environmentalists, humanitarian hucksters, bullying prevention, or political agitators of any kind—only a docile, compliant population of slaves ruled by the globalist elite.

After 241 years of American freedom, the world will be returned to the dystopian existence of masters and slaves because a willfully blind American public was seduced by the Humanitarian Hoax of Bullying Prevention advanced by leftist humanitarian hucksters promising protection and safety for their fragile intersectional selves. The humanitarian hoax will have succeeded in killing America with "kindness."

HOAX 6

The Humanitarian Hoax of Diversity

July 26, 2017

THE humanitarian hoax is the deliberate and deceitful tactic of presenting a destructive policy as altruistic. The humanitarian huckster presents himself as a compassionate advocate when in fact he is the disguised enemy.

Barack Obama, humanitarian huckster-in-chief, weakened the social fabric of the United States for eight years, presenting his crippling diversity policies as altruistic when in fact they were designed for destruction.

Diversity is an anthem for the leftist Democrat party. Democrats rail against Republicans as exclusionary racists, sexists, misogynists, and homophobic anti-immigration elitists insensitive to diversity. The Left's deceptive inclusionary message was codified in Hillary Clinton's 2016 campaign slogan, "Stronger Together." Let's examine the subjective reality of the leftist fiction of diversity being propagated by these humanitarian hucksters.

Government recognition of the importance of diversity began in 1948 when President Truman signed Executive Order 9981 that desegregated the military, making it illegal to discriminate on the basis of race, color, religion, or national origin. The Civil Rights Act of 1964 made discrimination in the workplace illegal and broadened the previous categories to include sex, making it now illegal to discriminate on the basis of race, color, religion, national origin, or sex.

In the mid-to-late twentieth century, diversity was still thought of only in terms of groups and group identities. What race are you? What color are you? What religion are you? Where were you born? Are you male? Are you female?

Diversity was an issue of differences between groups. Differences of *opinion* were not a consideration because our constitutional guarantee of freedom of speech implies freedom of thought. And then came radical socialist huckster-in-chief Barack Obama.

Obama sold political correctness to America gift-wrapped as progressive, compassionate, sensitive, and caring. Feelings replaced freedom as the metric of expression. In a stunning sleight of hand, Obama successfully perpetrated the Humanitarian Hoax of Diversity by pressuring conformity and silencing opposing voices. How language or actions deemed hurtful, marginalizing, insulting, or excluding to specific groups were socially stigmatized is fully discussed later in Hoax 29.

Barack Obama redefined diversity in America. Obama's leftist diversity embraces all races, colors, religions, national origins, sexes, and genders, but it is entirely intolerant of diversity of thought. Presenting himself as the agent of change and protector of all Americans, Obama publicly focused attention on diversity as identifiable differences between groups and concealed his covert attack on diversity of thought. Obama institutionalized political correctness in America and disguised his deceitful attack on freedom of speech. Publicly, Obama spoke of inclusive diversity and privately forced his leftist agenda into every sphere of American life. The echo chamber that he and Deputy National Security Advisor for Strategic Communications Ben Rhodes created in the White House extended to every mainstream media outlet and entertainment medium. The medium became the message.

There is virtually no distinction between Obama's radical leftist views and what is presented as educational curriculum and entertainment in the United States. Americans are being deceptively propagandized toward collectivism and socialism in the name of diversity.

There is no authentic media diversity when conservative political voices are not hired as political analysts or allowed to speak as guests. There is no authentic entertainment diversity on television or at the movies when conservative script writers, actors, and producers are not hired to present an alternative voice to the leftist agenda. There is no authentic academic diversity on campus when conservative voices are not hired or allowed to speak as guests. There is only leftist, politically correct groupthink.

Economist and social theorist Thomas Sowell famously remarked, "The next time some academics tell you how important diversity is, ask how many Republicans there are in their sociology department."

Georgetown University adjunct law professor <u>Preston Mitchum</u> recently tweeted, "Yes, ALL white people are racist. Yes, ALL men are sexist. Yes, ALL cis people are transphobic, we have to unpack that. That's the work."

Fomenting racism is a despicable pursuit that should never be tolerated under the guise of academic freedom. Imagine if Georgetown University hired an adjunct law professor who tweeted that all black people are racists. The outrage from the Left would be deafening. Preston Mitchum is a disgrace and should be fired and never allowed to teach on any campus. Reverse racism is still racism, and the *pretense* of diversity is not diversity.

Authentic diversity includes diversity of thought. It is incompatible with political correctness and the social stigma of expressing opposing ideas.

Authentic diversity requires the open and candid exchange of ideas debated on merit. Authentic diversity requires freedom of speech. The Humanitarian Hoax of Diversity is designed to dupe the public into rejecting diversity of thought, which is based on free speech. It is a deliberate effort to impose conformity to leftist groupthink and weaken America toward collectivism and socialism.

The globalist elite who fund the leftist humanitarian hucksters are using them as useful idiots to facilitate the great Humanitarian Hoax of Diversity to severely restrict freedom of speech in homes, at school, and in the workplace. The increasing pressures of political correctness are effectively changing America's cultural norms.

Obama and his leftist lemmings are too arrogant to understand that they are being used as puppets by the globalist elite, who have an end game of their own. One-world government is the goal and the underlying motive of the campaign to destroy America from within. If the globalist elite are successful in their efforts to weaken America and collapse freedom of speech through their deceitful form-and-no-content diversity campaign, overthrow the U.S. government of President Donald Trump, and transform America into a socialist country, the next step is global conquest and imposition of a one-world government.

After 241 years of American freedom, the world will be returned to the dystopian existence of masters and slaves because a willfully blind American public was seduced by the Humanitarian Hoax of Diversity advanced by leftist humanitarian hucksters promising protection and safety for their fragile victimized selves. The humanitarian hoax will have succeeded in killing America with "kindness."

HOAX 7

The Humanitarian Hoax of Transgender Transitioning in the Military

July 31, 2017

THE humanitarian hoax is the deliberate and deceitful tactic of presenting a destructive policy as altruistic. The humanitarian huckster presents himself as a compassionate advocate when in fact he is the disguised enemy.

Barack Obama, humanitarian huckster-in-chief, weakened the U.S. military for eight years, presenting his crippling transgender policies as altruistic when in fact they were designed for destruction.

LGBTQ rights are an anthem for Obama's leftist "resistance" movement, which publicly rails against Republicans as homophobes, racists, sexists, and misogynists. Their rants are emotionally charged "feel good" slogans designed to unify their base. Sloganism is a manipulative marketing strategy designed by the advertising industry to hype the products they are trying to sell. Leftist Democrat party slogans are hyping **transgender** inclusion to sell **transitioning** inclusion in the military. There is a pivotal difference.

Of course transgender individuals are as patriotic as any other American. Of course transgender individuals can shoot as straight as any other American. Of course transgender soldiers can be as effective as any other American soldier. Inclusion of transgender individuals in the military is not a matter of IF transgender individuals should be admitted; it is a matter of WHEN they should be admitted.

The time for gender assignment and gender choice is BEFORE entering the military. An individual's path to maleness or femaleness is a personal, private matter and not the military's concern. Any individual applying for military service must have matching gender, genitalia, and gender identification BEFORE becoming a soldier. Let's examine why.

Premature inclusion undermines cohesion.

The mission of the military is unequivocally national defense—the protection of America and the American people. The military is one of the few appropriate collectives in a democracy. The military is a unique culture with unique rules, where collective units, not individuals, are prioritized and where the mission supersedes the needs of the individuals who serve. The effectiveness of the military depends on group cohesion and the ability of the group to function effectively as a single unified lethal force under extreme pressure. Anything that threatens group cohesion is contraindicated in the military.

Obama and his leftist Democrat legacy party are deliberately trying to weaken and undermine group cohesion in the American military by disingenuously advocating for transgender inclusion BEFORE gender identity issues are resolved. Ambivalence, counseling, transitioning, surgeries, and any ancillary services during military service are contraindicated. Coed showering with undecided or transitioning individuals is contraindicated in the military. Obama's directive that our men in uniform prance around in high heels to identify with women and learn how women feel is a stunning example of his sinister intention to destabilize the military. Beyond making our military the laughingstock of the world, Obama is intentionally undermining the cohesiveness of the American military in its mission to preserve and protect America.

The leftist campaign for premature transgender inclusion in the military is designed to create chaos in order to weaken the military's readiness and cohesion.

If the American military is weakened and cannot protect American democracy, then all the individual rights guaranteed by our Constitution, including all the individual rights of the LGBTQ community, are sacrificed as well. Deceptive feel-good slogans chanted by noisy politicians do nothing to protect the rights of transgender individuals. It is the U.S. military that preserves, protects, and defends those rights, and military cohesion makes that possible.

Destabilizing the military with destructive, premature transgender policies is a humanitarian hoax presented as altruistic inclusion but actually designed to destroy the military.

The Democrat party presents itself as America's advocate but is in fact America's enemy.

The goal of the leftist Democrat party is to destroy American democracy and replace it with socialism. Transformative social change requires social chaos, and Obama's deceitful domestic policies were all designed to produce chaos. Chaos in the military, chaotic racial divisiveness, economic chaos, social chaos at home, and chaos among nations that view a chaotic America as an unstable ally. Destabilizing America through social chaos is the structural theory of socialist Saul Alinsky's *Rules for Radicals*—Obama's playbook.

One-world government is the goal and the underlying motive of the campaign to destroy America from within. By destroying the military's ability to perform its duties, Obama's disingenuous policies in the military destabilize and weaken America both domestically and internationally. Our allies no longer trust us and our enemies are emboldened.

The globalist elite who fund the leftist humanitarian hucksters are using them as useful idiots to facilitate the great Humanitarian Hoax of Transgender Transitioning in the Military in order to create the overwhelming social chaos necessary to internationalize the police force and impose their own special brand of a New World Order.

If the globalist elite are successful in their efforts to weaken America and destroy military cohesiveness through Obama's deceitful transgender/transitioning inclusion campaign, overthrow the U.S. government of President Donald Trump, and transform America into a socialist country, the next step is global conquest and imposition of a one-world government.

There is no social justice in a one-world government, no income equality, no leftists, environmentalists, humanitarian hucksters, transgender advocacy, diversity, or political agitators of any kind—only a docile, compliant population of slaves ruled by the globalist elite.

After 241 years of American freedom, the world will be returned to the dystopian existence of masters and slaves because a willfully blind American public was seduced by the Humanitarian Hoax of Transgender Transitioning in the Military advanced by leftist humanitarian hucksters promising protection and safety for their fragile victimized community. The humanitarian hoax will have succeeded in killing America with "kindness."

HOAX 8

The Humanitarian Hoax of Victimhood

August 21, 2017

THE humanitarian hoax is the deliberate and deceitful tactic of presenting a destructive policy as altruistic. The humanitarian huckster presents himself as a compassionate advocate when in fact he is the disguised enemy.

Barack Obama, humanitarian huckster-in-chief, weakened the United States for eight years, presenting his deceitful social policies featuring victimhood as altruistic when in fact they were designed for destruction.

The three basic tenets of leftist progressivism are political correctness, moral relativism, and historical revisionism. Leftist progressivism is an extremely regressive political structure that emphasizes victimhood and encourages childlike dependence on the government in its march toward socialism. Progressivism is an Orwellian doublespeak word designed to dupe the participant into believing he is moving society forward when in fact it is moving backward, toward eternal childhood.

Historical records present the humanitarian huckster with a conundrum. The history of our American republic is one of immense growth, development, and achievement. American history contradicts the negative message of the humanitarian huckster attempting to transform America into a socialist country. Destroying historical records, historical facts, and historical icons does not erase history—it simply leaves history open to historical revisionism. Obama's revisionist anti-American, pro-Muslim Common Core re-education curriculum was a start, smashing historical statues was an escalation, and violent anarchy is the ultimate leftist strategy to destroy American democracy.

Progressivism posits that objective reality does not exist—this in itself is an invitation for historical revisionism. For progressives there are only matters of opinion, and all opinions are equal. This means that the opinions of out-of-control screaming protesters at Evergreen College in Washington have the same status as the opinions of their professors. Progressives support subjective reality and deny objective reality in their self-serving need to preserve the fiction of their narrative. Here is the problem: saying something does not make it true. Objective reality exists whether the Left accepts it or not. Watching the Left is like watching a child insist he can fly. He is certain of it—but that does not make it a fact in objective reality.

George Orwell understood these dynamics seventy years ago when he created the dystopian society in his cautionary tale, *1984*. American society under Obama has devolved into an Orwellian nightmare of leftist political correctness, groupthink, and moral relativism designed to destroy the moral fabric of American society. When leftists insist that opposing points of view are intolerable hate speech, they hypocritically deny freedom of speech and a free society. The Left is convinced of its moral superiority because its narrative of moral relativism and political correctness insists it is superior and its groupthink mentality validates itself.

A civil society requires consensus. Normative behavior is consensus codified into laws that govern society. Multiculturalism challenges consensus. If one individual thinks "honor" killing is acceptable and society considers it murder, then there is a problem. Whose norms will prevail if everyone's opinions are equal? When everything is a matter of opinion and all opinions are equal, there can be no consensus. Without consensus, there are no accepted laws to abide—there is only anarchy and social chaos. But that is exactly the point: the Left *wants* anarchy and social chaos. Its leaders foment racial violence, religious violence, and violent anarchy because social chaos is the prerequisite for seismic social change.

Obama's "resistance" movement is trying to destroy American democracy and replace it with socialism. The Leftist/Islamist axis is attacking Judeo-Christian values and destabilizing society with the collaboration of the mainstream media. For the Left to embrace the barbaric tenets of Islamist Sharia law requires political correctness, moral relativism, historical revisionism, and the dreamscape of subjective reality where the stunning hypocrisy of the Leftist/Islamist alliance is deliberately ignored by the mainstream media.

The leftist demand for the destruction of American historical statues is an angry expression of victimhood. American democracy has made enormous strides since the Civil Rights Act was passed in the 1960s. Americans elected a black president to lead the country, but the Left intentionally ignores that reality and chooses to promote a victim mentality instead of an achievement mentality. The Left prefers to look backward instead of forward. Why? Because looking backward solidifies their base as victims of white exploitation and foments more racist violence. It is ironic that leftists call themselves "progressive" when everything they do is regressive.

The leaders of the Left understand that identity politics is tribal in nature. Leftist identity politics invites anyone who self-identifies as a victim to join the group and express their angry victimhood. Identification with the group promotes groupthink that concentrates on the WHO of behavior rather than the WHAT of behavior. If a member of the group does something, it is accepted; if a non-member of the group does the same thing, it is rejected. Groupthink is possible only when people surrender their critical-thinking skills and embrace the emotional sound bites repeated incessantly by other members of the group and the media.

Here is the problem. A victim identity may be a unifying force, but victimhood is a position of powerlessness, a childhood dependence promoted by leaders on the Left. Why do the leftist leaders insist on a regressive, dependent victim identity instead of an independent, achievement mentality? Why do the mainstream media collude with these leaders and advance the victim mentality that produces angry violence? Voices of divisiveness, voices of exploitation, voices of victimhood, voices of dependence, voices of angry powerlessness fomenting social chaos to destabilize and overthrow the democratic government of President Donald Trump are the voices we hear from the Left. This is extremely important to understand: the Left is deliberately inciting race wars, religious strife, and violent anarchy in the streets of America by selling victimhood.

Socialism suits the childish Left. Like children, they expect all the benefits of society without doing the work. Their leftist leaders have promised them free tuition, free food, free housing, free health care—complete cradle-to-grave dependence upon the government mommy and daddy, who will provide unconditional love and care for them forever. When their demands are opposed, like angry adolescents they go out of control and their temper tantrums become violent—they smash statues, shatter store windows, burn police cars, and physically assault the opposition. The violence in the streets of America is deliberately fomented by the Left to create the social chaos necessary for social transformation. But socialism is not the end game.

One-world government is the goal and the underlying motive of the campaign to destroy America from within. The globalist elite like George Soros who fund the leftist humanitarian hucksters are using them as useful idiots to facilitate the great Humanitarian Hoax of Victimhood in order to create the overwhelming social chaos necessary to internationalize the police force and impose their own totalitarian New World Order.

After 241 years of American freedom, the world will be returned to the dystopian existence of masters and slaves because a willfully blind American public was seduced by the Humanitarian Hoax of Victimhood advanced by leftist humanitarian hucksters promising protection and safety for their fragile dependent victimized selves. The humanitarian hoax will have succeeded in killing America with "kindness."

HOAX 9

The Humanitarian Hoax of Sanctuary Cities

October 1, 2017

THE humanitarian hoax is the deliberate and deceitful tactic of presenting a destructive policy as altruistic. The humanitarian huckster presents himself as a compassionate advocate when in fact he is the disguised enemy.

Barack Obama, humanitarian huckster-in-chief, weakened the United States for eight years by persuading America to accept his obstructive, politically correct sanctuary city policies as altruistic when in fact they were designed to destabilize and destroy civil society.

The term "sanctuary city" originated in the 1980s when San Francisco passed a city ordinance forbidding city police and city magistrates from assisting federal immigration officers in enforcing immigration policies that denied asylum to refugees from Guatemala and El Salvador. The mission of the sanctuary city was to protect innocent refugees from deportation—although these immigrants were in the United States illegally, they had not committed any other crimes.

Today, sanctuary cities are actually sanctuary jurisdictions because they include cities, counties, and, probably soon, states. Over <u>300 sanctuary jurisdictions</u> exist in America today, actively hindering federal authorities in their ability to seize illegal criminal aliens, rapists, murderers, terrorists, and drug dealers for deportation.

The shocking murder of twenty-one-year-old Kate Steinle on July 1, 2015, publicized the danger of sanctuary jurisdictions. The shooter, Juan Francisco Lopez-Sanchez, an illegal immigrant from Mexico with seven felony convictions, had been deported five times and intentionally sought shelter in San Francisco. Yet officials in "sanctuary city" San Francisco refused to turn him over to federal authorities for deportation and instead released him into society, enabling him to kill Kate Steinle.

The three Muslim migrant boys ages 7, 10, and 14 who sexually assaulted, raped, and urinated in the mouth of an innocent five-year-old girl in Twin Falls, Idaho, on June 24, 2016, were protected as well. No jail time, no deportation. Instead, according to a <u>courtroom observer</u>, they were found guilty of lewd conduct and placed on probation. These monsters were shielded by the mainstream media and local city officials, who tried to cover up the case and pretend that Twin Falls was a model for multiculturalism. Wendy Olson, Obama-appointed U.S. attorney for Idaho, stunned the country by threatening to prosecute Idahoans who spoke out about the heinous crime in ways SHE considered "false or inflammatory."

Judge Thomas Borresen issued an equally stunning gag order that denied the right of anyone in the courtroom to speak about the sentencing even AFTER the case ended. <u>Mathew Staver</u>, chairman and co-founder of the nonprofit legal assistance agency Liberty Counsel, says the ruling is completely illegal. "Case law is clear," he says. "You cannot gag someone after the case is over."

Twin Falls is one of two Muslim refugee relocation centers in Idaho. Rather than identifying itself as a "sanctuary city," Twin Falls has chosen the equally disingenuous name of "welcoming city" and declared itself to be a "neighborly community." REALLY? Protecting rapists and censoring free speech is definitely not neighborly for the victims!

The word sanctuary implies safety from a threat; it does not mean shelter for immigrant criminal felons, rapists, murderers, and terrorists who threaten the safety of law-abiding citizens. Why would any law-abiding citizen endorse the protection of these criminals, whether they are illegal aliens or legal citizens? The answer lies in the active participation by the mainstream media in the Humanitarian Hoax of Sanctuary Cities. The media have deliberately romanticized sanctuary cities as humanitarian havens for the oppressed instead of honestly reporting them as despicable safety zones for criminal aliens. The colluding media have duped the trusting American public and exploited their compassion and goodwill.

The original mission of sanctuary cities has been perverted from the protection of innocent refugees into the protection of guilty criminal aliens at the expense of public safety. Sanctuary cities in America continue to flagrantly defy federal law. Thirty years after San Francisco became the first sanctuary city, California seeks to become the first sanctuary state.

The protection of illegal aliens from deportation incentivizes illegal entry into the United States, which has enormous economic and political consequences. Illegal aliens overload our welfare system, cost American taxpayers a whopping $116 *billion* per year, and rob Americans of their jobs.

Barack Obama gave sanctuary jurisdictions the freedom to ignore detention orders from the federal agency Immigration and Customs Enforcement (ICE) with his June 2015 executive action establishing the Priority Enforcement Program, allowing local agencies to ignore ICE notifications of deportable aliens in their custody.

To understand Obama's motive, simply look at the benefits to Democrats of increasing the number of illegal aliens:

- Secures more Democrat votes for the leftist agenda. Elected leftist Democrats will grant illegals immunity to vote legally and eventually grant them citizenship, knowing they will vote Democrat and ensure Democrat leadership for the foreseeable future.
- Creates social chaos by importing populations with hostile cultural norms.
- Creates divisiveness by taking American jobs.
- Alienates legal citizens, who receive far fewer government benefits than do illegal aliens.
- Eventually collapses the economies of sanctuary jurisdictions.

Obama's executive action flagrantly violated 8 U.S.C. § 1373, a 1996 law requiring government entities and officials to cooperate with the Immigration and Naturalization Service, the predecessor of ICE.

Finally, in July 2016 Rep. John Culberson (R-Texas), chair of the Commerce, Justice, and Science Committee on Appropriations, took action against the danger and sent a letter to the Department of Justice demanding that federal law enforcement grants be denied to cities not in compliance with the 1996 law.

During the five years from 2011 to 2016, local and state governments received over $3.4 billion in federal law enforcement grants. Rep. Culberson gave sanctuary jurisdictions a choice: either continue to receive the grant money or protect dangerous illegal criminal aliens. They could no longer do both.

Sanctuary jurisdictions doubled down and continue to defy the law. San Francisco and Santa Clara counties challenged President Trump's policy in court. In April 2017 U.S. District Judge William Orrick, an Obama appointee, issued a temporary ruling that blocked the president's directive to withhold federal funding from cities that refuse to comply fully with federal immigration enforcement. The lawfare campaign designed to delay and disrupt President Trump's America-first agenda was launched.

No-go zones are geographic areas within a country that brazenly disregard the laws of the country. No-go zones establish a two-tier system of justice within a country because they observe a different set of laws. All across Europe, Islamists have established religious no-go zones that recognize Islamic Sharia law exclusively. All across America, leftists have created sanctuary jurisdictions that flagrantly defy federal law.

People will stand quietly and peacefully in long lines until one person jumps the line. It is a fascinating social dynamic that as long as members of a group abide by the same rules, the consequence is harmony. It is the unfairness of the line-jumper that creates anger and social chaos. Social chaos for seismic social change is the goal of the Leftist/Islamist axis that supports the two-tier system of justice created by secular sanctuary jurisdictions and religious no-go zones.

The globalist elite who fund the leftist humanitarian hucksters are desperate to block Trump's policies that defund sanctuary jurisdictions. The colluding mainstream media continue to deceitfully portray leftist sanctuary jurisdictions as altruistic, denying that protecting illegal criminals at the expense of law-abiding Americans is a sinister leftist political tactic designed to destabilize and destroy America.

If the globalists are successful, the world will be returned to the dystopian existence of masters and slaves because a willfully blind American public was seduced by the Humanitarian Hoax of Sanctuary Cities. The humanitarian hoax will have succeeded in killing America with "kindness."

HOAX 10

The Humanitarian Hoax of the Lone Wolf

October 6, 2017

THE humanitarian hoax is a deliberate and deceitful tactic of presenting a destructive policy as altruistic. The humanitarian huckster presents himself as a compassionate advocate when in fact he is the disguised enemy.

For fifty-four years, Americans have been expected to believe the "lone wolf" theory of murder—from President Kennedy's shocking assassination to the savagery of radical Islamic terror and now the horrifying mass murder of concertgoers in Las Vegas. In art and entertainment there is a term, "suspension of disbelief," defined as the willingness to suspend one's critical-thinking faculties and believe the unbelievable. Suspension of disbelief is the voluntary experience of sacrificing logic for the sake of enjoyment.

Suspension of disbelief in the fifties happened when we went to the movies and allowed ourselves to believe that Clark Kent was Superman. Faster than a speeding bullet! More powerful than a locomotive! Able to leap tall buildings in a single bound! Clark Kent, the mild-mannered reporter, was fighting a never-ending battle for truth, justice, and the American way.

Suspension of disbelief in 1963 was believing that President John F. Kennedy was killed by "lone wolf" Lee Harvey Oswald, who shot a magic bullet that changed trajectories in mid-flight. Oswald was then conveniently murdered by Jack Ruby, another "lone wolf." Skeptical Americans were very suspicious. After all, this was real life, not the movies. The government doubled down on suspension of disbelief and insisted that the public believe the Warren Commission's absurd conclusion that the assassination was accomplished by that "lone wolf" shooting his magic bullet. The public was considered far too fragile to handle the truth. Suspension of disbelief applied to real life was rationalized as altruism.

On September 11, 2001, the United States was attacked by Islamic terrorists who hijacked passenger planes and flew them into the World Trade Center and the Pentagon, killing over 3,000 Americans. No one could seriously posit the lone-wolf theory in this case, so instead Americans were expected to believe the lone-group theory, and al-Qaeda was the first enemy group to be identified. As the Islamic terrorist movement expanded, more groups were created and terrorist attacks that could not be linked to a specific group were dismissed as lone-wolf attacks.

Over and over again, experts in Islamic theology and men and women who had lived in Islamic countries told America that there are no Islamic lone wolves. Islam's supremacist expansionist ideology breeds and unites the pack. Even the terrorists themselves announced that Islam is Islam. There is no moderate Islam. Islamic terrorism is inspired by the commandments in the Koran that unite jihadis in violence against all infidels. Islamic terrorism is one of several jihadi tactics being used to establish the Islamic caliphate—a worldwide Islamic theocracy governed by religious Sharia law.

Western leftist politicians and the colluding mainstream media continue to insist that radical Islamic terror is not an existential threat to the West. Instead, they insist upon public suspension of disbelief and belief in the lone-wolf theory of murder. Why? Because it works!

Although it strains credulity, people WANT to believe the lone-wolf theory; it calms their fears and makes them FEEL safe and secure. The problem is that feelings are not facts. We are not living in a Hollywood movie that ends in two hours. Suspension of disbelief is dangerous in real life. Islamic terrorism is a real fact of twenty-first-century life and is an existential threat to America.

The murderous October 2, 2017, attack in Las Vegas is yet another call for suspension of disbelief. Here we go again. The American public is expected to believe the lone-wolf theory of murder—that a flabby sixty-four-year-old without military training managed to smash two windows of the Mandalay Bay hotel and shoot concertgoers 1,100 feet away for eleven minutes before conveniently killing himself. Eyewitness accounts of multiple shooters: immediately dismissed. Eyewitness accounts of shooters on lower floors: immediately dismissed. Gun expert assessments of the impossibility of this man being a lone wolf: immediately dismissed. Past military expert assessments of the impossibility of this man being a lone wolf: immediately dismissed. All hotel video evidence immediately confiscated by the FBI, and multiple YouTube videos challenging the lone-wolf theory immediately removed as hate speech!

Feeling safe is not the same as being safe. Whoever is demanding that the American public suspend their critical-thinking faculties and believe the unbelievable is a humanitarian huckster and an enemy of the state.

There are no lone wolves in real-life Islamic terrorist attacks. There are no magic bullets in real life. There is no Clark Kent in real life—but the never-ending battle for truth, justice, and the American way remains. If the American public chooses to willingly suspend its disbelief in the real-life battle for truth, justice, and the American way, we will have voluntarily surrendered ourselves to the real-life enemies of the state.

After 241 years, American freedom will finally be lost because a willfully blind American public was seduced by the Humanitarian Hoax of the Lone Wolf advanced by leftist humanitarian hucksters promising safety to a public too frightened to live in reality. The humanitarian hoax will have succeeded in killing America with "kindness."

HOAX 11

The Humanitarian Hoax of Gun Control

October 8, 2017

THE humanitarian hoax is the deliberate and deceitful tactic of presenting a destructive policy as altruistic. The humanitarian huckster presents himself as a compassionate advocate when in fact he is the disguised enemy.

Those who support gun control and those who oppose gun control are speaking two different languages.

The Second Amendment to the Constitution of the United States, guaranteeing the American people the right to bear arms, was passed by Congress on September 25, 1789, and ratified on December 15, 1791. The American Revolution had freed the colonists from British oppression, and our Founding Fathers were determined to prevent future tyranny by their newly formed federal government. The federal government would be armed, but so would the citizenry—it was a balance of power.

One hundred thirty-six years later, Chinese dictator Mao Tse-tung, speaking before the Central Committee of the Chinese Communist Party, famously declared, "Political power grows out of the barrel of a gun." Mao explained to Communist Party leaders how armed struggle is necessary to acquire political power:

> Whoever wants to seize and retain state power must have a strong army. Yes, we are advocates of the omnipotence of revolutionary war; that is good, not bad, it is Marxist. The guns of the Russian Communist Party created socialism. We shall create a democratic republic. Experience in the class struggle in the era of imperialism teaches us that it is only by the power of the gun that the working class and the laboring masses can defeat the armed bourgeoisie and landlords; in this sense we may say that only with guns can the whole world be transformed. We are advocates of the abolition of war; we do not want war, but war can only

be abolished through war, and in order to get rid of the gun it is necessary to take up the gun.

Mao Tse-tung was a communist revolutionary seeking to overthrow the
established rule of the Republic of China. He advocated arming his
supporters (the proletariat) against the opposition (the bourgeoisie).
Mao was successful, and the communist People's Republic of China took
power in 1949.

So, guns have been used both to take power from those who have
power (Mao) and also to balance the power of the federal government
(Second Amendment). These are the two languages of gun control.

The leftist radical Humanitarian Hucksters of Gun Control also know
that political power grows out of the barrel of a gun. They are disingenuously selling gun control as the altruistic answer to gun violence, but
in reality they seek to eliminate the Second Amendment and disarm its
supporters. Why?

The Second Amendment right to bear arms gives citizens the right to
defend and protect themselves against the tyranny of the armed federal
government. The Founding Fathers envisioned an independent America
with a federal government doubly restrained—by a tripartite checks-
and-balances structure and by the Second Amendment. Leftists today
envision a public completely dependent upon the federal government and
completely controlled by the federal government, and this leftist dream
requires dissolution of the Second Amendment.

Gun control is being disingenuously marketed as the solution to gun
violence. The fiction of the gun-control narrative is that gun control
will keep Americans safe from the gun violence that has plagued the
country. Here is the problem. Chicago, with its strict gun-control laws, is
a record-setter in homicides. Almost everyone killed in Chicago was shot
to death. So, how did gun control stop the gun violence in Chicago? It
didn't. Criminals will always find access to guns.

The horrifying and increasingly suspicious October 1, 2017, massacre of
innocent concertgoers in Las Vegas immediately and predictably triggered
emotional calls from the Left for gun control. Gun-control enthusiasts
focus on terrorism, mass shootings, and police-related shootings. A recent
study published by the *New York Times*' online magazine *FiveThirtyEight*
examined "Gun Deaths in America." Of the 33,000 annual fatal shootings

in America today the study shows that only a very small percentage involves mass-murder attacks. Almost two-thirds of the deaths are suicides, another third are homicides, and the rest are considered accidents.

A person committing suicide could take pills or jump off a building. A person committing homicide could use a knife or a hammer. A person committing mass murder could use poison. How would gun control affect the number of deaths in America? It wouldn't. So, why does the Left consistently focus on gun control? Because gun control is the argument that seeks to disarm the American public and dissolve the Second Amendment.

The leftist Democrat party is speaking Mao's Marxist/Communist/Socialist language: "Political power grows out of the barrel of a gun."

The Humanitarian Hoax of Gun Control presents restricting or eliminating the Second Amendment as the altruistic solution to gun violence, but it is really a sinister attempt to disarm the American public. Disarming America awards total control of the people to the federal government; preventing that possibility is specifically why our Founding Fathers ratified the Second Amendment. The Second Amendment is the fulcrum of American freedom, and those who defend it are speaking the language of American independence.

If the Left succeeds in eliminating the Second Amendment, then 241 years of American freedom will be lost because a willfully blind American public was seduced by the Humanitarian Hoax of Gun Control advanced by leftist humanitarian hucksters promising safety to a frightened public. The Humanitarian Hoax of Gun Control will have succeeded in killing America with "kindness."

HOAX 12

The Humanitarian Hoax of Community Organizing

October 12, 2017

THE humanitarian hoax is the deliberate and deceitful tactic of presenting a destructive policy as altruistic. The humanitarian huckster presents himself as a compassionate advocate when in fact he is the disguised enemy.

Barack Obama, humanitarian huckster-in-chief, weakened the United States for eight years, presenting his crippling community organizing tactics and strategies as altruistic when in fact they were designed for destruction. His legacy, the leftist Democrat party and its ongoing "resistance" movement, is the party of the humanitarian hoax, attempting to destroy American democracy from within and replace it with socialism.

Radical socialist Saul Alinsky wrote his 1971 m anual, *Rules for Radicals*, to instruct future generations of radical community organizers in effective tactics to transform a capitalist state into a socialist state. Obama became the quintessential community organizer.

In May 1966, *The Nation* published an article written by Alinsky's contemporaries at Columbia University, sociologists Richard Cloward and Frances Piven. "The Weight of the Poor: A Strategy to End Poverty" described the tactics necessary to destroy capitalism by overloading the government bureaucracy with unsustainable demands that push society into social chaos and economic collapse. Cloward and Piven took the termite approach to destruction: collapse structures from the inside out. They specifically targeted the U.S. public welfare system in order to instigate a crisis that would collapse welfare and replace it with a system of guaranteed annual income.

Freedom Center director David Horowitz explains that Alinsky and his followers deliberately "organize their power bases without naming the end game, without declaring a specific future they want to achieve—socialism, communism, or anarchy. Without committing themselves to concrete principles or a specific future they organize exclusively to build a power base which they can use to destroy the existing society and its economic system." With those words Horowitz has identified the Humanitarian Hoax of Community Organizing with great precision.

David Horowitz is a leftist apostate who warns the nation about the singular goal of the Left:

"Its intention is to destroy the constitutional foundations of American democracy, dismantle traditional American governance and replace traditional American values with the socialist ideals that underpin the structures of totalitarian states."

Cloward and Piven's strategy used poverty as the weapon of destruction that would collapse America and replace the government with their idealized totalitarian Marxist model. They succeeded in bankrupting New York City for a time, but there was not enough pressure to destroy the economy of the country. Supplying additional pressure required Barack Obama's particular skill set.

The Cloward-Piven experiment in New York City revealed the weakness of their strategy. Community organizing provided insufficient economic pressure—success required ideological politicians and a colluding media willing to disinform the public. Twenty-first-century politics has embraced an expanded three-step Cloward-Piven strategy that includes gun control advocacy in order to eliminate any serious resistance to the effort.

Step 1: Politicians must overburden governmental/social institutions to the breaking point.

Step 2: Politicians must incite social chaos through divisive policies to make the country ungovernable.

Step 3: Politicians must disarm the public so that they cannot oppose the leftist totalitarian state that will follow.

Leftist European leaders and America under Obama added uncontrolled immigration with divisive immigration policies to both overload their respective welfare systems and create social chaos. Obama, presidential humanitarian huckster-in-chief, spent eight years implementing the expanded Cloward-Piven strategy of economic chaos.

In 2007 there were 26 million recipients of food stamps; by 2015 there were 47 million. Obama's open-border policy and calls for amnesty flooded the country with illegal immigrants, further straining the system and creating economic chaos. Illegal aliens overload our welfare system, cost American taxpayers a whopping $116 *billion* per year, and rob Americans of their jobs. Obama's executive orders created extraordinary divisiveness by importing a population of immigrants with hostile cultural norms, including jihadi terrorists.

Illegal immigration, the ascendancy of the racist organization Black Lives Matter, and the hysterical demands for gun control are the current weapons used by the Left and reported dishonestly by the colluding mainstream media in their ongoing attempt to destroy American democracy.

The globalist elite fully support the Left's expanded Cloward-Piven termite strategy to destroy American democracy and replace it with socialism, the social structure they require for eventual world domination. But unknown to the Left, the globalists added their own fourth step to the expanded Cloward-Piven strategy:

Step 4: Internationalize the totalitarian states into their New World Order of one-world government that they themselves will rule.

If the globalist elite's deceitful efforts are successful, after 241 years of American freedom the world will be returned to the dystopian existence of masters and slaves because a willfully blind American public was seduced by Barack Obama, the quintessential community organizer, deceitfully promising "hope and change" for America. The humanitarian hoax of the termite king will have succeeded in killing America with "kindness."

HOAX 13

The Humanitarian Hoax of Socialism

October 15, 2017

THE humanitarian hoax is the deliberate and deceitful tactic of presenting a destructive policy as altruistic. The humanitarian huckster presents himself as a compassionate advocate when in fact he is the disguised enemy.

The distinguishing feature of fascism, communism, and Islamism is totalitarianism. All power is vested in a central government and all aspects of life are controlled by its foundational ideology whether secular or religious.

In contrast, the United States is a constitutional republic with a power-sharing arrangement between its three branches of government. What distinguishes the governing structure of the United States is *de*centralization of power and the separation of church and state. The U.S. government was designed by our Founding Fathers to specifically deny totalitarian rule to any political party or particular religion.

The Constitution is the supreme law of the United States and codifies the framework of our government. Interpretation of the Constitution and tensions between the federal government, state governments, and individual rights are integral to American politics and fluctuate according to the political party in power. Government agencies and institutions were designed to function as nonpartisan components of the bureaucratic whole.

Probably the greatest source of political tension is disagreement over the role of government in American life. In totalitarian governments there is no private property. The state owns all means of production and the people are basically employees of the state. There are two classes of people—the ruled and the rulers (masters and slaves). The decentralization of power in America and the individual freedoms guaranteed by our Constitution allowed private ownership of the means of production, where people own, operate, and work for private businesses. Private ownership incentivized a strong, extremely productive middle class, and by World War II the United States of America was the most powerful country in the world.

Private ownership and a strong middle class provide the greatest defense against totalitarian rule, which is precisely why enemies of the United States are determined to destroy the middle class and private ownership of the means of production. This is where socialism enters the picture.

Socialism is a soft sell. Russian-born American author Ayn Rand wrote extensively about the dangers and sinister nature of collectivism. Rand famously said, "There is no difference between communism and socialism, except in the means of achieving the same ultimate end: communism proposes to enslave men by force, socialism, by vote. It is merely the difference between murder and suicide."

Ayn Rand also compared socialism and fascism:

> The difference between [socialism and fascism] is superficial and purely formal, but it is significant psychologically: it brings the authoritarian nature of a planned economy crudely into the open. The main characteristic of socialism (and of communism) is public ownership of the means of production, and, therefore, the abolition of private property. The right to property is the right of use and disposal. Under fascism, men retain the semblance or pretense of private property, but the government holds total power over its use and disposal.

The humanitarian hucksters selling socialism in America deceitfully market it as the system that empowers the people by providing public ownership of the means of production. They disingenuously insist that the workers own the means of production without mentioning that the state manages the property. Under socialism, the state has the power—not the individual.

Venezuela is a prime example of socialism's failure. Venezuelan socialist president Hugo Chavez nationalized the private sector of a once wealthy nation through confiscation and expropriation and destroyed the economy of Venezuela. Today, the local currency is worthless and the people are hungry.

Fascism, communism/socialism, and Islamism are all totalitarian systems that have been or continue to be enemies of the United States. Theoretically, all promise their adherents social justice and income equality provided by their centralized governments. Here is the problem—the application of fascism, communism, socialism, and Islamism exposes them as tyrannical and oppressive for all except the elite ruling class.

So, why do people choose the fiction of the promise instead of the reality of the application? Why do people ignore the words of real people who have escaped the tyranny and oppression of totalitarianism?

The answer is that centralized governments are an escape from freedom. Their cradle-to-grave care appeals to the most dependent, regressive, emotional parts of ourselves at the expense of our adult strivings for individual rights, freedom, and liberty. The government mommy and daddy control infantilized citizens.

Decentralized governments provide freedom and appeal to the most independent, rational, adult parts of ourselves. Decentralized governments offer adult independence and freedom, but they also require adult responsibility. The enemies of America did not go quietly into the night after World War II. They were determined to infantilize America and offer cradle-to-grave socialism in order to destroy the middle class.

America's enemies understood that the United States could never be conquered from outside; it would have to be defeated from within. They launched a deliberate effort to reverse traditional American strivings for adulthood, freedom, and independence in an effort to infantilize the American public and move the country toward socialism. Cry-bullies on campus who now require safe spaces to protect themselves from unwelcome ideas are a glaring example of the success of the effort. Infantilized students at the University of California at Berkeley have similarly declared free speech dead on campus, opposing ideas apparently too threatening to their fragile egos.

Leftist radical socialist Barack Obama, the quintessential humanitarian huckster, politicized every American government institution during his two lawless terms. Activist judges, activist lawyers, activist politicians, activist teachers, activist curriculum developers, activist administrators, activist IRS, CIA, FBI, CDC. Activists are not just a bunch of out-of-control college students; they are also men and women in positions of power intent on destroying American democracy and replacing it with socialism.

Activists are a broad, seemingly disparate genus joined by their activist ideology. The reason they are so dangerous is that they embrace a lawless, ends-justify-the-means mentality. So, now the country is confronted with whole institutions that lawlessly pursue a political agenda antithetical to American democracy. The censorship and disabling of accounts on social media are particularly disturbing examples.

In his famous <u>1961 farewell address</u> President Eisenhower warned America against the "unwarranted influence" of the military-industrial complex. He advised the public to "guard against the grave danger that public policy itself could become the captive of a scientific-technological elite."

Eisenhower understood how the increasing power of the military-industrial complex could threaten the decentralized power-sharing arrangement of the U.S. government. His words echoed the words of English aristocrat Lord Bertrand Russell in his 1952 book, *The Impact of Science on Society*. Eisenhower's words were a warning; Russell's words were a promise of the New World Order and a one-world government.

Both men anticipated the power of the scientific-technological elite. Both could imagine industry (means of production) being consolidated into the hands of fewer multinational conglomerates. But neither could have imagined the application of science and technology in a digital age of information wars, where manipulating and censoring information could direct public opinion worldwide and destabilize governments, including our own, via the Internet and the World Wide Web.

Neither man could have imagined the globalist elite being in control of both the means of production AND a weaponized, politicized worldwide information industry. Globalism is a clear and present danger to the United States of America today. It is the existential threat of the expanded military-industrial complex capable of creating a worldwide echo chamber that controls public opinion completely.

Leftist radical socialist Barack Obama opened the door to the globalist elite by soft-selling socialism to America. Globalism requires socialist nations that manage the means of production in order to internationalize them into their New World Order of a one-world government.

Eisenhower's parting hope for America that our democracy would "survive for all generations to come, not to become the insolvent phantom of tomorrow" will perish if Obama's presidential campaign pledge to fundamentally transform America succeeds.

After 241 years of decentralized government and American freedom, the world will be returned to the dystopian existence of masters and slaves because a willfully blind American public was seduced by Barack Obama, the quintessential humanitarian huckster, deceitfully promising "hope and change" for America. The Humanitarian Hoax of Socialism will have succeeded in killing America with "kindness."

HOAX 14

The Humanitarian Hoax of George Soros

November 6, 2017

THE humanitarian hoax is the deliberate and deceitful tactic of presenting a destructive policy as altruistic. The humanitarian huckster presents himself as a compassionate advocate when in fact he is the disguised enemy.

Billionaire George Soros is the consummate humanitarian huckster. He is the man behind the curtain who finances the radical leftist agenda of the Democrat party in the United States through his disingenuously named Open Society Foundations (OSF). Money buys political influence, and George Soros has a lot of money to spread around. This is the way it works.

The Open Society Foundations funnel money into hundreds of smaller organizations with <u>deceptively positive names</u>, such as:

- Advancement Project
- Alliance for Justice
- Bill of Rights Defense Committee
- Center for American Progress
- Democracy Alliance
- New Israel Fund
- Psychologists for Social Responsibility
- Southern Poverty Law Center

One must enter the world of deception to fully understand what these organizations actually do. It is essential to remember that an organization with a humanitarian name does not make it a humanitarian organization. The primary focus of Soros's Open Society Foundations and its funding goals is to destroy American democracy and replace it with socialism. The long-term ambition is an internationalized one-world government that the globalist elite like Soros will rule.

Soros's Open Society Foundations was named after Viennese philosopher Karl Popper's 1945 book, *The Open Society and Its Enemies*. Popper believed that "open societies" possess moral codes based on universal principles that benefit all mankind. Open societies recognize no ultimate truths and particularly disdain any society claiming superior cultural norms. Popper criticized American confidence in its Declaration of Independence, which boldly states, "We hold these truths to be self-evident." Soros considered Popper's greatest philosophical contribution to be his insistence that "the ultimate truth remains permanently beyond our reach."

Popper's philosophy is a very convenient foundation for the leftist tenets of political correctness, moral relativism, and historical revisionism. The Soros/Popper philosophy denies objective reality (facts) and substitutes subjective reality (opinions). For Popper and Soros, facts and opinions are equivalent, because without factual certainty everything is a matter of opinion. The fallacy of Popper's philosophy is exposed when he acknowledges that there are limits to tolerance. In *The Open Society and Its Enemies* he argues that unlimited tolerance necessarily leads to the disappearance of tolerance. He claims, in the name of tolerance, the right not to tolerate the intolerant. Apparently, the self-destructiveness of tolerating the intolerant is an "ultimate truth" that is not "beyond our reach." Another hypocritical convenience for the elitists who intend to rule this utopia of harmonious existence.

So, what does all of this mean?

To a theoretical philosopher, the ideal society (subjective reality) is a world without borders, national sovereignty, or laws—a world of tolerance, harmony, income equality, and social justice. It is the idealized unified world romanticized in John Lennon's countercultural anthem, "Imagine."

To a practicing profiteer like George Soros, the ideal society as described by Popper is a world without borders or national sovereignty that offers a lucrative, unrestricted global marketplace. The actual, factual certainty of a world without borders or national sovereignty is a world of chaos (objective reality)—precisely what is required to destabilize governments and collapse prices so that Soros can buy countries' assets on the cheap. Social chaos is an extraordinary opportunity for exploitation by profiteers.

Soros is unapologetic about his desire to change the world, and particularly the United States, according to his vision of social justice. The reality of Soros's vision of change is disguised by misleading descriptions of his "philanthropy." Soros's stated ambition to be the conscience of the world by using his charitable foundations is sociopathic considering the reality of his Open Society Foundations and its attempts to destabilize America. For a profiteering megalomaniac the goal is power and control, and George Soros is arguably the world's most successful manipulator on the world stage—he is the great pretender. This is how the Soros humanitarian hoax works.

Soros is a heavy contributor to liberal mainstream media outlets. Media Research Center reports that since 2003, "Soros has spent over $48 million funding media properties, including the infrastructure of news—journalism schools, investigative journalism and even industry organizations. . . . The Soros media empire truly spans the globe, but few even realize it because it's decentralized under numerous organizations, funded in turn by more than 30 Open Society Foundations." The supposed watchdog agency Organization of News Ombudsmen—"a professional group devoted to monitoring accuracy, fairness and balance"—is supported exclusively by the Open Society Foundations, formerly the Open Society Institute.

George Soros understands the psychodynamics of objective reality (what is factually true) and subjective reality (what is perceived to be true) and applies the disparity to financial markets. The scheme is consummately dishonest, manipulative, and wildly successful. Soros uses his media empire to manipulate subjective reality (investor perceptions) to change objective reality (markets). Consider the following.

Media outlets disseminating fake news deliberately manipulate public opinion and, therefore, public behavior. If Soros wants to drive stock prices down, his television lackeys ominously predict a serious downturn and the public predictably responds with panic selling—the false prediction of a downturn results in a real downturn (reflexivity) and Soros goes on a buying spree. When stock prices return to their appropriate levels, Soros sells the stock and makes millions more so he can finance the ambitions of his deceitful Open Society Foundations.

Reflexivity in economics is the theory that a feedback loop exists in which investors' perceptions affect economic fundamentals, which in turn changes investors' perceptions. Reflexivity theory states:

Investors don't base their decisions on reality, but rather on their perceptions of reality instead. The actions that result from these perceptions have an impact on reality, or fundamentals, which then affects investors' perceptions and thus prices.

The same principle of reflexivity applies in society, where the staggering power of the media to manipulate public opinion and behavioral responses becomes clear. Consider the media coverage of leftist causes such as Black Lives Matter, LGBTQ organizations, open-border immigration activists, and anti-Israel groups, including the Council on American-Islamic Relations (CAIR), the Muslim Brotherhood, Muslim Advocates, and the Arab American Association of New York. Soros's donations to these causes are marketed as humanitarian, but their purpose is to create social chaos. Social chaos is exactly what the globalist vulture George Soros wants and he is masterful at disguising his will to power in "humanitarian" labels.

Islamists call it taqiyya—lying in the service of Islam. Multiple Islamic "charitable" organizations with humanitarian-sounding names (see above) are funneling money to terrorist organizations. There is no equivalent word in the English language for this deliberate deception, so I have coined a new word in "honor" of Saul Alinsky, Alinskiyya—lying in the service of socialism. The Arab world is familiar with taqiyya because it is a tactic encouraged to promote Islam. The West has never had an equivalent word because the Enlightenment did not teach deception—it taught truth, freedom, pluralism, and the free exchange of ideas in order to debate the relative merits of issues.

In October 2017 Soros quietly transferred $18 billion to his Open Society Foundations. Eighteen billion dollars buys a lot of reflexivity in the world of Soros. It buys politicians, media properties, media pundits, leftist propaganda spewed by anti-American organizations, and educational disinformation designed to collapse America.

George Soros is a multi-talented humanitarian huckster who disguises his destructive reflexivity policies as philanthropy. Soros is not America's advocate. He is an enemy of the state attempting to destroy America from within by funding radical leftist causes designed to replace our representative democracy with socialism.

We simply cannot allow the Humanitarian Hoax of George Soros to kill America with "kindness."

HOAX 15

The Humanitarian Hoax of Unconditional Love

November 25, 2017

THE humanitarian hoax is the deliberate and deceitful tactic of presenting a destructive policy as altruistic. The humanitarian huckster presents himself as a compassionate advocate when in fact he is the disguised enemy.

Unconditional love is the Holy Grail for millennials. They talk about it, dream about it, want it, need it, and are outraged if anyone dares to question its value. Unconditional love is, after all, "settled" science among millennial "experts" whose opinions are accepted and observed with religious conformity by their devotees.

Wikipedia defines unconditional love as "affection without any limitations or love without conditions." The current demand for unconditional love is consistent with the leftist campaign to value feelings over facts and effort over achievement as metrics for what is good in society. So, let's examine unconditional love.

First, an appropriate season for unconditional love exists during infancy and early childhood. Parents accept anything and everything that babies do; we love them for just being. Babies and young children lack the ability for self-control, so we do not expect standards of behavior—anything goes. Unconditional love separates the individual from his or her behavior, which is entirely appropriate for infants and young children. When the demand for unconditional love is extended into adulthood, however, the individual inappropriately demands to be loved without regard for his or her behavior in the same way an infant is loved.

Relationships are structured with written, spoken, and unspoken rules and standards of behavior. Family relationships, social relationships, business relationships, professional relationships, sexual relationships are all organized on some level by rules that participants are expected to follow.

Societies are similarly organized by their infrastructure of rules and laws that citizens are expected to observe. What makes the period of infancy and early childhood so exceptional is its distinguishing "no rules" formula, when society temporarily accepts the separation of the individual from his or her behavior. But what happens when a society refuses adulthood and instead strives for permanent childhood?

When the no-rules formula is protracted and adulthood is rejected, the result is an infantilized population and social chaos. Consider the consequences to society of adults who refuse to abide by laws—traffic laws, property laws, family laws, contract laws. All rules and regulations are considered anathema to chronological adults living in the subjective reality of no-rules infancy, including college campus policies that no longer respect the constitutional guarantee of free speech. Fragile, infantilized students require "safe spaces" and "trigger warnings" to protect them from ideas they disagree with. College students have historically been considered future leaders, but how can a leader lead a pluralist society if he or she cannot even listen to an opposing point of view?

The demand to restrict free speech and the need for safe spaces demonstrate the dependency and failure to thrive that the demand for perpetual childhood has created. Valuing feelings over facts and effort over achievement, redefining free speech as hate speech, and demanding unconditional love are all hallmarks of an infantilized society.

Who has fueled and financed the descent of our adult society into eternal childhood, and what is the purpose?

Children are easily manipulated because childhood is a state of being dependent and powerless. A society of adults who think and behave like children is therefore easily manipulated and easily controlled. A regressed society is the unaware and compliant citizenry required by leftists for socialism to advance in America.

Children live in a world of subjective reality and magical thinking. They believe whatever they are told without questioning blatant inconsistencies or ambiguities. College students who demand free speech for themselves do not acknowledge the glaring hypocrisy of denying free speech to opposing voices and relabeling oppositional views as hate speech. Their hypocrisy exposes the childishness of their stance. Attempts to rationally argue or debate the inconsistencies are as futile as trying to convince a three-year-old that he cannot fly. The problem, of course, is that these students are chronological adults—they are virtual children, not actual children, and their temper tantrums are dangerous.

Students who are virtual children are being recruited on campuses by anarchist groups funded by George Soros's Open Society Foundations to become soldiers in the leftist war on America. The leftist war on America targets the three pillars of our society that support the dreams of our Founding Fathers: family, church, and patriotism. The leftist intention is to destroy America from within and replace our representative democracy with socialism.

The attack on the family is rooted in the destructive demand for unconditional love by infantile adults. Parents are disrespected with the same arrogance that authority figures including teachers, religious leaders, and the police are disrespected. Attacks against traditional authority are deliberately designed to make society ungovernable and families unsustainable.

Free speech is labeled hate speech by students on campus who view oppositional speakers as enemies who must be silenced. Parents with opposing views are considered toxic by adult children who choose estrangement in order to secure silence. Their childish, all-or-nothing perspective rejects the mature option of discussion and/or agreeing to disagree. Tyrannical demands to accept the unacceptable shatter relationships, families, and, ultimately, societies.

In the upside-down world of leftist politics, the infantile demand for unconditional love remains the Holy Grail. Free-speech activists remain as baffled as parents of estranged adult children until they realize that destroying free speech and shattering families are both goals and tactics in the leftist war on America.

If America is to survive, we must continue to love our infants and young children unconditionally but insist upon growth, respect, and self-control from adults in society. We must reject the subjective reality of virtual children and be resolute that our children grow up emotionally and accept the responsibilities and standards of adult behavior, because a society of infants is unsustainable. If we do not protect free speech and reserve our unconditional love only for infants and young children, the leftist war on America will have succeeded.

If the Left prevails, then 241 years of American freedom will be lost because an infantilized American public was seduced by leftist humanitarian hucksters promising eternal dependence and unconditional love to a public too frightened to grow up and live in objective reality as responsible adults. The Humanitarian Hoax of Unconditional Love will have succeeded in killing America with "kindness."

HOAX 16

The Humanitarian Hoax of Relativism

December 6, 2017

THE humanitarian hoax is the deliberate and deceitful tactic of presenting a destructive policy as altruistic. The humanitarian huckster presents himself as a compassionate advocate when in fact he is the disguised enemy.

Relativism is defined as the belief that there is no absolute truth, only truths that a particular individual or culture happens to believe. People who believe in relativism accept that different people can have different views about what is moral and what is immoral. So far, so good—a society can tolerate multiple opinions on the relative merits of a thing or an idea. Here is the problem: civilized society requires consensus on the *existence* of that thing or idea. It requires agreement on what is real. Objective reality is the foundation for the laws and rules that regulate public behavior in a society.

In my article "The Mathematics of the Culture War on America," I introduced the problem of multiple realities inherent in Kurt Lewin's Change Theory with the example of a man walking down a street.

A man is walking down a street. Four people are nearby. The first person says there is a man walking down the street. The second person says there is a person walking down the street. The third person says I'm not sure who is walking down the street. The fourth person says there is a woman walking down the street.

The objective reality is that a man is walking down the street regardless of the observers' perceptions. *Objective* reality is rooted in facts and exists independent of the perceptions of those facts. *Subjective* reality, on the other hand, tolerates conflicting multiple realities because it is rooted in perceptions and informed by opinions. So, in subjective reality the fourth person's observation that a woman is walking down the street is accepted. The consequence, of course, is that societal acceptance of multiple realities ultimately creates chaos because there is no agreement on what is real.

Joseph Backholm, director of the Family Policy Institute of Washington (FPIW), is a 5'9" white male. In April 2016 he interviewed eight diverse students on campus at the University of Washington to see if they would accept or reject his self-identification as a woman, a child, 6'5", and Chinese. The answers were shocking. Backholm began by asking if the students were aware of the debate over males and females using the same bathrooms, locker rooms, or spas based on gender identity.

He asked the first student, "If I told you that I was a woman, what would your response be?" She answered, "Good for you. Okay." Then he asked two male students the same question. The first said, "Nice to meet you." The second, "Really?" Next Backholm asked, "What if I said I was seven years old?" The student answered that if he felt as if he was seven years old at heart, then so be it—good for him. She actually accepted an adult male's self-identification as a seven-year-old child. When asked if it would be okay for him to enroll in a first-grade class, another student answered that as long as he wasn't hindering society and causing harm to other people, it should be okay. Not hindering society? Not causing harm to other people?

Backholm continued, "What if I told you I was a Chinese woman; what would you say?" One student answered that it was not her place as another human being to say he was wrong and to draw lines or boundaries. Another said that if he believed he was taller than he was, it was not harmful, so it was not a problem for her—but she would not tell him he was wrong. Only one student out of eight white, black, male, and female students rejected Backholm's self-description as 6'5", saying he was not 6'5" even though she accepted his saying that he was a Chinese woman. These students confirmed that their reality is firmly rooted in subjective feelings and opinions, not in objective facts.

The students interviewed demonstrate the leftist narrative that says all opinions are equal. That narrative has moved beyond differences of opinion and debates about the merits of ideas into the realm of different realities. Leftist relativism is presented as humanitarian and respectful. These students did not consider accepting a 5'9" white adult male as a seven-year-old child or as a 6'5" Chinese woman to be hurtful to another person or a hindrance to society. They live in the dreamworld of subjective reality, where time, space, and facts are entirely absent. In dreams, anything goes. In the conscious world, the destruction of our societal standard of objective reality is beyond hurtful; it is catastrophic because without consensus on what is real, there is no infrastructure for the laws and rules that regulate public behavior. Eventually there is only chaos.

Consider the shift in the definition of mental health. Historically, mental health was a metric of being in touch with objective reality. Any student accepting a 5'9" white adult male as a seven-year-old child or a 6'5" Chinese woman would be diagnosed as delusional because he or she was clearly out of touch with reality. Today, according to the <u>World Health Organization</u>, an agency of the United Nations, "Mental health is a state of well-being in which every individual realizes his or her potential, can cope with the normal stresses of life, can work productively and fruitfully, and is able to make a contribution to his or her community." No mention of being in touch with objective reality. So, students who accept a 5'9" adult white male as a seven-year-old child or a 6'5" Chinese woman are considered mentally healthy as long as they reach their potential, cope with stress, work productively, and contribute to society.

What is the purpose of this change? Who benefits from the shift? Kurt Lewin's Change Theory, mentioned above, offers an explanation.

Lewin's three-step theory can be visualized as follows:

1.   UNFREEZE—a block of ice that melts

2.   CHANGE—into a puddle of water

3.   REFREEZE—and is then reshaped into a cone.

The Culture War on America is a political war between objective reality and subjective reality. The leftist narrative based on feelings and opinions seeks to collapse the established authority of objective reality based on facts. Through its educational and media indoctrination, the Left has already unfrozen established American cultural norms that required consensus and objective reality. Society is being indoctrinated to willingly accept multiple realities as normal and embrace feelings over facts. America is currently in a state of transition—the puddle of water—when college students, our future leaders, are comfortable accepting unreality as reality.

The Left is using Lewin's model to fundamentally transform the infrastructure of America from one of objective reality into one of subjective reality. The leftist pressure to accept subjective reality is their primary weapon of destabilization. The Left is driving society crazy by demanding that people accept unreality as reality.

The Left seeks to refreeze America into a cone of subjective reality based on feelings, not facts—where the entire population, not just college students, will accept a white 5'9" male as a 6'5" Chinese woman. Why? Because the psychosocial Culture War on America will determine the course of our country.

The Humanitarian Hoax of Relativism is a purposeful, methodical, coordinated psychological operation designed to drive society into subjective reality and create social chaos.

The end game of the cone of subjective reality is social control. Social chaos is followed by government suppression that restores order. Civil liberties are suspended and the government acquires total control. The end game of the leftist psychosocial Culture War on America is total government control. It is the political difference between a block and a cone.

HOAX 17

The Humanitarian Hoax of Net Neutrality

December 17, 2017

THE humanitarian hoax is the deliberate and deceitful tactic of presenting a destructive policy as altruistic. The humanitarian huckster presents himself as a compassionate advocate when in fact he is the disguised enemy.

Barack Obama, humanitarian huckster-in-chief, weakened the United States for eight years, presenting his crippling policies as altruistic when in fact they were designed for destruction. The late-term passage of his FCC regulation 15-24, the Report and Order on Remand, Declaratory Ruling, and Order in the Matter of Protecting and Promoting the Open Internet, deceitfully named Net Neutrality, was no exception.

By a 3–2 vote, Democrat majority commissioners legalized censorship by establishing the Federal Communications Commission (FCC) as the sole regulator and arbiter of the structural basis of the Internet.

In his dissenting opinion, Republican FCC Commissioner Michael O'Reilly said, "Today a majority of the Commission attempts to usurp the authority of Congress by re-writing the Communications Act to suit its own 'values' and political ends."

Humanitarian hoaxes are deceitfully given positive-sounding names that disguise their negative intent and mislead the trusting public. The Affordable Care Act was not affordable, the Southern Poverty Law Center maligns legitimate advocacy centers, George Soros's Open Society Foundations fund anarchy all over the world. So, "Net Neutrality" sounds constructive and fair, but it is actually a leftist attack on Internet freedom designed to restrict freedom of speech—particularly the speech of conservatives and libertarians. This is how it works.

The World Wide Web for nongovernmental commercial use has been an open and unrestricted American business since its launch over twenty years ago. The Web is the twenty-first-century public square for global information sharing. Internet business is divided into two separate sections: Internet *service* providers (ISPs) such as Comcast, Verizon, and AT&T; and Internet *content* providers such as Google, Microsoft, Facebook, Amazon, and Twitter.

In 2015 Obama disingenuously decided to "protect" the open Internet and vigorously supported passage of regulation FCC 15-24, deceptively tagged Net Neutrality and derisively referred to as Obamanet. Republican political consultant Roger Stone has written a scathing article on the subject exposing what it all means. In the article, published by the *Daily Caller* on December 8, 2017, and titled "UNCENSORED: Time for Real Net Neutrality," Stone exposed the deceit of Obama's Humanitarian Hoax of Net Neutrality.

To summarize, FCC 15-24 awards the Federal Communications Commission exclusive authority to apply rules or not to apply rules—it can choose who to regulate vigorously and who to disregard. The new rules, written under a Title II provision of the Communications Act of 1934, reclassified broadband Internet *service* providers as common carriers. These providers were previously classified under Title I as information services.

Classifying broadband service providers, such as Comcast, Verizon, and AT&T, as common carriers means that they are then regulated by the FCC as common carriers. This distinction is critical because the new rule stipulates that broadband Internet service providers are to be bound by Net Neutrality. So, Net Neutrality binds Internet *service* providers to the FCC 15-24 rules, but exempts the Internet content providers, such as Google, Microsoft, Facebook, and Twitter. The exemption is a bonanza for content providers, awarding them complete freedom to curate and restrict content.

The Tech Left was instrumental in the formulation of Net Neutrality and helped write the new rules. The unsurprising consequence is that the leftist content providers who currently dominate the Web are, according to Stone, "free to restrain content by censoring out all conservative and libertarian views at will, without so much as an explanation to anyone why the objectionable views were banned." It is complete censorship and very dangerous. It is the Humanitarian Hoax of Net Neutrality.

The leftist elite in Silicon Valley, funded generously by George Soros, embraced Canadian philosopher Marshall McLuhan's famous saying, "The medium is the message." Leftists have understood for a long time that political control is possible only with communication control—control the medium and you control the message. The purpose of Net Neutrality was control of the Internet in order to control its ideological content.

In legalizing censorship by Internet content providers, Net Neutrality is a serious stealth attack on free speech in the cyber public square. The leftist narrative already dominates American universities, the entertainment sector, and the mainstream media. Net Neutrality is a power grab for the World Wide Web. Without freedom of speech, there is no freedom. If the leftist behemoths are free to regulate and censor content on the Internet, then we no longer are living in a free society or a free world—we are living in the dystopian society described by George Orwell in his famously prescient book *1984.*

Republican Commissioner Ajit Pai, President Trump's designated chair of the Federal Communications Commission (FCC), was the second dissenting vote on the 2015 passage of FCC 15-24. In his remarks on President Trump's <u>Restoring Internet Freedom Order</u>, Pai endorsed the president's initiative to roll back Obama's "heavy-handed micromanagement" and return to the pre-2015 light-touch regulatory framework.

President Trump's action to reverse FCC 15-24 was predictably misreported by the media and consequently misunderstood by the public. Restoring Internet Freedom generated hysterical criticism like that articulated by actor Mark Ruffalo: "Taking away #Net Neutrality is the Authoritarian dream. Consolidating information in the hands of a few controlled by a few. Dangerous territory." Pai responded by saying, "These comments are absurd. Getting rid of government authority over the Internet is the exact *opposite* of authoritarianism. Government control is the defining feature of authoritarians, including the one in North Korea."

Pai pointed out that the Internet grew and thrived for nearly twenty years before the implementation of Net Neutrality under pressure from the Obama White House. "For one thing, there was no problem to solve. The Internet wasn't broken in 2015," said Pai. "We were not living in some digital dystopia. To the contrary, the Internet has been one thing, perhaps the only thing in American society, that we can all agree has been a stunning success. Not only was there no problem, the solution hasn't worked."

The FCC is directed by five commissioners appointed by the president and confirmed by the Senate for five-year terms. The current Republican-majority FCC successfully ended Obama's Humanitarian Hoax of Net Neutrality on December 14, 2017, with a 3–2 vote that repealed FCC 15-24. Of course the Left immediately began challenging the outcome with its predictably hysterical "end of the world" cries that are exactly the OPPOSITE of what the repeal of Net Neutrality will accomplish. Consider the following leftist predictions, courtesy of conservative website *Breitbart News* dated December 14, 2017:

1. It's the end of the Internet as we know it!

2. The end of Net Neutrality means the "silencing" of gays and "marginalized communities."

3. The end of Net Neutrality is an attack on "reproductive freedom."

4. SUICIDE! ABUSE! MENTAL HEALTH! ANOREXIA! BUZZWORD!

5. The end of Net Neutrality will lead to a new civil war.

6. The end of Net Neutrality is the end of free speech on the Internet.

7. The end of Net Neutrality means the end of democracy.

8. It means we'll be paying $14.99 a month for Twitter!

Net Neutrality is a signature Obama humanitarian hoax, promising Internet fairness but delivering Internet unfairness and legalized censorship. Only in the leftist Orwellian world of subjective reality is censorship considered "fair" and truth labeled "hate speech." In the real world of objective reality, censorship remains against the law in America and freedom of speech protects the truth. Obama's Net Neutrality is a deceitful attempt to bypass the Constitution and award exclusive control of Internet content to the leftist behemoths that currently dominate the World Wide Web.

Barack Obama continues to lead the leftist Democrat party and its "resistance" movement. It is the party of the humanitarian hoax attempting to destroy American democracy and replace it with socialism. The single greatest threat to America is the abolishment of freedom of speech—the precise goal of Obama's Humanitarian Hoax of Net Neutrality. Be glad that FCC 15-24 has been rescinded. It is not the end of the world; it is the beginning of a new era of deregulation and renewed protection of our precious freedoms under the leadership of President Donald J. Trump.

HOAX 18

The Humanitarian Hoax of Sanctuary States

January 5, 2018

THE humanitarian hoax is the deliberate and deceitful tactic of presenting a destructive policy as altruistic. The humanitarian huckster presents himself as a compassionate advocate when in fact he is the disguised enemy.

Barack Obama, humanitarian huckster-in-chief, weakened the United States for eight years by persuading America to accept his ruinous, politically correct sanctuary-city policies as altruistic when in fact they were designed to destabilize and destroy civil society. His legacy, a leftist Democrat party starring sycophant California Governor Jerry Brown, is the party of the humanitarian hoax attempting to destroy the capitalist infrastructure of American democracy and replace it with socialism. This is how it works.

The Humanitarian Hoax of Sanctuary Cities—Hoax 9 discussed how the Left deliberately perverted the original sanctuary mission of protecting innocent refugees to protecting criminal aliens at the expense of public safety. In defiance of federal immigration laws, sanctuary cities provide safe haven for criminal illegal aliens and establish a reprehensible two-tier system of justice that protects the illegals.

Why would any American patriot support such an anti-American policy?

The extremely anti-American motive for supporting sanctuary cities was introduced in The *Humanitarian Hoax of Community Organizing—Hoax 12*. This chapter detailed radical socialists Richard Cloward and Frances Piven's strategy of using poverty as a weapon of destruction to destroy capitalism by overloading the government bureaucracy with unsustainable demands that push society into social chaos and economic collapse.

The two deceitfully destructive humanitarian hoaxes were married when California became the first sanctuary state on January 1, 2018, with Jerry Brown as the officiant. The married status of "sanctuary state" is an open invitation for illegal aliens to come to California and exploit its generous welfare benefits, free medical services, free educational benefits, free or subsidized housing, free vocational training, and immunity from prosecution for crimes.

The law signed by Governor Brown bars local police from asking about immigration status and from participating in federal immigration enforcement procedures. This means that if an illegal alien gets arrested for rape or murder in Los Angeles County, agents from Immigration and Customs Enforcement (ICE) are not allowed in the jail to question that person. LA County will not share information with ICE or accept ICE detainers authorizing the continued detention of illegal aliens. ICE acting director Thomas Homan says, "In denying to detain criminals, sanctuary cities end up putting them back on the street where they will re-offend and prompt ICE agents to take the dangerous step of tracking them down."

The extraordinary benefits awarded to illegal aliens cost the legal taxpaying residents of California money, jobs, medical services, and educational opportunities. A 2017 study by the Federation for American Immigration Reform (FAIR) lists the cost of illegal immigration to U.S. taxpayers as a staggering $116 *billion* per year, with the tax burden falling disproportionately on state and local taxpayers by a ratio of 2 to 1.

So, the hard-working legal taxpaying residents of California are subsidizing the illegal non-working immigrant population that has been invited to overwhelm the government bureaucracy with unsustainable demands designed to push society into social chaos and economic collapse. Sound familiar? It is the Cloward-Piven strategy on steroids, promoted by leftist political leaders who consider California too big to fail and assume there will be a federal bailout that will eventually collapse the nation's economy, especially if New York and Illinois follow California's egregious example.

The Cloward-Piven-Brown strategy may have worked while Obama was in office or may have been the plan for a Hillary Clinton presidency, but President Donald Trump is an American patriot. He is not about to participate in a federal bailout of the state of California, which would encourage even more unrestrained, irresponsible spending and defiance of federal immigration laws. By defying laws and establishing California as a sanctuary state, the leftist Democrat party is fomenting anarchy and social chaos. What is the motive?

Cloward and Piven's socialism is only the short game. The long game is a one-world government. Socialism, with its complete government control, is the prerequisite social structure for the globalist elite to internationalize the country, internationalize the police force, and impose a one-world government. One-world government is the overarching goal and the underlying motive to destroy America from within.

The capitalist infrastructure of American democracy, with President Donald Trump as its leader, is the single greatest existential threat to a one-world government. The globalist elite and their leftist lackeys are desperate to stop President Trump because his America-first policies have disrupted the advancement of a one-world government.

America is being marched toward anarchy and social chaos with Obama's ongoing anti-American "resistance" movement and Governor Brown's illegitimate establishment of a sanctuary state.

America is at a pivotal time in history when the decision must be made to either preserve our individual freedoms, liberty, and rule of law or surrender to radical socialist political bullies like Obama and Brown. Both are dangerous enemies of the state who arrogantly impose their leftist ideology on America with blatant disregard for our Constitution. They foment divisiveness, disorder, turmoil, and lawlessness.

In a _Newsweek_ article on June 28, 2017, ICE's Thomas Homan explained, "Sanctuary jurisdictions pose a threat to the American public by refusing to work with ICE and allowing egregious criminal offenders back into the community to put the lives of the public at risk."

Homan continued, "We gotta take [sanctuary cities] to court, and we gotta start charging some of these politicians with crimes." Homan believes in political responsibility, saying, "Politicians who pushed sanctuary city legislation should be held 'personally accountable' for their actions."

Yet sanctuary cities, increasing exponentially across the United States, and now our first sanctuary state are proudly supported by the Left and marketed as humanitarian and altruistic.

Making California a sanctuary state was not a humanitarian mission to protect innocent refugees; it was a humanitarian hoax designed to protect illegal criminal aliens at the expense of law-abiding Americans, create divisiveness and social chaos, collapse the nation's economy, deny the authority of the president, and nullify the Constitution of the United

States of America. It is time to prosecute anyone who attempts to usurp the power of the presidency and Congress with seditious plans to overthrow the government and defy constitutional laws. And that means anyone, including Barack Obama and Jerry Brown.

HOAX 19

The Humanitarian Hoax of Common Core

January 14, 2018

THE humanitarian hoax is the deliberate and deceitful tactic of presenting a destructive policy as altruistic. The humanitarian huckster presents himself as a compassionate advocate when in fact he is the disguised enemy.

Barack Obama, humanitarian huckster-in-chief, weakened the United States for eight years, presenting his crippling Common Core State Standards (CCSS) advocacy as altruistic when in fact it was designed for destruction.

Common Core is a deliberate information war targeting American children. It is a deceitful campaign to undermine established American Judeo-Christian cultural norms celebrating patriotism, the meritocracy, and American sovereignty. The Leftist/Islamist axis is using Common Core to promote collectivism in preparation for a one-world government. This is how it works.

Serious educational reform enacted by the No Child Left Behind Act (NCLB) of 2001 was designed to provide high standards and measurable goals in order to improve individual outcomes in education. Federal funding was correlated to test performance. Rather than improving education, however, the net effect of NCLB was education reformatted to teach to the tests. Education critic Alfie Kohn argued that the "NCLB law is 'unredeemable' and should be scrapped—its main effect has been to sentence poor children to an endless regimen of test-preparation drills." There were loud calls for reform.

Enter Common Core State Standards (CCSS), launched under Obama in 2009, deceptively marketed by a propaganda campaign emphasizing the positive benefits of national standards and uniformity in curriculum guidelines, with measurable effectiveness for American public education

K-12. Common Core State Standards (CCSS) are mistakenly understood to be a derivative of the No Child Left Behind Act, but they aren't.

Obama's 2009 <u>Race to the Top</u> program was introduced as a competitive grant program that awarded points to states for satisfying performance-based evaluations of teachers and principals based on measures of educator effectiveness. Sound familiar? It should, because "measures of educator effectiveness" = student test scores. Even though Race to the Top did not mandate adoption of Common Core, in order to receive federal stimulus money states had to "commit" to adopting Common Core standards. Forty-two states now operate public and private education under the Common Core program.

What makes Common Core a humanitarian hoax? Let's review.
<u>Common Core State Standards Mission Statement</u>:

> The Common Core State Standards provide a consistent, clear understanding of what students are expected to learn, so teachers and parents know what they need to do to help them. The standards are designed to be robust and relevant to the real world, reflecting the knowledge and skills that our young people need for success in college and careers. With American students fully prepared for the future, our communities will be best positioned to compete successfully in the global economy. . . . These Standards do not dictate curriculum or teaching methods.

Sounds great, doesn't it? The problem is the deceptive language referring to the "real world" and the "global economy," and the misleading statement that the Standards do not dictate curriculum or teaching methods. The reality is that Common Core State Standards are not a derivative of America's No Child Left Behind Act. Common Core State Standards are a derivative of the United Nations' <u>Global Education First Initiative</u> (GEFI). <u>The 3 Priorities</u> of GEFI are:

Priority 1: Put Every Child in School

Priority 2: Improve the Quality of Learning

Priority 3: Foster Global Citizenship

It is <u>Priority 3</u> that is the most alarming and the basis for the Humanitarian Hoax of Common Core.

Obama's Common Core is not teaching American children about the world and how to be effective and competitive in a global marketplace. Obama's deceitful Common Core initiative is propagandizing American children toward collectivism, globalism, and one-world government with its anti-American, anti-Judeo-Christian, pro-Islamic bias. American public/private education no longer advocates American patriotism, the meritocracy, American exceptionalism, or American sovereignty. America is no longer in control of American education. This is how it happened.

Obama made a speech in Cairo in 2009 that launched an eight-year initiative to Connect All Schools that was fraudulently presented as a program to help different people who believe different things communicate and understand one another.

Political analyst Bethany Blankley's stunning April 2015 article, "Common Core Ties Libya, Qatar, Saudi Arabia," exposed Obama's Common Core as "originating from the One World Education concept, a global goal orchestrated by the Connect All Schools program to globalize instruction. Its origin is funded by the Qatar Foundation International (QFI). The director of QFI's Research Center for Islamic Legislation and Ethics is Tariq Ramadan, grandson of Muslim Brotherhood founder, Hassan al-Banna."

Internet news site *World Net Daily* reported that in 2011 the Qatar Foundation International "partnered with the Department of State and the U.S. Department of Education to facilitate matchmaking between classrooms in the U.S. and international schools through . . . the 'Connect All Schools' project." QFI proudly states on its website that the initiative was founded in response to Obama's 2009 Cairo speech, where representatives of the Muslim Brotherhood were prominently seated in the front row.

The conspiracy of the Leftist/Islamist axis to re-educate American children away from America-first patriotism toward global governance and Islam is well under way and well funded.

Qatar Foundation International unapologetically states its mission of advancing global citizenship through educational curricula on its Q&A page:

Why is your global presence limited to a select few countries?

While QFI's mission is dedicated to connecting cultures and advancing global citizenship through education, our current focus is K-12 public and charter schools in the United States, Canada, and Brazil. To find out if a school near you is a QFI partner, see our map. To find other resources that may help your child learn Arabic, visit Al Masdar.

Most parents have no idea what their children are learning in school unless their child asks for help with homework or relates an experience at school. Parents in any of the forty-two states that have adopted Common Core State Standards need to start reading their children's textbooks immediately. It is up to parents to decide if they support American sovereignty and fair trade in the global marketplace or global citizenship and a globalized curriculum promoting a one-world government. It is a matter of informed consent.

This brings us to UN Agenda 21, initiated in 1992 and described in a lengthy report titled United Nations Sustainable Development. The entire document can be summarized in one sentence:

UN Agenda 21 is a plan for a New World Order that internationalizes the entire world into a global society under its own UN global governance—for our own good, of course.

Its lofty Preamble reads like the lyrics of John Lennon's song "Imagine." In the old days power grabbers for world domination were not so soft spoken. Hitler, Stalin, and Mussolini did not sing lullabies of peace, but the twenty-first century requires a different approach. We have "Imagine" and the UN's updated Agenda 21, Transforming Our World: The 2030 Agenda for Sustainable Development.

The Culture War is an insidious psychosocial information war being waged on America through the political correctness, moral relativism, and historical revisionism embodied in the informational materials supplied by the pro-globalism enemies of national sovereignty at the United Nations. Stealth jihad is quietly being fought in classrooms with the educational propaganda of the World Core Curriculum.

In 1989 the United Nations Educational, Scientific and Cultural Organization (UNESCO) awarded its prize for peace education to the father of global education and creator of the World Core Curriculum (WCC), Dr. Robert Muller. In accepting his award Muller said, "I dream that UNESCO will study and recommend by the year 2000 a world core curriculum for adoption by all nations."

Most people understand the mission of the United Nations to be promotion of mutual respect and understanding between sovereign nations with differing cultures. Were we mistaken or misled? Was the goal of the United Nations always universal citizenship? Muller says, "In the final analysis . . . the main function of education is to make children happy, fulfilled, and universal human beings." Universal human beings??

In November 2010 Obama's secretary of education, Arne Duncan, addressed <u>UNESCO</u>, praising universal education without ever mentioning educational content. Educating the world's children is a laudable goal. Putting every child in school and improving the quality of learning is an altruistic undertaking. The problem is that most people naively assume that universal education advances literacy and do not realize that it is a propaganda tool designed to advance global governance. It is a seismic humanitarian hoax.

In a world of technology, where hard-copy books are increasingly being replaced with software and lessons taught on computers, it is incredibly simple to alter, censor, and manipulate original texts. Having the world's children literate and able to read about the world to better understand other cultures and live together in peace is not the same thing as having the children of the world literate so they can be propagandized by manipulative curriculum content.

There are 193 <u>member states</u> in the United Nations and less than half, 86, are full-fledged democracies. The Group of 77 (G77) has grown to a coalition of 134 developing nations (69 percent of member states) and functions to advance the economic well-being of the Third World, including several Islamic nations. The Organization of Islamic Cooperation (OIC) is the largest single subset of both the G77 and the Non-Aligned Movement (NAM), originally the bloc of countries that would remain neutral during the Cold War. The G77 is the single largest voting bloc at the United Nations, where every country, democratic or undemocratic, gets one vote. So, it should surprise no one that pro-Muslim UN educational objectives supporting a globalized world are antagonistic to traditional American educational objectives emphasizing national sovereignty and separation of church and state.

Curriculum content for American educational materials must be developed *by* Americans *for* Americans with an unapologetic America-first foundation. Parents endorsing the Common Core State Standards are unwittingly endorsing the pro-Muslim, anti-American globalized educational products designed by British publishing giant <u>Pearson Education</u>. Pearson Education supplies <u>educational materials</u> to the Connect All Schools program.

When the UK froze <u>Muammar Gaddafi's</u> assets in 2011, <u>The Sov-</u>

ereign Fund of Libya had a 3.27 percent stake in Pearson. Libya was the second-largest shareholder in Pearson Education. The Council on American-Islamic Relations (CAIR), designated a terrorist organization by the United Arab Emirates, was also an investor. The anti-American, anti-Semitic, pro-Muslim Pearson educational products must not be allowed to propagandize American students.

Words matter. It is essential that Americans understand what a one-world government and global citizenship mean in the Arab world. To Qatar and the Islamic world, both terms mean re-establishing the Islamic caliphate that will rule the world under Islamic Sharia law. It is equally important for Americans to understand what a one-world government means to the secular globalist elite.

Neither the secular nor the religious version of a one-world government is the fulfillment of John Lennon's iconic song "Imagine." Both are regressive returns to feudal infrastructures consisting of the few ruling masters, the mass of ruled slaves, and an army of soldiers to enforce the pyramid. Both Islamists and secularists see the United Nations as their instrument for imposing and managing their own version of global governance.

If American parents do not become actively involved in discovering what their children are learning in school, they will be unable to oppose the radical education initiative currently transforming their children and all the other children of the world into "green" or "global citizens" prepared for the New World Order. The Humanitarian Hoax of Common Core will successfully propagandize American children to reject American citizenship and become citizens of a world dictated and governed by the United Nations. Ignorance is not bliss, and willful blindness is not a position of strength—it is submission.

HOAX 20

The Humanitarian Hoax of DACA

January 23, 2018

THE humanitarian hoax is the deliberate and deceitful tactic of presenting a destructive policy as altruistic. The humanitarian huckster
presents himself as a compassionate advocate when in fact he is the disguised enemy.

Barack Obama, humanitarian huckster-in-chief, weakened the United
States for eight years, presenting his pernicious Deferred Action for Childhood Arrivals (DACA) advocacy as altruistic when in fact it was designed
for destruction. His legacy, the leftist Democrat party and its ongoing
"resistance" movement, is the party of the humanitarian hoax attempting
to destroy the capitalist infrastructure of American democracy through
deceitful immigration reforms. This is how it works.

DACA was the 2012 product of Obama's illegal executive overreach.
The lesser-known DAPA, Deferred Action for Parents of Americans, was
Obama's 2014 expansion program that legalized illegal-alien parents
whose children had become legal American citizens through "birthright
citizenship." DACA and DAPA, both enacted by executive order, illegally
circumvented immigration laws and congressional authority with an
unconstitutional exercise of authority by the executive branch.

Birthright citizenship is a derivative of the Civil Rights Act of 1866
granting citizenship to freed slaves after the American Civil War, and of
the Fourteenth Amendment, adopted July 9, 1868, confirming the 1866
legislation. The first sentence of the Fourteenth Amendment, the Citizenship Clause, states that "All persons born or naturalized in the United
States, and subject to the jurisdiction thereof, are citizens of the United
States and of the State wherein they reside."

According to a December 28, 2017, *Breitbart* article, John Binder
reports, "The number of United States-born children who were given

birthright citizenship despite at least one of their parents being an illegal alien living in the country now outnumbers one year of all American births."

This process "anchors" illegal aliens and their families in the United States forever. There are an estimated 4.5 million "anchor babies" in the country who, according to Binder, "are able to eventually bring an unlimited number of foreign relatives to the U.S. through the process of 'chain migration.' Every two new immigrants to the U.S. bring an estimated seven foreign relatives with them."

The Citizenship Clause of the Fourteenth Amendment has been exploited to encourage anchor babies, chain migration, and "birth tourism," where pregnant foreign nationals visit the United States to deliver their babies on U.S. soil.

Expanding amnesty programs for illegal immigrants guaranteed Democrat votes, but Obama had a problem selling the idea to Congress even though Democrats had control of both houses. Illegal aliens needed a new image. No problem for Obama—his leftist image-makers went to work.

Soon, illegal aliens became undocumented aliens, then undocumented workers, then unauthorized immigrants, then undocumented immigrants, and finally, the loftiest brand of them all—Dreamers. Obama's rebranded illegal aliens were transformed into Dreamers, and protecting them was merchandised as the humanitarian imperative for America. Millennials signed on in droves, but here is the problem.

Rebranding is a marketing tool used by advertisers to sell products that don't sell. Rebranding changes the name, but it does not change the product. Dreamers are still illegal aliens. Obama needed the positive image of Dreamers to sell DACA and DAPA as altruistic programs to a compassionate American public. He needed to rebrand DACA and DAPA to disguise the underlying Democrat deceit of using Dreamers to tip Republican "red states" to Democrat "blue states." It was always about the votes.

USA Today reports that, according to the Migration Policy Institute, 3.6 million Dreamers live in the United States today—not the oft-repeated number of 800,000. "The 3.6 million estimate of undocumented immigrants brought to the U.S. before their 18th birthday comes from the Migration Policy Institute, a non-partisan, non-profit think tank that studies global immigration patterns. That is roughly a third of all undocumented immigrants in the country and does not include millions of their immediate family members who are U.S. citizens."

The Democrat narrative is that deportations of illegal aliens would be immoral and an economic calamity. The reality is that under-educated, non-working unauthorized immigrants, whether Dreamers or not, do not improve the economy, they drain it. The undisclosed underbelly of the leftist narrative is that most illegal aliens living in Republican states, if awarded amnesty, would vote Democrat and tilt red states to blue. If amnesty and bills to legalize chain migration pass, the additional Democrat votes would put several red states in play, particularly Florida, Arizona, Georgia, and North Carolina.

Michael Cutler, writing on the website *Front Page Magazine*, warned us about the consequences of DACA to national security and argued that DACA is the Immigration Trojan Horse. Cutler contended that "The Immigration Reform and Control Act of 1986 (IRCA) created a massive amnesty program that ultimately led to the greatest influx of illegal aliens in the history of our nation. It has been said that insanity is doing the same things the same way and expecting a different outcome."

So it is with DACA. Millions of illegal immigrants awarded amnesty will vote to elect a Democrat president who will open the borders and flood the country with more immigrants who will be granted voting rights and vote Democrat. This chain of events will achieve the leftist goal of destroying our constitutional republic and replacing it with socialism. The United States of America is the greatest experiment in individual freedom and upward mobility the world has ever known. Preserving our republic is the essence of President Trump's America-first policies.

President Trump issued executive orders revoking DAPA in June 2017 and ending DACA in September 2017, saying, "The legislative, not the executive, branch writes these [immigration] laws." Yet DACA continues to be discussed and marketed to a trusting public by Obama's "resistance" movement as the altruistic responsibility of compassionate American citizens.

For 241 years America has said NO to monarchies, NO to oligarchies, NO to totalitarianism, NO to authoritarianism, and NO to illegal immigration. We are a country of LEGAL immigrants, not illegal aliens. We have fought to preserve our constitutional republic with its checks and balances on power codified in our Constitution to protect our individual rights and way of life. Socialism is the great leftist scam being perpetrated on the American people and implemented through destructive leftist immigration policies.

Millennials have no idea what socialism is in practice. Socialism is most definitely not the Bernie Sanders fantasy of free stuff or the John Lennon song "Imagine" that they are being indoctrinated with. Socialism is an infantilizing political structure in which there is no private property and the government owns all means of production. Citizens are wards of the state, subject to the whims of the government. The government tells its dependent subjects what they can have and how much they can have. There is no freedom or upward mobility in socialism because there is no private ownership. There are only the ruling elite and the enslaved population who serve them. The American dream is dead in socialism.

Unrestricted immigration, particularly Dreamers and chain migration, will ultimately transform America the Beautiful into a socialist state. The American Dream will be sacrificed to DACA Dreamers. Why? The answer is that socialism is the prerequisite political infrastructure to internationalize sovereign countries in preparation for a one-world government. Globalism's one-world government is the hidden motive for leftist Democrat policies that endorse the Humanitarian Hoax of DACA and chain migration.

Socialism is deceitfully marketed as the great equalizer—the social system that will provide social justice and income equality. Socialism is the big lie of the twenty-first century because in reality socialism benefits only the elitists who rule the country. All anyone has to do is look at Cuba and Venezuela, where the rulers live like kings and the ruled suffer shortages, deprivation, and poverty.

We cannot allow DACA Dreamers to tilt America toward leftist socialism that will rob all Americans of their liberty except the elitists in power. Choosing the Dreamers' dreams over the American Dream is a lethal choice that will end our constitutional republic. But that was always the point of the Humanitarian Hoax of DACA—to kill America with "kindness."

HOAX 21

The Humanitarian Hoax of Collectivism

January 30, 2018

DECEMBER 7, 1941, the date of infamy when Japan attacked Pearl Harbor, killing 2,400 Americans and wounding 1,178. President Franklin D. Roosevelt responded decisively by addressing Congress and unambiguously seeking a formal declaration of war on Japan.

September 11, 2001, the date of infamy when nineteen mostly <u>Saudi al-Qaeda Muslims</u> living in the United States attacked New York City, killing 3,000 Americans and wounding 6,000. President George W. Bush responded ambiguously by addressing the nation and declaring a War on Terror without naming the enemy. Instead, he disarmed America by assuring the country that Islam is a religion of peace.

Roosevelt's War on Japan was far more successful than Bush's War on Terror. Why?

In 1941, Americans had not yet been attacked by political correctness, moral relativism, and historical revisionism—the three basic tenets of radical leftist liberalism that support collectivism. Americans unapologetically loved their country, their families, and their God. Roosevelt's America was still the land of the free and the home of the brave.

Individualism, the foundation of America, values freedom for individuals over collective or state control. Individualism is the infrastructure that supports our Constitution and protects our right to live freely with minimal government interference. Individualism encourages independence, adulthood, personal responsibility, and allegiance to the United States of America. Individualism and the meritocracy incentivize production and created the most powerful and freest country in the world.

In 1941, collectivism was in its nascent stages in America. Collectivism is the practice of giving a group priority over each individual in the group. Collectivism encourages dependence, perpetual childhood, government control, and allegiance to a world community without national borders or national sovereignty. Collectivism is the enemy of individualism. Collectivism is the enemy of a free and sovereign United States.

After World War II the enemies of the United States did not go quietly into the night. My December 1, 2017, article, "The Mathematics of the Culture War on America," explains how our enemies adjusted to military defeat by shifting strategies. Instead of targeting soldiers and military installations, they targeted civilians and cultural institutions in order to destroy America from within by shattering the infrastructure of American individualism—no bullets required. This is how it works.

"The Re-education of America," my August 7, 2017, article, describes the long-term information/indoctrination war targeting the entire population of children and adults. From its inception, the information war was a Culture War on America designed to eliminate patriotism, minimize family influence, and eradicate the religious authority of the church—the cultural pillars that support individualism. To win an information war it is necessary to indoctrinate and propagandize the children as early as possible and the adults as much as possible. "Birdman and the Reality Revolution—Part 1," my October 27, 2017, article, details the psychologically devastating leftist assault on reality.

The re-education of America began after World War II with a marketing campaign designed to sell collectivism to adults through the media. The effort required rebranding in order to sell it to Americans, who were culturally averse to collectivism and committed to individualism. Communism was renamed socialism and socialism was sold as globalism. Collectivism was falsely advertised as a compassionate, selfless political system that provides social justice and income equality.

Patriotism was disingenuously rebranded as nationalism and associated with Hitler's supremacism. Academia seized the opportunity to teach collectivist cultural Marxism as the preferable alternative to free-market capitalism. Television programming, films, editorialized news, all participated in the mass social-engineering effort to indoctrinate America away from its traditions of individualism and move it toward collectivism.

Every traditional American cultural norm was attacked in the media and on campus, including religious norms, sexual norms, family norms, and patriotic norms. The sixties romanticized drugs, sex, and rock and roll, culminating in Woodstock, the most visible group orgy in American history. John Fogerty, lead singer of the rock group Creedence Clearwater Revival, described the Woodstock scene at 3:30 a.m. just before the band went on stage:

"We were ready to rock out and we waited and waited and finally it was our turn . . . there were a half million people asleep. These people were out. It was sort of like a painting of a Dante scene, just bodies from hell, all intertwined and asleep, covered with mud."

Woodstock became the symbol of the collectivist counterculture. The Culture War continued for decades and escalated exponentially under Barack Obama's collectivist tenure, with the help of the Internet. The war against America continues to revile the most powerful traditional influences supporting American individualism: patriotism, family, and the church.

The Common Core initiative under collectivist-in-chief Obama institutionalized early-childhood educational indoctrination toward collectivism and advanced its spread throughout the country. *The Humanitarian Hoax of Common Core—Hoax 19* is a deceitful scheme perpetrated by collectivists to undermine individualism and bring socialism to America.

The Humanitarian Hoax of Socialism—Hoax 13 is a sinister war tactic that presents collectivism as altruistic. Globalism is the culmination of collectivism on a worldwide scale. A globalized world ruled by totalitarian global governance through the United Nations is the ultimate goal of collectivism. This matter is discussed fully in my September 20, 2017, article "Globalism: The Existential Enemy of Sovereignty, Security, and Prosperity."

Individualism, the infrastructure of independence and sovereignty, was the foundation of American social and military policy that was capable of defeating our enemies in World War II. The leftist Culture War on America spent six decades re-educating Americans toward collectivism. Collectivism, the infrastructure of dependency, subjective reality, political correctness, moral relativism, and historical revisionism, transformed our social and military policy, rendering a victory in the War on Terror impossible.

American psychiatrist Dr. Lyle Rossiter has written an extraordinary book titled *The Liberal Mind: The Psychological Causes of Political Madness*, which explores the psychodynamics of collectivism. Dr. Rossiter explains the overwhelmingly destructive pressure toward psychological regression that the "progressive" liberal agenda encourages. The political polarization of America is a consequence of this regression and is an existential threat to our ordered liberty and constitutional republic.

President Trump's initiative to make America great again is a total rejection of collectivism and a return to the individualism and objective reality that made America great. Trump's commitment to American sovereignty is an existential threat to worldwide collectivism and a one-world government.

President Trump is the leader of the effort to recommit America to individualism and national sovereignty. He is being vehemently and viciously attacked by the collectivist army arrayed against him that seeks global governance. Obama's "resistance" movement of radical leftist Democrats, establishment Republicans who support collectivism, the "progressive" educators indoctrinating our children toward collectivism, the colluding globalist mainstream media, the Hollywood glitterati "faux" socialists, and the propagandized millennial protesters are all united in their ideological collectivism. The "resistance" movement to drive President Trump from office is a collectivist campaign to drive individualism out of America—the individualism that made America undefeatable in World War II.

America is at a tipping point. We can choose individualism and make America great again, or we can choose collectivism and surrender our individual freedoms, power, and national sovereignty to global governance. The humanitarian hoax is the deliberate and deceitful tactic of presenting a destructive policy as altruistic. The Humanitarian Hoax of Collectivism promises equality and delivers subjugation.

Freedom and liberty are the products of individualism—both are destroyed by collectivism and replaced with indentured servitude to the government and allegiance to the world. President Donald Trump's effort to make America great again protects our precious freedoms, guarantees our liberty, and affirms our allegiance to a sovereign United States of America—the land of the free and the home of the brave.

HOAX 22

The Humanitarian Hoax of 'For Your Own Good'

February 18, 2018

THE humanitarian hoax is the deliberate and deceitful tactic of presenting a destructive policy as altruistic. The humanitarian huckster presents himself as a compassionate advocate when in fact he is the disguised enemy.

Professional politicians are a breed of humanitarian hucksters selling policies and products that benefit themselves rather than the American public they are entrusted to serve. Politicians are necessary in our representative government, but career politicians are not. Term limits are necessary to protect the public against abuses of power created by career politicians living insulated lives inside Washington, DC, where their self-serving deals have become normative.

Our Founding Fathers never intended service in Congress to become a career. Politicians began as citizen legislators who provided short-term patriotic service to the country. They were citizens from all walks of life, bringing a variety of perspectives to Washington in service to their constituents. What happened? LOBBYISTS.

Lobbyists spent $1.45 billion in 1998. In 2017, lobbyists spent $3.34 billion. How is that money spent? What do lobbyists expect to receive for the billions of dollars they spend? Who benefits? LOBBYISTS, CLIENTS, and POLITICIANS—with policies "for our own good," of course.

Opensecrets.org reports data on lobbying, lobbyists, and lobbying recipients. A lot of money is changing hands, and in the 2016 election season Hillary Clinton's name was at the top of the list. Lobbyists are not charities distributing to the poor; lobbyists spend billions of dollars on politicians to convince the politicians to vote in favor of whatever the lobbyist is peddling.

The problem is that what the lobbyist is selling is always beneficial to the lobbyist, the lobbyist's client, and the politician—but rarely beneficial to the public. The longer the politician remains in office, the longer he or she is tempted by the myriad of enticements offered by the lobbyist to provide favorable outcomes for the lobbyist's generous clients. Lobbying is a business, and lobbyists are extremely candid and unapologetic about their business goals.

Lobbyists are employees of special-interest groups including ideological groups, corporations, nonprofit organizations, school districts, anyone with enough money to pay to influence politicians to vote or introduce legislation favorable to themselves. Lobbyists are advocates for their clients, period. There are no ethical conflicts of interest for the lobbyist; the lobbyist's job is to influence politicians. "For our own good," of course.

Defenders of lobbying argue that it is a free-speech issue. Why shouldn't individuals be able to approach public officials and try to persuade them to vote in their favor? So, is lobbying free speech or is it bribery? Good question.

James Madison worried about special interests, which in the eighteenth century were called factions. Whatever they were called, it became abundantly clear that lobbying was lucrative, highly effective, and had a staggering potential for corrupting politicians. By the early twentieth century, Herbert Hoover complained about the "locust swarm of lobbyists" filling the halls of Congress. The debate over lobbying as free speech and lobbying as bribery escalated.

Eventually the ethics of lobbying were litigated as a free-speech issue. The 1953 Supreme Court case *Rumely v. United States* settled the matter by protecting lobbying as free speech. The predictable result was that the lobbying industry increased exponentially.

Lobbyists who used to spend their money on politicians only after elections began spending before elections. Vast sums of money are now contributed directly and indirectly on behalf of special-interest clients to get preferred politicians re-elected. This marriage of lobbyists to career politicians has empowered the Washington swamp that must be drained.

The more money spent on election campaigns, the more money required to compete. A House seat that cost $86,000 in 1976 cost $1.3 million in 2006. Political Action Committees (PACs) have existed since 1944, but Super PACs are a result of *Speechnow v. FEC* in 2010. The creation of Super Pacs altered the relationship between money and politics in the United States. The impact is explained in a *DifferenceBetween.net* article, "Difference Between PAC and Super PAC":

> While PACs had and have some restrictions on the amount of money they can receive from donors (be they private citizens, corporations, or other political action committees), Super PACs are allowed to receive unlimited donations (from corporations, individuals, financial institutions, labor unions, trade associations, etc.) to use for their purposes, but they cannot directly donate money to candidates and parties.

> The shift from PACs to Super PACs—even though the original Political Action Committees still exist—has allowed private organizations to spend unlimited funds to subject opposing candidates to attacks and to advocate for the election of their chosen candidate.

Why is so much money being spent by special-interest groups to get preferred candidates elected? Lobbying is a business transaction. If you want to know the motive, look at the result and follow the money. As of October 2016, sixty members of the U.S. Senate had held elected office for more than twenty years and thirty-six had held office for more than thirty years. Politicians who come into office with a modest net worth are paid $175,000 in salary and leave office as millionaires. How does that happen? LOBBYISTS.

The Ballotpedia Personal Gain Index is a stunning two-part study examining the extent of U.S. congressional personal gain during tenure. The findings are nonpartisan, and they are disturbing. For the first time in American history, the majority of elected officials are millionaires at the same time that the majority of Americans are living from paycheck to paycheck. No wonder then–Democrat Minority Leader of the House Nancy Pelosi said a $1,000 tax rebate is crumbs—for her it is.

Presidential term limits were ratified in 1951 with the Twenty-Second Amendment: "No person shall be elected to the office of President more than twice." Presidents are limited to two terms; why not all of Congress as well? And while we are at it, why not end the self-serving lifetime pensions members of Congress awarded themselves, even for one-term representatives and senators, and also insist that Congress live by the same laws they created for the rest of us "for our own good."

A May 18, 2015, *Zero Hedge* article, "79 Members of Congress Have Been in Office for at least 20 Years," summarized the issue:

No matter which political party you prefer, this should greatly disturb you. Our founders certainly never intended for a permanent class of elitists to rule over us. But that is what we have. We are supposed to have a government of the people, by the people, and for the people. Instead we have a government of the elite, by the elite, and for the elite. Most people do not realize this, but today most members of Congress are actually millionaires. The disconnect between members of Congress and average Americans has never been greater than it is right now, and I think that is a very troubling sign for the future of this nation. *So is there a solution to this problem?*

The answer to the question is Yes.

Lobbying is a for-profit business. For-profit businesses expect returns on their investments, and lobbyists invest in politicians. Term limits will help limit the obscene pay-to-play influence peddling that has become normative in American politics.

On January 3, 2017, Senator Ted Cruz (R-Texas) and Rep. Ron DeSantis (R-Fla.) proposed an <u>amendment</u> to the U.S. Constitution to impose term limits on members of Congress. The amendment would limit senators to two six-year terms and members of the House of Representatives to three two-year terms. Let's hope they are successful in this effort.

Term limits will not stop all the graft and influence peddling in American politics, but making a career of graft and influence peddling will no longer be possible. Political humanitarian hucksters pretending their self-serving deals benefit the public must no longer be permitted to kill America with "kindness"—for our own good, of course.

HOAX 23

The Humanitarian Hoax of Multiple Realities

February 23, 2018

THE humanitarian hoax is the deliberate and deceitful tactic of presenting a destructive policy as altruistic. The humanitarian huckster presents himself as a compassionate advocate when in fact he is the disguised enemy.

The ideological strivings of our Founding Fathers were rooted in freedom, liberty, limited government, and the separation of church and state. They sought to create a more perfect union—a society of individuals cooperating by mutual consent. Psychiatrist Lyle Rossiter's stunning book *The Liberal Mind: The Psychological Causes of Political Madness* details America's extraordinary achievement of ordered liberty, how its infrastructure complements the nature of man, and how the collectivist liberal narrative is pathologically antithetical to ordered liberty.

The ideological moorings of ordered liberty require consensus on what is real. This is no small matter. Language is based on consensus of what is real. Laws are based on consensus of what is real. Without agreement on what is real, there is no societal order, only chaos.

Senator Patrick Moynihan famously remarked, "Everyone is entitled to his own opinion but not his own facts." Well said. Opinions are based on the subjective reality of feelings; facts are based on the objective reality of actuality. Feelings are not facts.

This is worth repeating. Objective reality is defined by facts and subjective reality is defined by feelings. The leftist Culture War on America is attacking the ideological strivings and ideological moorings of ordered liberty by attacking its most basic requirement—consensus on what is real. My article "Birdman and the Reality Revolution" exposes the leftist attack strategy seeking to replace factual, objective reality with subjective multiple realities based on feelings. This is how it works.

Tom, a thirty-year-old, 6'2" white male, FEELS like a fifty-year-old, 5' Asian woman named Tuyen. Shall society accept Tom's self-identification as Tuyen? Existing laws in society are based on a consensus of what is real. Conservatives insist that Tom is a thirty-year-old, 6'2" white male no matter how Tom feels. The left demands that society accept Tom as the fifty-year-old, 5' Asian woman Tuyen—Tom *is* Tuyen because Tom *feels* as if he is Tuyen.

The Left is demanding that Tom's feelings be accepted as fact. What if Tom self-identifies as George Soros? Would über-leftist George Soros accept Tom's self-identification and allow Tom to live as the actual George Soros? I think not. What is instantly apparent is that the leftist demand for society to accept self-identification as fact has serious limitations and convenient self-serving exclusions.

The hypocrisy of the self-serving exclusions is obvious. If Tom can be Tuyen in a ladies' bathroom, why can't Tom be George Soros at the bank?

If self-identifying is not universally applicable, why is the Left so insistent that it become normative? If you want to know the motive, look at the result.

The goal of the leftist campaign to have feelings accepted as facts is the Humanitarian Hoax of Multiple Realities, designed to disrupt our ordered liberty. As described in my article "The Mathematics of the Culture War on America," if the Left can shatter the reality-based foundation of language and laws, then it has succeeded in shattering our ordered liberty and the morality that supports it. The laws that govern Western society by mutual consent reflect a reality-based consensus on what is right and what is wrong. In America it is both illegal and morally wrong to impersonate another human being. That is because in our ordered society each individual owns his selfness and the rights to his own property.

Our Founding Fathers dreamed a society consistent with psychiatrist Lyle Rossiter's notion of the innate bipolar nature of man—his individualism and his need for mutual consent. Dr. Rossiter's theory on the nature of man, discussed in Hoax 21, affirms that unless a man is living on a desert island by himself, his survival requires mutual consent for living with others on the island. So it is in modern society. Harmonious living requires both individualism and mutual consent. The most basic requirement for both is ownership of one's self and one's property.

Collectivism denies ownership of one's self and one's property and is, therefore, inconsistent with the fundamental nature of man. Collectivism awards all ownership to the state. The collectivism being sold to America by humanitarian hucksters avoids this inconvenient truth. It disingenuously promises egalitarian social justice and income equality, but without individualism and mutual consent there are only masters and slaves.

The secret that lies beneath every humanitarian hoax is that the elite always take care of the elite. This is how it works.

Imagine the leftist collective dream as reality. Does anyone actually think that George Soros, Bill Gates, Mark Zuckerberg, Eric Schmidt, the Rockefellers, the Kennedys, Hillary Clinton, Nancy Pelosi, Barack Obama, Jeff Bezos et al. plan to live an egalitarian life? History has taught us that leftist promises of social justice and income equality through collectivism are humanitarian hoaxes. Cuba and Venezuela are cautionary tales. Their citizens are conned into surrendering their individual freedoms to the "revolution," whose leaders soon become the ruling elite and exploit the people like slaves.

There is no egalitarianism in collectivism. The elite always take care of the elite.

Historically, the world's populations were divided into rulers and ruled until our Founding Fathers sought to create a more perfect union of individualism and mutual consent. It was an extraordinary experiment in individual freedom that produced a thriving middle class, upward mobility, and the freest, most powerful nation on Earth. The leftist globalist elite selling collectivism are freedom's enemy.

The leftist campaign to destroy Western consensus on what is real is a deliberate strategy to collapse the language and laws of our ordered liberty and produce chaos. Why?

Chaos provides the lawlessness necessary to federalize the police and socialize the country. Socialism, with its complete government control, is necessary to internationalize America into a global community ruled by—you guessed it—the globalist elite.

The globalist dream of a one-world government cannot come true without first destroying America's consensus on what is real. English aristocrat Lord Bertrand Russell, member of the globalist political elite, detailed the shameless strategy in his shocking 1952 classic, *The Impact of Science on Society*:

> Education should aim at destroying free will so that pupils thus schooled, will be incapable throughout the rest of their lives of thinking or acting otherwise than as their schoolmasters would have wished. . . . Influences of the home are obstructive; and in order to condition students, verses set to music and repeatedly intoned are very effective. . . . It is for a future scientist to make these maxims precise and to discover exactly how much it costs per head to make children believe that snow is black. When the technique has been perfected, every government that has been in charge of education for more than one generation will be able to control its subjects securely without the need of armies or policemen.

The first step in the sinister effort to make people believe that snow is black is the acceptance of multiple realities—the acceptance as real that Tom is really Tuyen. Multiple opinions, multiple experiences, and multiple perspectives can be debated in a free society. But without an accurate reference to test reality, there is only madness, chaos, and disorder. America is split between those still insisting upon a standard of objective reality and those demanding subjective reality. Freedom and ordered liberty require the infrastructure of objective reality.

If the leftist Humanitarian Hoax of Multiple Realities is successful in America, we will be reduced to a feudal society of masters and slaves. The globalist elite's dream of a New World Order can only become a reality if America surrenders its commitment to objective reality. To remain free, we must insist that Tom is still a thirty-year-old, 6'2" white male, no matter how Tom feels.

The Humanitarian Hoax of Globalism

April 8, 2018

THE humanitarian hoax is the deliberate and deceitful tactic of pre-senting a destructive policy as altruistic. The humanitarian huckster presents himself as a compassionate advocate when in fact he is the dis-guised enemy.

The Humanitarian Hoax of Globalism requires clarification. Globalism is the internationalizing of sovereign nations into a federated one-world government ruled by the globalist elite. Globalism is internationalized collectivism.

Globalism is NOT to be confused with global trade. Global trade is the import and export of goods and services by sovereign nations across international boundaries.

Why is understanding the distinction between globalism and global trade so important? Because the globalist humanitarian hucksters are busy conning the American public with promises of cheaper goods through global trade deals in order to disguise their sinister underlying motive of collapsing the American economy. Globalism requires a collapsed Amer-ica in order to internationalize our country into the globalist New World Order that the humanitarian hucksters intend to rule.

The Humanitarian Hoax of Globalism is based on <u>asymmetric infor-mation</u>—Joseph Stiglitz's theory of economics in which one party to an economic transaction possesses greater material knowledge than the other party. The globalist humanitarian huckster relies on asymmetric information to sell global collectivism to an unsuspecting public.

<u>Wikipedia explains</u> the differences between two asymmetric infor-mation models. "In adverse selection models, the ignorant party lacks information while negotiating an agreed understanding of or contract to the transaction, whereas in moral hazard [models] the ignorant party

lacks information about performance of the agreed-upon transaction or lacks ability to retaliate for a breach of the agreement."

Globalism exemplifies both the <u>adverse selection</u> model and the moral hazard model. This is how it works.

Collectivism, whether it is socialism, communism, Islamism, or globalism, denies freedom of speech and the ownership of personal property. In theory, collectivism means giving a group itself priority over the individuals who form the group. In practice, however, collectivism awards all the power and privilege to the ruling elite. This is discussed in my May 18, 2017, article <u>Connecting the Dots: Islamism . . . Socialism . . . Globalism</u>. Equality simply cannot exist in collectivism because of its asymmetric power structure.

A free society requires free speech and the ownership of personal property—both are fundamental to American life and are rights guaranteed by our Constitution. The Culture War on America is an asymmetric information war against both freedom of speech and ownership of personal property. Collectivism as an economic theory awards control of both production and distribution to the group. Collectivism as a political reality enslaves the population and establishes a master/slave infrastructure, since collectivism is the absence of individual freedom. The ruling elite have absolute power over production and distribution with centralized social and economic control over the group. The globalist elite know this and they are duping the American public with asymmetric information.

Asymmetric information succeeds in an environment of controlled, curated, censored information. The current concentration of information by mainstream media giants of television and the Internet is a system of asymmetric information that is indoctrinating the public toward collectivism by eliminating free speech in the public square.

So, why is it necessary to eliminate free speech and private property in collectivism? Because without these two elements there is no upward mobility and no middle class. There is only the ruling class and those who serve them.

America's thriving middle class is a direct impediment to collectivism. People often think it is big businesses that support jobs in America, but in fact it is small businesses that employ the vast majority of workers. Trade deals unfavorable to American businesses drive jobs offshore, making the unemployment rate go up and more people dependent on the government. Bill Clinton's North American Free Trade Agreement (NAFTA), Obama's Trans-Pacific Partnership (TPP), and Obama's excessive rules and regulations are all job killers designed to drive businesses out of America. Why?

Besides the obvious national security threat of driving essential businesses offshore, the small-business closures destroy the middle class, leaving the top and bottom of the social pyramid intact—exactly what the globalists need to socialize and then internationalize America.

The socioeconomic infrastructure of collectivism is cradle-to-grave dependence upon the power of a centralized government. Collectivism is a return to the feudal pyramid of the ruling class, their enforcers, and the general public. There is no social justice or economic equality in collectivism. There is only childish dependency upon the ruling elite.

Wars are won and lost on the basis of information. The Culture War on America is an asymmetric information war being waged by globalists against American sovereignty. These humanitarian hucksters are using asymmetric information to persuade Americans that life in their globalist collective will be different from life in socialist Cuba, socialist Venezuela, communist Russia, or Islamist Iran. It won't be. Collectivism by any other name is still collectivism.

BUYER BEWARE! Asymmetric information is conning you. Cheap goods are very expensive. They are destroying manufacturing jobs, businesses, and the middle class in America. Cheap goods will eventually cost you your freedom.

The hysteria over President Trump's tariffs is pure political theater and deliberate asymmetric information deceitfully circulated by the globalists in their war on American sovereignty. Globalist humanitarian hucksters are America's mortal enemies, using both the adverse selection model and the moral hazard model of asymmetric information to destroy America from within. The Humanitarian Hoax of Globalism is a power grab by the globalist political elite designed to rob you of your freedom. Do not let them!

HOAX 25

The Humanitarian Hoax of the Federal Reserve System

April 24, 2018

THE humanitarian hoax is the deliberate and deceitful tactic of presenting a destructive policy as altruistic. The humanitarian huckster presents himself as a compassionate advocate when in fact he is the disguised enemy.

Most Americans do not realize that the Federal Reserve is NOT constitutionally part of the government of the United States—and is not even a bank! It is a system. International banker Marilyn Barnewall explains that the <u>Federal Reserve System</u> is a privately held corporation owned by bankers and it is most definitely not part of our federal government.

The Federal Reserve Act that created the Federal Reserve System (the Fed) was passed by Congress on December 22, 1913, and signed into law by President Woodrow Wilson the next day. In Barnewall's July 8, 2014, *NewsWithViews* article, "What is the Federal Reserve," she describes the dramatic effects of its passage:

> <u>The Act</u> transferred the right to print currency from the United States Congress to an independent and privately-owned entity calling itself a bank but which is not a bank—changing the Constitution, which cannot be changed without amending it. The Fed is somewhat federal in form, but is very privately owned and operated. President Wilson lived to regret signing the Federal Reserve Act and on his deathbed is quoted as saying:

"I am a most unhappy man. I have unwittingly ruined my country. A great industrial nation is controlled by its system of credit. Our system of credit is concentrated. The growth of the nation, therefore, and all our activities are in the hands of a few men."

So, who are these men and why was President Wilson so remorseful about signing the Federal Reserve Act? And why is the Federal Reserve

System so disingenuously named that the average citizen assumes it is a banking institution that is part of the federal government?

Sometimes it is necessary to look back in order to understand the present and anticipate the future.

Banking in the world has a long history that began with merchant trading. People living in small, isolated agricultural communities exchanged pigs for goats or wheat for milk. Personal bartering among members of the community was enough to satisfy their survival needs—there was no need for currency or banking. As populations grew and trade between communities began, currency was introduced to make commerce more efficient. Currency was assigned a monetary value, and buying and selling with money replaced bartering as the preferred form of commerce.

Determining the value of currency and the relative value of the goats, pigs, wheat, and milk being bought and sold was the beginning of banking. Currency use requires that people trust the banknotes and coins to represent an actual and real valued commodity. Gold was chosen as the standard that backed the currency, and banks became repositories for both. Today we use fiat currency—money without gold backing—as the medium of exchange and it is the taxpayers' labor that backs it.

Think about it. As long as the federal government can tax its citizen labor force and confiscate its money to pay its debts, it is the taxpayers who are actually backing the currency. We the people are the twenty-first-century gold standard!

Banking is and always has been a for-profit business, and the Federal Reserve Bank is no exception.

The United States had two central banks prior to 1913—both non-governmental entities. The First Bank of the United States (1791–1811) was chartered by the First Congress in 1790 and modeled after the Bank of England. Thomas Jefferson opposed the First Bank as an engine for speculation, financial manipulation, and corruption. When its twenty-year charter expired, it was not renewed.

Its successor bank, the Second Bank of the United States (1816–1836) was also a private bank with public duties, and Andrew Jackson, like Thomas Jefferson, opposed the Second Bank as an engine of corruption. Jackson, who became president in 1828, was unable to get the bank dissolved but refused to renew its charter. President Jackson required all federal land payments to be made in gold or silver, which produced the <u>Panic of 1837</u> when buyers were unable to come up with the gold and silver required. Runs on the banks, bank failures, and economic depression followed. The panic unleashed riots and domestic unrest, ultimately resulting in more state policing and more professional police forces.

The depression lasted five years, until 1842, when the American economy began to rebound. In 1848 the California gold rush boosted the economy and by 1850 the U.S. economy was booming again. Still, a national system was required to facilitate banking between regions and avert another financial crisis. When President Wilson signed the 1913 Federal Reserve Act, the current central banking system of the United States was created. Twelve U.S. cities were chosen as locations for one of twelve Federal Reserve District Banks. This is how it happened.

A secret gathering took place on <u>Jekyll Island</u> in November 1910 that laid the foundation for the Federal Reserve System in the United States. In attendance were:

- <u>Senator Nelson W. Aldrich</u>, chair of the U.S. Senate Finance Committee and chair of the National Monetary Commission, the study group commissioned by the Aldrich-Vreeland Act of 1908 after the Panic of 1907
- Abram Piatt Andrew, assistant secretary of the U.S. Treasury and special assistant to the National Monetary Commission
- Charles D. Norton, president of the First National Bank of New York, a bank dominated by American financier J. P. Morgan

Frank Vanderlip, president of National City Bank

- Henry P. Davison, senior partner at banking firm J. P. Morgan & Co.
- Benjamin Strong, representing J. P. Morgan
- Paul Warburg, partner at Kuhn, Loeb & Co., an investment bank founded in 1867 by Abraham Kuhn and his brother-in-law Solomon Loeb

The clandestine 1910 Jekyll Island meeting produced <u>draft legislation</u> for the creation of the U.S. central bank, and the Aldrich Plan was incorporated into the 1913 Federal Reserve Act.

Why is the <u>Jekyll Island</u> history so important? Why was the meeting so clandestine? Because the secret meeting at Jekyll Island failed to disclose its connections to the Bank of England.

J. P. Morgan & Co., and Kuhn, Loeb & Co. are the New York representatives of the Rothschilds' Bank of England, which means that the American Federal Reserve system is under the control of the Bank of England. The howling anti-Semitic memes that Jews control banking is deliberate and misleading. The Federal Reserve Cartel, comprising the Rothschild (Jewish), Rockefeller (Baptist), and Morgan (Episcopalian) families, are globalist, multireligious, and nondenominational.

The Humanitarian Hoax of the Federal Reserve System is evident in its deliberately deceptive name. There is an enormous public misconception that the Federal Reserve System exists to protect and serve America. It does not. The Fed is a for-profit corporation of globalist world bankers seeking to internationalize the world for their own power and profit. The Fed is NOT an advocate of American sovereignty or America-first policies. The Fed is not altruistic—it is an economic humanitarian hoax.

President Donald Trump is an American patriot committed to American sovereignty and is, therefore, an existential enemy of the Fed. So is International Banking Consultant Marilyn Barnewall. In a fascinating February 19, 2012 interview appearing in *The Daily Bell*, "Marilyn Mac-Gruder Barnewall on the Problems of Central Bank 'Debt Capitalism' and the Promise of US-Style State Banking," she offers a stunning solution.

Barnewall supports the establishment of a bank owned by each state as a means of replacing and eliminating the Federal Reserve System. State banks put the power of the American economy back in the hands of the people and returns our economic engine to growth rather than debt. It is called credit-driven banking.

Daily Bell: What is "credit-driven private banking"?

Marilyn MacGruder Barnewall: There are two types of private banking, and it is different than what you might think. Traditionally, private banking is and always has been the management of other people's money or assets. The one I created was a *credit-driven* form of private banking.

Basically, credit-driven private banking is done in a way that strengthens and broadens the middle class. During my time as a bank advisor, I basically created a concept of banking that enabled lenders to make business purpose loans based on personal assets and cash flow. So a business-purpose loan, a commercial loan, depends for repayment on the purpose of the loan. If the purpose of the loan is to make cars, then the source of repayment comes from the sale of those cars, the dealers or the public. In other words, individuals can't do that because they aren't in the business of selling cars or building condominiums. It's recognizing all the potential available.

The globalist elite use our Federal Reserve System to manipulate world economies through their banking malfeasance. By raising interest rates, lowering interest rates, and printing money, they control the availability of funds to their member banks, which make loans to individuals and businesses. World banking is based on the U.S. dollar, so Fed decisions in America affect inflation, employment, and production worldwide.

Both raising and lowering interest rates have political consequences.

When the Fed raises interest rates in America, the interest rates go up on consumer credit cards, car loans, and mortgages, making it harder for American consumers to get credit. This causes the U.S. economy to shrink in the private sector. Raising interest rates makes business loans more expensive, increases unemployment, and degrades productivity, which shrinks the U.S. economy in the business sector. Most threatening is that raising interest rates increases the U.S. national debt, increasing the difficulty of servicing the debt and repaying the loans.

Conversely, the Fed can lower interest rates, which floods the market with cheap money to artificially stimulate the economy.

The power of the Federal Reserve System to collapse the American economy is held by a private corporation of international globalist bankers whose long-range political goals are to internationalize the world and establish a New World Order of one-world government—ruled, of course, by themselves.

Individuals who cannot repay their debts go bankrupt, and so do countries.

The existential threat to American sovereignty is GLOBALISM. Globalism's goal is a one-world government with one bank, one police force, one army, one flag, one language, one educational curriculum, one currency, one world with only one ruling class—the globalist elite. Make no mistake: globalism is a catastrophic return to a master/slave feudal infrastructure.

Globalism is a nondenominational power grab by the globalist elite using anti-Semitism as a strategic sideshow. Sideshows are diverting incidents or issues designed to distract attention away from bigger issues.

The Fed is manipulating world economies while its globalist armies have boots on the ground indoctrinating America to accept collectivism and one-world government via the mainstream media, the educational system, Obama's "resistance" movement, and an unremitting assault on American traditional values.

If the Humanitarian Hoax of the Federal Reserve System continues, our republic and the constitutional freedoms our forefathers created will cease to exist. The globalist New World Order will be imposed by the ruling class of globalist elite who coordinate the world economic systems through international banking systems that include planned failures.

The sycophants who support the globalist elite power grab and the anti-Semitic memes that reinforce it are the same useful idiots marched toward slavery in Goethe's famous quote: "None are more hopelessly enslaved than those who falsely believe they are free as they are marched into servitude."

The Humanitarian Hoax of the Muslim Brotherhood

May 6, 2018

THE humanitarian hoax is the deliberate and deceitful tactic of presenting a destructive policy as altruistic. The humanitarian huckster presents himself as a compassionate advocate when in fact he is the disguised enemy.

Ikhwan, Arabic for Muslim Brotherhood (MB), is an organizational humanitarian hoax being perpetrated on the American people to establish Islam in America. Islam in America would not be problematic if it were a religion, like Christianity, Judaism, or Buddhism—but it isn't. Islam is a comprehensive sociopolitical, military, all-inclusive way of life with its own governing supremacist religious Sharia laws that are antithetical to Western cultural norms and America's governing secular constitutional laws.

The Muslim Brotherhood is an enemy of the United States.

The goal of Islam is to convert the world to Islam. The purpose of the Muslim Brotherhood in America is SETTLEMENT, not assimilation. Settlement is the incremental process of making Islam familiar, acceptable, and normative, ultimately replacing secular American constitutional law with supremacist religious Islamic Sharia law.

The treasonous conspiracy of the Muslim Brotherhood and its offshoot organizations is fully documented in its 1991 mission statement, _An Explanatory Memorandum: On the General Strategic Goal for the Group in North America (Explanatory Memorandum)_, which clearly states its political goal and the tactical requirement of organizational acceptance. The Muslim Brotherhood understood that America is structured by organizations, so the MB has spawned hundreds of offspring organizations with the same subversive settlement goal and the same deceitful operating principles.

The *Explanatory Memorandum* explicitly states:

> The process of settlement is a "Civilization-Jihadist Process" with all the word means. The Ikhwan [Muslim Brotherhood] must understand that their work in America is a kind of grand jihad in eliminating and destroying the Western civilization from within and "sabotaging" its miserable house by their hands and the hands of the believers so that it is eliminated and God's religion is made victorious over all other religions.

The Muslim Brotherhood's menacing mission statement is crystal clear: Islam intends to subjugate (settle) host populations in North America and replace host religions and cultures with supremacist Islam and Islamic Sharia law. So, where is the hoax?

The *Explanatory Memorandum* was a secret strategic document for internal use only and certainly not intended for public consumption by its targeted society—the United States of America. The Memorandum describes in chilling detail the overarching deceit required to present the Muslim Brotherhood and every one of its hundreds of offshoots as peaceful organizations when their stated objective is to destroy Western civilization and replace it with Islam. The MB disguises itself as a compassionate advocate for peace and Muslim tolerance when in fact it is America's existential enemy. The Muslim Brotherhood is a dangerous humanitarian hoax.

In the 1970s, American radical leftist Saul Alinsky instructed his followers to cut their hair, blend in, and destroy the American capitalist system from within. So did the Muslim Brotherhood. The Arabic word for this deception is taqiyya—lying in the service of Islam. There is no equivalent word in English, only the equivalent deceit. Like Alinsky's guidebook for leftists *Rules for Radicals*, the Muslim Brotherhood's *Explanatory Memorandum* details the seditious steps necessary to overthrow the American government from within by blending in, keeping a low profile, and becoming part of the organizational/political infrastructure.

Former Turkish radical Muslim Isik Abla describes how she was taught to believe that as a Muslim, she had a responsibility to use every way to Islamize the world. Now an international Christian evangelist, Abla warns America of the Muslim Brotherhood's treasonous conspiracy to Islamize America. She describes eight deceptive types of Islamic jihad currently being waged against the West in Islam's campaign to rule the world under Sharia law:

- Population jihad—championing open borders and mass migration of Muslims into Western countries
- Media jihad—buying media channels and directing content to promote the deceit that Islam is a religion of peace
- Education jihad—buying university chairs and directing curriculum content to promote the deceit that Islam is a religion of peace
- Economic jihad—investing in Western banks, properties, businesses, and stocks in order to buy cultural influence promoting the deceit that Islam is a religion of peace
- Physical jihad—killing nonbelievers until everyone left is either Muslim or recites the Muslim declaration of faith
- Legal jihad—bringing Sharia tribunals, councils, and courts to the West
- Humanitarian jihad—Muslim "humanitarian" organizations requiring registration as a Muslim in order to receive humanitarian aid and then further requiring prayer meetings and enrollment in Muslim schools in order to continue receiving humanitarian aid
- Political jihad—Muslim politicians in office downplaying the role of Islam in violence and terror

The Muslim Brotherhood, a Sunni Islamist organization founded in Egypt in 1928, has been declared a terrorist group by Egypt, Saudi Arabia, Russia, Kazakhstan, and the United Arab Emirates. Why not by the United States?

The biggest criticism after 9/11 was that the security services failed to connect the dots. In 2001, President George W. Bush disingenuously tried to separate Islam from terrorism by announcing that Islam is a religion of peace. Fifteen of the nineteen 9/11 hijackers were Saudi, yet Bush allowed Saudi nationals to fly back to Saudi Arabia when no other airplanes were allowed to fly. WHY?

America has a complex connection to Saudi Arabia and so does the Muslim Brotherhood. Saudi Arabian oil was first discovered in commercial quantities by Americans in Dhahran, Saudi Arabia, in 1938. The United States went into business with Saudi Arabia, and in 1943 the Arabian American Oil Company (ARAMCO) was formed. Oil revenues became the primary source of wealth for Saudi Arabia, replacing its tourist income derived from pilgrimages to Mecca. Oil made Saudi Arabia rich—very rich.

America needed a guaranteed source of oil and Saudi Arabia needed its oil wells protected, so a deal was made.

The Muslim Brotherhood arrived in Saudi Arabia in the 1950s, with the thousands of Egyptian teachers recruited to work in Saudi Arabia's new public schools. The Egyptian teachers who supported the Muslim Brotherhood began organizing themselves into branches in the kingdom. The Saudis refused to allow the Brotherhood to use religion for political purposes, knowing it posed a threat to the Saudi royal family.

A deal was reached and the Brotherhood was free to export its expansionist political tactics outside Saudi Arabia, but prohibited from using them inside the kingdom. This restrictive arrangement preserved the traditional structure of the ruling monarchy controlling foreign policy and politics, and the religious establishment controlling culture and religious affairs.

In 2011, the Muslim Brotherhood celebrated the election of Mohammad Morsi in Egypt and stunned the Saudis by openly supporting uprisings in other Arab countries. In March 2014, Saudi Arabia designated the Muslim Brotherhood a terrorist organization.

The discovery of the Muslim Brotherhood's *Explanatory Memorandum* in a hidden sub-basement of the Virginia home of Ismael Elbarasse in 2004 was shocking. Elbarasse, a member of the Muslim Brotherhood's Palestine Committee, was a founder of the Dar Al-Hijrah mosque in Falls Church, Virginia. The *Explanatory Memorandum* should have been enough to declare the Muslim Brotherhood and every one of its offshoots in America terrorist organizations—including the Council on American-Islamic Relations (CAIR), the Islamic Circle of North America (ICNA), the Islamic Society of North America (ISNA), and the Muslim Student Association (MSA)—but that did not happen. WHY NOT?

Pro-oil president George W. Bush protected the Muslim Brotherhood throughout his presidency by repeating the deceit that Islam is a religion of peace. Even after 2004, when the discovery of the Muslim Brotherhood's *Explanatory Memorandum* left no doubt that Islamists intended to settle America and replace the U.S. Constitution with religious Sharia law, Bush protected the Brotherhood at the expense of America's security.

Pro-Muslim president Barack Obama went much further by embracing the Muslim Brotherhood in America and seeding the government with seditious MB operatives. Together, Obama and the Brotherhood, along with CAIR, conspired to prevent any mention in the media of Islam, jihadis, or the stated political goals of Islam and the Muslim Brotherhood to conduct civilization jihad and destroy America from within. Obama and the Brotherhood weaponized accusations of "Islamophobia" and effectively restricted free speech in America.

Pro-Muslim huckster-in-chief Obama successfully conned America into believing that the Muslim Brotherhood is a peaceful, moderate voice of Islam. Americans were so enamored with Obama that they actually believed his subversive lies. Terrorism expert Rachel Ehrenfeld has written a comprehensive article supporting the argument for President Trump to classify the Muslim Brotherhood as a terrorist organization. Dissident Egyptian author and political analyst Cynthia Farahat, a Fellow at the Middle East Forum, has written an exposé about current Islamists with ties to terrorism lobbying Congress.

Islam's victims, experts, dissidents, and apostates have connected the dots and are warning America that it is necessary to equate terrorism with treason. The attack on 9/11 was the beginning, not the end, of Islamic jihad against America. The Muslim Brotherhood and every one of its vile offshoots are terrorist organizations that should be designated as such. Every member of Congress should be required to read the Muslim Brotherhood's *Explanatory Memorandum*, which clearly states the purpose of the MB in America—to destroy America from within and settle it under supremacist Islamic Sharia law. After reading the *Explanatory Memorandum*, any member of Congress who refuses to designate the Muslim Brotherhood as a terrorist organization is either too corrupt or too indoctrinated to hold office. Terrorism is treason. It is that simple.

The Humanitarian Hoax of the Muslim Brotherhood cannot be allowed to continue in the United States. A March 21, 2018, Reuters article, "Saudi Arabia Purges Muslim Brotherhood Influence from Schools," reported that Saudi crown prince Mohammed bin Salman was revamping the Saudi educational curriculum to eradicate any trace of the Muslim Brotherhood.

It is time for the United States to reverse Obama's Muslim Brotherhood infestation and follow the Saudi prince's lead, to eradicate the Muslim Brotherhood from America. Let's begin by removing Obama's pro-Muslim training manuals from all security and law enforcement training.

Former FBI special agent John Guandolo publishes an online magazine, *Understanding the Threat* (UTT). In the August 28, 2017, edition Guandolo answers the question, "How can US Leaders NOT Know About Islam?"

> In 2011, there was a directed purge of all training materials inside the Department of Justice, FBI, DHS, and the military after known Muslim Brotherhood groups the Islamic Society of North America (ISNA), the Muslim Public Affairs Council (MPAC), and Hamas doing business as the Council on American Islamic Relations (CAIR) complained to the White House about "offensive" materials being included in government training discussing Islam. FBI Director Mueller, DHS Secretary Napolitano and Chairman of the Joint Chiefs General Martin Dempsey (US Army) all ordered the "offensive" materials purged.

> The MB controls the narrative by controlling the information our national security professionals receive as it relates to "terrorism" and related matters. Inside the government, there is no training which provides employees of the State Department, FBI, CIA, DHS, DIA, National Security staffs, Pentagon, military commands, or other key components of the government factual information about Sharia (Islamic Law) and its role in this war. Nor is there substantive training related to the massive jihadi network in the United States, primarily led by the Muslim Brotherhood.

> The primary Islamic advisors regarding the Islamic threat inside the White House, State Department, CIA, FBI, DHS, national security staffs, and others are Muslim Brotherhood (MB) operatives or Muslims ideologically aligned with the MB.

> The factual basis for understanding the enemy threat doctrine—Sharia—is nowhere to be found in the US government, and so the very people charged with protecting American citizens remain ignorant of the threat of Islam.

To expunge Obama's treasonous stain on America, we must remove the subversive Muslim Brotherhood and its disinformation personnel and materials from the government. We cannot allow Obama and the Humanitarian Hoax of the Muslim Brotherhood to succeed in its treasonous campaign to settle America and make America Muslim.

HOAX 27

The Humanitarian Hoax of 'Convenient' Google Chromebook Education

June 11, 2018

THE humanitarian hoax is the deliberate and deceitful tactic of presenting a destructive policy as altruistic. The humanitarian huckster presents himself as a compassionate advocate when in fact he is the disguised enemy.

Convenience is one of the highest priorities in twenty-first-century life. Electronic devices that communicate with each other are marketed with the flattering descriptor of "smart" devices. Futuristic smart homes feature everything smart—appliances, lighting, heating, air-conditioning, TVs, computers, entertainment audio and video systems, security, and camera systems that can communicate with each other and be operated remotely from any location in the world via phone or Internet.

So, how smart is it to have a *smart home*? That depends upon how much you value your privacy and how smart you think it is to allow your metadata to be collected and possibly sold to a third party. Metadata is defined as data about data—it is not the actual data. The risk to consumers is that the metadata becomes more important than the data itself. If your metadata is tracking your online purchasing, it is also creating a profile of your buying habits and movements including the device you are using, your location, and time of day. Just in case you're wondering whether or not the convenient devices you've plugged in are collecting data on you—they are. Technology reporter Kashmir Hill and data reporter Surya Mattu conducted an experiment. They outfitted Hill's apartment with eighteen Internet-connected devices and Mattu built a special router to monitor the devices that were monitoring Hill. The report on the hidden server feedback results were published in a February 8, 2018, article for technology website *Gizmodo* titled "The House That Spied on Me."

Mattu and Hill's conclusions are extremely disturbing:

Mattu: Overall, my takeaway is that the smart home is going to create a new stream of information about our daily lives that will be used to further profile and target us. The number of devices alone that are detected chattering away will be used to determine our socioeconomic status. Our homes could become like internet browsers, with unique digital fingerprints, that will be mined for profit just like our daily Web surfing is. If you have a smart home, it's open house on your data.

Hill: What our experiment told us is that all the connected devices constantly phone home to their manufacturers. You won't be aware these conversations are happening unless you're technically savvy and monitoring your router like we did. And even if you are, because the conversations are usually encrypted, you won't be able to see what your belongings are saying. When you buy a smart device, it doesn't just belong to you; you share custody with the company that made it.

That's not just a privacy concern. It also means that those companies can change the product you bought after you buy it. So your smart speaker can suddenly become the hub of a social network, and your fancy smart scale can have one of its key features taken away in a firmware update.

What do smart homes have to do with the "convenience" of Google Chromebooks?

Chrome is Google's proprietary cross-platform (PC or Mac) Web browser first released by Google in 2008. The browser is the main component of Google's operating system, Chrome OS, and is currently the preferred browser for desktops, with a staggering 66.87 percent worldwide market share.

Chromebook, Google's laptop/tablet computer, uses Google's Chrome-based operating system to run apps so they are faster and less expensive than traditional laptops that use hard drives. Chromebooks store documents in the cloud, they can be shared among students, and school administrators have an online dashboard that can manage thousands of laptops remotely at once. The benefits of Google Chromebooks and Apps for Education are advertised as convenient "innovative technologies that enhance teaching and increase student engagement by bringing the power of the Web to the classroom."

Google's Chromebooks are replacing textbooks in classrooms across

America. So, let's examine how smart it is to use a "smart" twenty-first-century Chromebook.

In a dismissive statement describing traditional teaching methods, Google Education Team member <u>Cassi Caputo</u> said, "We are no longer limited to learning by solely listening to a lecture or reading a book. All students do not learn the same way, and we now have the resources to accommodate different types of learners." What Ms. Caputo fails to mention is that Google Apps for Education are extremely manipulative and politically biased toward the radical Left.

A July 7, 2018, <u>YouTube video</u> of *Infowars* reporter David Knight interviewing an anonymous high school teacher from Georgia is particularly chilling and has been deleted from the Internet. The interview exposes what Ms. Caputo is concealing. The resources Ms. Caputo praised include an Orwellian system of grouping. Students are categorized according to their intellectual abilities—high flyers, average students, and low performers. Google's "personalized" curriculum covertly guides the high flyers toward leadership positions with intensely political anti-American, pro-communist content. High flyer exams include questions on gay marriage, wearing the hijab, and the gender wage gap. Customized content for average students guides them toward skilled-labor career pathways of welding, plumbing, and agriculture. Low performers are steered into computer programs where they earn meaningless diplomas by taking tests repeatedly until they pass; they will become manual laborers.

Google is ideologically committed to global governance. Its radical leftist perspective promotes collectivism, dependence, and universal education in opposition to the individualism, independence, and upwardly mobile American educational meritocracy. Google's educational suites deliver radical leftist student indoctrination on a massive scale—for your "convenience," of course.

Leo Goldstein, Russian-born mathematician, political analyst, and editor of *DefyCCC*, writes about the chilling similarities between the ideological Left in America and the Communist Party in the Soviet Union. His September 2017 research paper, "<u>Google's Search Bias Against Conservative News Sites Has Been Quantified</u>," methodically reveals how it is done. Search queries, the words and phrases people type into a search box, are divided into three basic levels, transactional for purchasing, informational for general inquiries, and navigational for going to a specific website. The term PGSTN in the following quote means Percent of Google Search Traffic Net [navigational], which measures percentage of new users sent to a domain by Google:

> Google Search uses self-appointed "fact checkers," including *snopes.com* and *politifact.com*, [both of which] have [a] PGSTN [of] about 50%. That gives ground to the suspicion that they had been hand-picked by Google for prioritization. Another two sites with suspiciously high PGSTN are *sourcewatch.org* (PGSTN = 50.1%) and prwatch.org (PGSTN = 40.9%). These two sites grossly exchange links (they refer to each other as the source), have overlapping content, and are known to Google to belong to the same organization, the Center for Media and Democracy. These are well-known signs of spam—yet Google has not only failed to downrank them as spam, but likely manually prioritized them.

According to *Influence Watch.org*, the Center for Media and Democracy is principally funded by leftist foundations. It receives substantial funding from the Schuman Center for Media and Democracy and from George Soros's Foundation to Promote Open Society. Goldstein concludes that "Google Search is biased in favor of left/liberal websites against conservative websites, and is extremely biased in favor of climate alarmism against climate realism."

Google provides a curated one-world curriculum preloaded onto its Chromebooks. Consistent with the United Nations' Agenda 21 goals for the twenty-first century of one world, one language, one culture, one flag, Google Chromebook facilitates one-world education that strives to create global citizens prepared for the sustainable New World Order.

What this means is that our children and grandchildren are being propagandized, without parental consent, away from the traditional American values of individualism, national sovereignty, patriotism, and the merit system. They are being taught to embrace collectivism, dependence, and a New World Order of a globalized world. They are being pressured toward groupthink rather than independent thought. The educational focus on collaborative learning rather than independent achievement is a mask for globalized groupthink.

Tobacco companies once advertised their products with beautiful images of sophisticated men and women smoking cigarettes—not horrific pictures of people dying from lung cancer. It took decades for the public to become aware of the health risks of cigarettes that were well known to tobacco manufacturers. Today, Google products are advertised with pictures of smiling children in classrooms around the world gazing happily at their Chromebook screens—not pictures of enslaved children mindlessly reciting the same words in robotic synchrony.

Lest you think that these observations are wild conspiracy theories, please remember that since 1992 the United Nations and world leaders have unapologetically affirmed the need to transform the existing world order and create a top-down, deliberate, restricted society that rejects national sovereignty, individual liberty, Judeo-Christian values, and Western traditions. These are the foundational principles of the United Nations' Agenda 21 that are indoctrinating our children.

Congress never approved Agenda 21, although presidents George H. W. Bush, Bill Clinton, and Barack Obama all signed executive orders implementing it. Leaders from 178 other countries agreed to it at the 1992 United Nations Conference on Environment & Development in Rio de Janeiro, where it was developed. The current Agenda 2030 is a reboot of Agenda 21 plus the 17 Sustainable Development Goals (SDGs) intended to be achieved by 2030. On September 25, 2015, all 193 countries of the UN General Assembly adopted the 2030 Development Agenda titled "Transforming Our World: The 2030 Agenda for Sustainable Development."

Google's twenty-first-century Chromebooks are propaganda boxes disguised as legitimate education. Parents unwittingly enter into a shared-custody arrangement with Google when their school districts buy Google Chromebooks. Parents need to know that their children are being inculcated with radical leftist political correctness, moral relativity, and historical revisionism. Chromebook "facts" can be altered with the tap of a key on an administrative keypad, obliterating historical accuracy—just like the "smart" devices plugged in at your home.

Curriculum content is the single greatest indoctrination force in education, and it has been weaponized to serve the radical leftist Culture War on America. The educational initiative against America began decades ago. A 1999 book titled *The Deliberate Dumbing Down of America: A Chronological Paper Trail*, written by Charlotte Thomson Iserbyt, records the deliberate effort by American social engineers to destroy the intellect of American children for the purpose of leading America into a socialist world government. It is the actualization of Bertrand Russell's shameless strategy described in Hoax 23. The program teaches students WHAT to think, not HOW to think. Google's Chromebook is its current delivery system.

Just as smart homes are marketed "for your convenience," without exposing the manufacturers' ulterior motive of data mining, so it is with Google products. Chromebooks and Apps for Education are marketed for your convenience, without exposing Google's ulterior motive of indoctrinating your sons and daughters with lessons designed to mold them into citizens of the world and subjects of planetary governance.

Educational curricula will determine our children's future and the future of our nation. Apathy is not an option. Parents must become informed, proactive soldiers combating Google's sinister social engineering. If not, one more generation of students using Google's weaponized Chromebooks will fundamentally transform American children from future citizens of a free and sovereign America into subjects of a New World Order ruled by the globalist elite. The Culture War against American sovereignty will be won at the ballot box when the next generation of propagandized students turn eighteen and vote their indoctrinated consciences—no bullets required. The Humanitarian Hoax of "Convenient" Google Chromebook Education will have successfully shattered the American ideals of national sovereignty and individual liberty. Cancer kills.

HOAX 28

The Humanitarian Hoax of Illegal Immigrant Family Separation at the U.S. Border

June 22, 2018

THE humanitarian hoax is the deliberate and deceitful tactic of presenting a destructive policy as altruistic. The humanitarian huckster presents himself as a compassionate advocate when in fact he is the disguised enemy.

Children are the future of every nation and culture on Earth, which makes them the most valuable natural resource in the world. Water, air, land, coal, natural gas, phosphorus, oil, minerals, iron, soil, forests, and timber are all subjects of worldwide conservation efforts. What about children?

Wars are fought over natural resources in competition for power and dominance. So it is with children. The leftist exploitation of illegal immigrant children is a political dirty trick being played for the hearts and minds of compassionate American voters. This is how it works.

President Trump's America-first policies are demonstrably positive for America and threaten the narrative of Barack Obama's leftist collectivist destruction. President Trump's insistence on our national sovereignty is an existential threat to Obama's battle for internationalized globalism. Obama's promise to transform America has been exposed as a promise to destroy America from within and replace our infrastructure with socialism in preparation for the epitome of collectivism—planetary governance.

The Left is exploiting ILLEGAL immigrant children in a desperate attempt to delegitimize President Trump before the midterm elections. A midterm victory is necessary for leftist Democrats to start impeachment proceedings against the president. Tear-jerking appeals for reunification of ILLEGAL immigrant families are completely disingenuous. They are pure political theater—a desperate humanitarian hoax designed to engage compassionate voters and ensure a Democrat midterm election victory, for the following reasons:

- Mueller's investigation into Russian collusion in the 2016 presidential election fell apart and served only to expose serious malfeasance of Obama's FBI, DOJ, CIA, and State Department.
- Sensationalized news is an effective political weapon designed to stigmatize Trump and offset his stunning economic victories before the midterm elections.
- Reunification of immigrant families deflects attention away from the damning June 14, 2018, inspector general's report recommending more investigations into FBI improprieties during the Hillary Clinton email scandal, which will ultimately expose Obama's participation.

The colluding leftist mainstream media deliberately refuse to include the essential word ILLEGAL in their reports. There would be no issue of separated families if the families came to the United States LEGALLY, the type of immigration that President Trump is in favor of. Leftist attempts to deny that reality and present POTUS as anti-immigration are typical of the deceit that has come to characterize the leftist Democrats under Obama.

Rich Lowry explains the history, legal complications, and false accusations leveled against President Trump regarding separation of illegal immigrant children from their families at our southern border. Lowry's article "The Truth about Separating Kids," published in the *National Review* on May 28, 2018, begins by noting that in the last decade illegal immigration has shifted from single males to women, children, and family units.

> The Trump administration isn't changing the rules that pertain to separating an adult from the child. Those remain the same. Separation happens only if officials find that the adult is falsely claiming to be the child's parent, or is a threat to the child, or is put into criminal proceedings.
>
> It's the last that is operative here. The past practice had been to give a free pass to an adult who is part of a family unit. The new Trump policy is to prosecute all adults. The idea is to send a signal that we are serious about our laws and to create a deterrent against re-entry. (Illegal entry is a misdemeanor, illegal re-entry a felony.)

What the Democrats do not mention is that if the adult chooses to go home, he/she is immediately reunited with the child and returned home as a family unit. If the adult files an asylum claim, the Flores Consent Decree from 1997 is activated. Flores requires the removal of unaccompanied minors from detention as quickly as possible. The Ninth Circuit Court decision in the subsequent 2016 _Flores v. Loretta Lynch_ case created the illegal alien family separation debacle by ruling that both accompanied and unaccompanied minors had to be removed from detention within 72 hours. So, if the government could not process the immigration/asylum case within 72 hours, the minors were separated from their families. _Conservative Daily News_ summarized the outcome:

> The Obama administration decided to release both the suspected criminal alien and the accompanied minors into the United States pending trial to satisfy the court decision although the action failed to enforce U.S. law. Less than 10 percent of those released bother to show up for their court dates.

> The conclusions of the court in _Flores v. Loretta Lynch_ are as follows:

> 1. The Flores Dissent Decree applies to accompanied and unaccompanied minors.

> 2. The Flores Dissent Decree does not require the release of accompanying parents or guardians.

> This basically creates the situation where, if immigration laws are enforced and these decisions adhered to, the minor must be moved to a non-secure, licensed facility, but the parents will remain in a secure detainment facility awaiting trial. That is where the separation of illegal alien families originates—a legal agreement during the Clinton administration and a court decision during Obama's term. Only Congress can make a law or set of laws to remedy this.

In a stunning June 22, 2018, article in the _Jerusalem Post_, political analyst Carolyn Glick exposed the deceitfulness of the media in their outcry over the U.S. government policy of separating illegal immigrant minors from their illegal immigrant parents:

> The policy is cruel. Indeed, recognizing its cruelty, Trump signed an executive order banning the practice.

> But the policy isn't new. This was the Obama administration's policy following a court order prohibiting children from joining their parents in detention.

> Rather than soberly acknowledge that law enforcement, including immigration law, is often a cruel business and recognize that to remain a state

of laws sometimes authorities undertake difficult and harsh actions, the anti-Trump media ignored reality and went straight for the kill. David Remnick, Frank Bruni, and countless others didn't care that the Obama administration separated children from their parents, placed them in cages, and wrapped them in aluminum foil. As far as they are concerned, the continuation of the same cruel policy under Trump is proof that Trump is a Nazi.

Gen. Michael Hayden, former director of the NSA and the CIA, posted a photo of the entrance to Auschwitz on his Twitter feed with the caption "Other governments have separated mothers and children."

Immigration legal authority Hans von Spakovsky identified more media deceit in his June 21, 2018, article, "Who's Responsible for Separating Alien Kids from Their Parents? Many People, but Not Trump." Here are two particularly instructive quotes from his article that absolve President Trump of wrongdoing:

In other words, it is the Ninth Circuit's misinterpretation of the Clinton administration's settlement agreement that doesn't allow juvenile aliens to stay with their parents who have been detained for unlawful entry into the country.

The Obama administration provided a huge incentive for illegal aliens to smuggle children across the border, since a child acted as a get-out-of-jail-free card for avoiding detention and prosecution for the adult accompanying the child. As the Department of Homeland Security correctly says, this policy "incited smugglers to place children into the hands of adult strangers so they can pose as families and be released from immigration custody after crossing the border, creating another safety issue for these children."

War makes strange bedfellows, and the current Culture War on America led by Obama's anti-American "resistance" movement has allies in its attempt to delegitimize and overthrow President Donald Trump. The economy is booming under President Trump. Unemployment for black Americans is the lowest in history. The optimism of small business owners is skyrocketing. Negotiations over fair trade are in America's favor. President Trump is making America great again, and the leftist Democrat predators, in collusion with the mainstream media including Internet giants Google, Facebook, and Twitter, are desperate to stop his party from winning the 2018 midterm elections.

It is abusive for illegal immigrant parents to subject their children to separation at the U.S. borders and equally abusive for leftist political predators to exploit the practice in a vile attempt to swing the midterm elections. Photographs of crying children tug at American hearts, but the photographs are fraudulent and are pure political theater—a seismic humanitarian hoax! It is time for the leftist/media/Internet alliance to stop abusing and exploiting children.

Americans must understand the malfeasance, purpose, and value of politicizing illegal immigrant children at the border. Leftist child abuse and exploitation create the sinister leftist humanitarian hoax that misrepresents the facts of illegal immigrant family separation begun under Clinton, continued under Obama, and blamed on President Trump in a deceitful campaign to delegitimize POTUS before the midterm elections.

The Trump administration wants the Flores Consent Decree reversed. Rich Lowry concludes:

> Congress can fix this. Congress can change the rules so the Flores Consent Decree will no longer apply, and it can appropriate more money for family shelters at the border. This is an obvious thing to do that would eliminate the tension between enforcing our laws and keeping family units together. The Trump administration is throwing as many resources as it can at the border to expedite the process, and it desperately wants the Flores Consent Decree reversed. Despite some mixed messages, if the administration had its druthers, family units would be kept together and their cases settled quickly.

The mainstream media and Internet behemoths are deliberately colluding to misrepresent Clinton and Obama's abusive family separation policies as belonging to President Trump. Americans believe in fairness. They do not appreciate being manipulated into believing leftist political propaganda masquerading as truth. If the Humanitarian Hoax of Illegal Immigrant Family Separation at the U.S. Border is successful, then leftist Democrats will have duped America into blaming President Trump for the inhumane practices of Bill Clinton and Barack Obama.

HOAX 29

The Humanitarian Hoax of Political Correctness

May 6, 2019

THE humanitarian hoax is the deliberate and deceitful tactic of presenting a destructive policy as altruistic. The humanitarian huckster presents himself as a compassionate advocate when in fact he is the disguised enemy. Political correctness is a humanitarian hoax, a deceitful end run around the First Amendment guarantee of freedom of speech. This is how it works.

The freedoms guaranteed by the U.S. Constitution award citizens the right to disagree with anyone about anything without fear of reprisal. American civil society is predicated upon the freedom to express disagreement, and is diametrically opposed to the politically correct demand for avoidance of language that might be offensive or hurt someone's feelings.

The freedoms guaranteed by our Constitution are impervious to feelings. Political correctness, on the other hand, is defined exclusively by feelings. Political correctness is a severe prohibition on free speech disguised as courtesy.

Political correctness, PC, is marketed by its devotees as progressive, compassionate, sensitive, and caring. It is defined as the avoidance of language or actions that are seen as excluding, marginalizing, or insulting to groups of people who are seen as disadvantaged or discriminated against, especially groups defined by sex or race. In America, PC has been embraced by leftists with religious fervor. The problem, of course, is deciding WHO will determine what is insulting.

Historically, political correctness was associated with the Communist Party and dogmatic Stalinists. The term was used disparagingly by Socialists, who considered themselves morally superior and more egalitarian than the Communists they were competing with. Not much has changed. Today, the leftists who adhere to PC consider themselves morally superior to conservatives, who refuse to surrender their freedom of speech. The leftists have conveniently appointed themselves the definitive authority on what is considered hurtful, offensive, insulting, or hateful, all of which they term "hate speech."

The staggering hypocrisy of leftist inclusion is evident by leftists' embrace of superficial differences—tall, thin, short, fat, black, brown, gay, straight, bisexual, transsexual, etc., etc. What leftists do not tolerate is anyone who *thinks* differently; there is no place for opposing views in leftism. Equally hypocritical is the PC restriction on free speech based on hurt feelings, since it applies only to leftist hurt feelings. Leftism is a supremacist ideology.

The Left has introduced secular tyranny to America disguised as inclusion.

The U.S. Constitution guarantees my rights to freedom of religion, freedom of speech, freedom of the press, freedom to assemble, and freedom to petition my government for redress of grievances. The most fundamental of these rights is speech. Without freedom of speech, there is no freedom at all. That explains why any attempt to abridge or curtail freedom begins with restrictions on speech and also explains why every despotic regime, including the Left in America, necessarily prohibits free speech.

The Humanitarian Hoax of Political Correctness is that it promotes the lawless disregard for the First Amendment guarantee of free speech as altruistic. PC most definitely "abridges" freedom of speech; it is not altruistic, it is supremacist and repressive.

In a complex society of millions of people, there are many who have ideas and beliefs that will be offensive to others. The First Amendment guarantees that they are free to think and say their thoughts, but they most definitely are not free to act upon them if they would harm others or break laws. The Constitution acknowledges the differences between thinking, saying, and doing.

Children in kindergarten are taught the distinction between words and actions. They learn that "sticks and stones may break my bones, but words will never hurt me." They are taught to tolerate offensive speech even when it hurts their feelings.

We are witnessing in twenty-first-century America a regressive blurring of boundaries between words and actions. In the world of adult *objective* reality, hurting people's feelings with words is not the same as breaking their bones with sticks and stones. The politically correct leftist demand to restrict free speech because it might hurt someone's feelings drives people into a world of infantile *subjective* reality.

In America, morality, good taste, civility, courtesy, and common sense have traditionally been the societal pressures applied to convince people to conform to cultural norms of acceptable speech. Today, the leftist Culture War on America is using the extraordinary social power of peer pressure to demand conformity to its tenets of political correctness. PC is the leftists' instrument for creating divisiveness, silencing opposition, and destabilizing the country.

When people are no longer free to express their opinions without being censured or ridiculed, when students are no longer free to argue their ideas in classrooms, when conservative speakers are no longer allowed on campuses, we are no longer living in a free society. We are living under the tyranny of leftist groupthink peer pressure.

The Left idealizes the restriction of free speech as altruism. Consider the ongoing conflict about what is permissible speech regarding Islam in America under the influence of the seditious Muslim Brotherhood. In my April 2019 article "The Squeaky Wheel Gets the Grease" I describe how the Council on Islamic-American Relations (CAIR) presents itself as a civil rights organization, but functions as the propaganda arm of the Muslim Brotherhood to facilitate Sharia law in America.

Islamists are straightforward—they tell you that it is against Sharia law to criticize Muhammad or Allah and the punishment for doing so is death. Islamists unapologetically reject the authority of the U.S. Constitution and the secular laws in America that guarantee free speech. Islamist Sharia law is based on its supremacist religious ideology.

Instead of protecting free speech, leftists protect the Muslim Brotherhood and whine that criticizing Muhammad or Allah hurts Muslims' feelings, making them feel marginalized and insulted. They have even invented a word for it: Islamophobia. Leftists have joined the Islamists and are equally unapologetic about not recognizing the authority of the secular laws in America that guarantee free speech, including criticizing Muhammad and Allah.

Consider the current restrictions on free speech and creeping Sharia law in America:

I am an American and free to criticize my government.

I am an American and free to criticize Jesus.

I am an American and free to criticize Yahweh.

I am an American and NO LONGER FREE to criticize Muhammad or Allah.

Any movement, whether secular or religious, that refuses to recognize the established laws of the U.S. Constitution is seditiously promoting anarchy.

It is simply untrue that all ideas and norms are equal. Every civil society has cultural norms that determine what is and what is not acceptable behavior. Consider cannibalism. If some people embrace cannibalism, they are free to live in parts of the world that still support cannibalism, but in the United States cannibalism is strictly forbidden—it is an idea without value in our culture.

What about child marriage? In Muslim cultures the marriage of an older man to a nine-year-old girl may be acceptable, but in the West we call it pedophilia and it is strictly forbidden. Sharia law supports the killing of homosexuals, female genital mutilation, "honor" killings, and a myriad of other repressive and culturally abhorrent practices forbidden by our Constitution.

Societies that embrace the politically correct narrative that all ideas are equal are necessarily accepting the unacceptable. Americans are being asked to accept the unacceptable today.

Public debate about Islam is no longer allowed in PC America. There is no open exchange of different opinions on the subject, no criticism of Islam permitted, and no discussion of the glaring conflicts between Islamic Sharia law and the U.S. Constitution. The Leftist/Islamist axis, including the colluding Internet behemoths, has unapologetically silenced any discussion about Islam and the existential threat it poses to America.

Secular and religious censorship is dismantling the First Amendment, using political correctness disguised as courtesy. The freedoms guaranteed by our Constitution award citizens the right to disagree. Freedom of speech guarantees the right to verbally express that disagreement. The future of our Republic depends upon our ability to speak freely. There is no freedom without freedom of speech.

The leftist Culture War on America is designed to destroy America from within and replace our government with Marxist socialism.

The Muslim Brotherhood's War on America is designed to destroy America from within and replace our government with Islamic Sharia law.

We must remember the kindergarten lesson of sticks and stones and restore the distinction between words and actions. The regressive Left has deliberately blurred that boundary to restrict free speech and demand compliance with their increasingly repressive standard of what is acceptable speech. Leftists are using the magical thinking and fearfulness of childhood to persuade America that words can break bones.

Americans must choose. We must decide whether we will tolerate hurt feelings in order to preserve freedom of speech or accept the unacceptable tyranny of leftist censorship and Islamic intolerance. It really does not matter whether forbidden speech is religious (criticizing Muhammad and Allah) or secular (criticizing political correctness). Free speech guarantees the right to express disagreement and opposing ideas without fear of reprisal.

Without freedom of speech there is only conformity, fear, and enslavement. We can live free by restoring objective reality and honoring the adult distinction between words and actions articulated in our Constitution. Or we can allow ourselves to be duped by the Humanitarian Hoax of Political Correctness and forfeit our freedom of speech to the insanity of the regressive leftist world of subjective reality, where words can magically break bones.

We must choose between sanity and insanity. It is the choice between freedom and enslavement.

HOAX 30

The Humanitarian Hoax of Pearson Education

May 15, 2019

THE humanitarian hoax is the deliberate and deceitful tactic of presenting a destructive policy as altruistic. The humanitarian huckster presents himself as a compassionate advocate when in fact he is the disguised enemy.

Pearson plc, a public limited corporation, is a British multinational, multibillion-dollar publishing powerhouse and the largest education company in the world. Pearson Publishing's reported 2017 share in global revenues was $8.2 billion, with a staggering 60 percent control of U.S. textbook sales. It listed the Libyan Investment Authority as its largest financial contributor. Pearson is an anti-American, pro-globalism, anti-Christian, anti-Semitic, pro-Muslim globalized education provider that is indoctrinating our children.

Pearson is the premier global educational humanitarian huckster hawking its anti-American message of globalism to K-12 students and teachers in America. Its globalized curriculum comports with Obama's pet Common Core State Standards (CCSS) initiative. Globally, Common Core originated from the One World Education concept, a global goal orchestrated by the Connect All Schools program. The creation of One World Education was funded by the Qatar Foundation International and supported by United Nations Agenda 2030. This is how it works.

Obama appointed Vartan Gregorian, board member of the Qatar Foundation International (QFI), to the prestigious and influential President's Commission on White House Fellowships. The QFI partnered with the U.S. Department of State and the Department of Education in 2011 to integrate classrooms in the United States and international schools through a program called Connect All Schools.

Obama's dream of a globalized, internationalized, pro-Muslim education was facilitated courtesy of the Qatari government, Qatar Foundation International, and the Libyan Investment Authority's major Islam-promoting donors:

- Turkey
- Saudi Arabia
- Muslim Brotherhood
- Council on American-Islamic Relations (CAIR)

The stated goal of humanitarian huckster-in-chief Barack Obama's Connect All Schools initiative was to "connect every school in the U.S. with the world by 2016." Sounds great, just like "hope and change" sounded great until it was exposed as a sinister humanitarian hoax designed to shatter the Judeo-Christian norms and sovereignty of the United States of America. Let's review.

Our American children are being indoctrinated to be self-loathing Americans by pro-Muslim, anti-American Muslim Brotherhood propaganda, courtesy of Barack Obama's Connect All Schools initiative. The transnational Muslim Brotherhood has the singular goal of spreading Islam worldwide and is "educating" our children with its propaganda. In its own words, the Muslim Brotherhood's *An Explanatory Memorandum: On the General Strategic Goal for the Group in North America* makes it crystal clear that indoctrination of American students through textbooks is a primary political tactic of Islamists to settle the United States of America and make it Muslim.

Obama's deceitful Race to the Top program, described in more detail in *The Humanitarian Hoax of Common Core—Hoax 19*, bribed school districts to accept destructive Common Core standards in exchange for federal grants that also affected teacher certification. New York State no longer evaluates its teachers—Pearson Education does. Pearson Education took over teacher certification for New York State in 2014 with its Teacher Performance Assessment (TPA) and is the sole administrator and evaluator of the assessment.

A 2012 article written by New York Hofstra University educator Alan Singer asks the question, "Pearson 'Education'—Who Are These People?" It is a pivotal question.

Singer writes:

The question that must be addressed is whether the British publishing giant Pearson and its Pearson Education subsidy should determine who is qualified to teach and what should be taught in New York State and the United States? I don't think so! Not only did no one elect them, but when people learn who they are, they might not want them anywhere near a school —or a government official.

In a particularly egregious example of Pearson's ideological bias, many accelerated advance placement students used a 2018 textbook published by Pearson titled *By the People: A History of the United States*. The final section, "The Angry Election of 2016," depicts President Trump as mentally ill and his supporters as racists. A Pearson spokesperson defended the textbook, insisting it had undergone "rigorous peer review to ensure academic integrity." This is the predictable outcome of globalist ideology and globalist revisionism disguised as scholarship.

Pearson is unapologetically committed to globalism and is a signatory to the United Nations Sustainable Development Goals discussed in Hoax 19. In Pearson's own words:

> The good news is that the world has agreed on a plan to put us on a more sustainable path and ensure that no one is left behind. UN Member States have adopted the 2030 Agenda for Sustainable Development, including its 17 Sustainable Development Goals (SDGs) and the Paris Agreement to tackle climate change. We have an opportunity and a responsibility to play our part in delivering these landmark agreements. By supporting the SDGs, we will help create a better world in which our business can grow and we can more effectively achieve our mission to help people improve their lives through learning.

In February 2019 Pearson sold its U.S. K-12 courseware business to Nexus Capital Management LP for $250 million in its planned shift from textbooks to digital content. Pearson claims the sale is part of its ongoing work to become a simpler, more efficient company. That is company-speak for its move toward higher education and *digital* delivery of its globalist educational curriculum. Pearson is going to college! In its own words:

> The broader U.S. K-12 market remains an important area of focus for Pearson and we are continuing to invest in faster growing digital services such as virtual schools and building on our strong position in U.S. student assessment. We will continue to provide Higher Education courseware for Advance Placement programmes in K-12 schools.

The odd terms of the deal gave Pearson only $25 million up front, but after the balance is paid Pearson will retain 20 percent of future cash flow from the business and is entitled to 20 percent of the sale price if Nexus sells. So, what is Nexus Capital, and who is behind it? What did the company buy? Why the odd deal?

Nexus is a Los Angeles–based private equity firm and member of Emerging Markets Private Equity Association (EMPEA). EMPEA is a consortium of globalist companies that share information in their singular objective of creating unfettered world markets for their goods and services. "Sustainable" is the watchword. Sustainable is the abracadabra, open-sesame key that begins with private equity firms in emerging markets and ends in one-world government.

Tariq Ramadan, director of Qatar Foundation International's Research Center for Islamic Legislation and Ethics, is the grandson of Hassan al-Banna, founder of the Muslim Brotherhood. At a 2011 fund-raiser in Dallas for the Islamic Circle of North America (ICNA), he openly called for young Muslims to colonize America. Canadian philosopher Marshall McLuhan coined a phrase that has become famous: "The medium is the message." In this case, Pearson/Nexus is the medium and Muslim supremacy is the message.

The Muslim Brotherhood's *Explanatory Memorandum* should be required reading for every American parent and every American educator, in order to fully understand the depth, breadth, and commitment of the movement to colonize America and make it Muslim. Most Americans scoff at the idea of such a seemingly outlandish objective. They have not read the *Explanatory Memorandum*. What many Americans fail to remember is that aspirational world domination is neither new nor unfamiliar; it appears in different forms at different times in different places.

Globalism is the modern-day ambition for world domination. It is deceitfully marketed as progress—the New World Order of global citizenship ruled by the globalist elite under the auspices of the United Nations—to help us improve our lives, of course.

Americans have been lulled to sleep by the security of our unparalleled freedoms, the vastness of our country, and the oceans that surround us. The Islamic menace will not conquer America by land or sea, and neither will the leftist menace. The globalists will eventually conquer America through Obama's sinister textbook initiative that indoctrinates American children and produces self-loathing voters who will willingly choose one-world government over sovereignty—no bullets required. We must wake up and stop them.

A 2015 *EdTech* article exposes the overarching threat that the sinister Humanitarian Hoax of Pearson Education poses. The article, titled "Do School Districts Need Their Own Data Centers Anymore?" explains how school districts are moving their entire educational databases online to Google Apps and Chromebook, and moving all their files to Google Drive for cloud storage.

Google Drive is an integrated file storage and synchronization service that allows users to store files on Google servers, synchronize files across devices, and share files. Pearson will host PowerSchool, its own unified education technology software, instead of school districts hosting their own data. Marketed for convenience, PowerSchool's stated mission is to power the education ecosystem with unified technology. School districts that move their entire educational databases online to Pearson's Power-School and Google Drive are awarding the companies absolute control over educational content.

In January 2019 Pearson announced that Pearson Realize, its single digital platform, is now a Google for Education Premier Partner. Google for Education is a service from Google that provides independently customized versions of several Google products using a domain name provided by the customer. This means that Pearson's globalist propaganda package will be indoctrinating American children digitally. Political correctness, historical revisionism, and moral relativity are now mainstream digital learning tools for social engineering that prepare American children for global citizenship and one-world government.

The Pearson/Nexus globalist indoctrination toward one-world government is either not known and recognized as an existential threat, or known and embraced by ideologues that support its objective. In either case, it is up to parents—not a foreign company with an anti-American globalist agenda—to decide the curriculum content and how their children will be educated.

The Humanitarian Hoax of Pearson Education must be exposed and eliminated. American textbooks and digital content must be provided by American patriots who are committed to our glorious Constitution and the extraordinary freedoms it provides. Freedom is never free. We must wake ourselves up to the clear and present danger of the triple menace of the Islamist/Leftist/Globalist axis and its apologists, who seek to destroy America from within. If we want to remain free, we must be willing to oppose globalism and stand up for our national sovereignty.

Islamist leaders strive for a worldwide religious Islamic caliphate that will rule an infantilized population without free will. Leftists strive for a secular world of international socialism that will provide an infantilized population with cradle-to-grave care. The globalists, who own, operate, and continue to expand their global control of the private sector and the Internet, use Islamists and leftists as useful idiots to create the chaos required for total globalist domination and one-world government.

President Donald J. Trump is the existential enemy of the entire Islamist/Leftist/Globalist axis that has conspired and colluded in common cause to overthrow his patriotic America-first government. Unlike his adversaries, President Trump's policies and objectives require adult awareness of the humanitarian hoaxes that threaten our freedom and sovereignty.

Freedom requires adulthood. If we choose freedom, we cannot allow the Humanitarian Hoax of Pearson Education to kill America with kindness in the disingenuous names of progress, multiculturalism, and convenience.

We are the land of the free and the home of the brave. We must free ourselves from Pearson/Nexus, the Muslim Brotherhood, and globalists, all of whose propaganda controls our schools, if we are to remain free, sovereign, and independent.

HOAX 31

The Humanitarian Hoax of Five-Times-a-Day Islam

June 8, 2019

THE humanitarian hoax is the deliberate and deceitful tactic of presenting a destructive policy as altruistic. The humanitarian huckster presents himself as a compassionate advocate when in fact he is the disguised enemy.

Islam is a comprehensive sociopolitical movement with a religious wing whose objective is to establish a worldwide caliphate ruled by Islamic Sharia law. The stated and unapologetic strategy is settlement. What does that mean?

Settlement means war against America.

Settlement is the opposite of assimilation. For centuries, the United States has welcomed immigrants from every continent to legally enter America and become Americans through assimilation.

Becoming an American is more than possessing a document—it is a commitment to an open and free society where citizens have the unalienable right to free speech without fear of reprisal. It is a commitment to diverse opinions and the freedom to express them. The U.S. Constitution guarantees our rights and defines American culture by stipulating what is and what is not legal in America. The Constitution articulates our fundamental principles and is the supreme law of the land.

Our Founding Fathers embraced the Judeo-Christian principles embodied in the Ten Commandments, which provided the ethical foundation for the Constitution and outlined moral standards for life in America.

Historically, American life was structured around a workweek with Sunday religious observance for Christian Americans and Saturday religious observance for Jewish Americans. The arrangement was designed to be efficient and effective. Religious moral and ethical lessons were delivered in weekly sermons that were expected to be practiced by congregants throughout the workweek. The separation of church and state was observed. Americans were expected to work while at work and pray at religious services during nonworking hours.

All Americans are expected to live by the laws of the Constitution regardless of race, creed, religion, or sexual orientation. The U.S. Constitution is the common denominator that makes all Americans part of one American family. This means that all Americans, including Muslims, are required to observe the separation of church and state.

The conflict for Muslims in America is threefold:

- In Islam there is no separation of church and state.
- Islamic Sharia law governs Muslims and is incompatible with our Western norms and secular laws.
- Islam recognizes the authority of Islamic supremacist Sharia law exclusively, and does not recognize the authority of the U.S. Constitution.

So, Muslims in America are confronted with two choices. Either embrace the Constitution and assimilate to become Americans. Or embrace Sharia law and try to settle America and make America Muslim.

Islam is a replacement ideology and its strategy for settlement is to incrementally eliminate the separation of church and state and eventually collapse the Constitution. The Constitution does not recognize the authority of Sharia law in America. The settlement plan deliberately challenges constitutional authority by demanding special religious accommodations for Muslims.

Muslim demands for religious accommodations that violate the Constitution are tactical weapons in Islam's war against America; they are the battleground where the limits of tolerance and multiculturalism are manifest. When accommodations are made to accept Sharia's religious authority, an unconstitutional two-tier system of justice is established in America.

Consider the following:

Honor killings are legal in Sharia-compliant countries. If we tolerate honor killings in the United States, we are saying that it is acceptable for a Muslim to kill his disobedient wife or daughters and we have allowed Sharia law to supersede American law. Honor killings, child marriage, forced female genital mutilation, killing homosexuals—all are examples of legal Sharia behaviors that are illegal in the United States. Five-times-a-day prayer is another intrusion into American life that challenges the constitutional separation of church and state.

Everywhere in the world, Islam requires prayers five times a day. This is an intentional structure that signals the importance of Islamic religious observance and demonstrates the expectation that Islam be the primary focus and commitment of Muslim life. Quintuplet prayers pose no threat to Sharia-compliant countries, where five-times-a-day prayer are normative and part of the social structure. But what about in the West?

The accommodations to Islam's five-times-a-day prayer routine is a humanitarian hoax designed to settle America. This is how it works.

In order to accommodate five-times-a-day prayer, special arrangements have to be made for Muslims. Workers must be excused from work five times a day, students must be excused from their studies five times a day. Classrooms and workplaces have to be segregated in order to accommodate prohibitions against males and females working, studying, or praying together.

- Accommodations made for Muslim students in the name of multiculturalism violate the separation of church and state.
- Accommodations made for Muslim workers in the name of multiculturalism violate the separation of church and state.
- Accommodations made for Muslims affect all of America because they restructure American life at work, school, and play. And that is the intention.

Multicultural accommodations are not how Muslims assimilate—they are how Islam will settle America and make America Muslim. It's all in the numbers.

Dr. Peter Hammond's book _Slavery, Terrorism, and Islam: The Historical Roots and Contemporary Threat_ explains the process in detail. According to Hammond,

> Islam is not a religion or a cult. It is a complete, total, 100 percent system of life. Islam has religious, legal, political, economic, social, and military components. The religious component is a beard for all of the other components. Islamization (settlement) begins when there are sufficient Muslims in a country to agitate for their religious privileges.

When Muslim numbers are small, there are no demands for special accommodations. As their population numbers increase, their demands for special treatment increase. In large countries like the United States, Muslims tend to concentrate in smaller communities where their numbers are proportionally large enough to make such demands. The Muslim populations in <u>Dearborn, Michigan</u> (54,000) and <u>Minneapolis, Minnesota</u> (74,000) are two such examples.

Islamization is an incremental process that begins with making Islam familiar, because familiarity brings acceptability and disguises its settlement objective.

The Muslim Brotherhood's 1991 mission statement, <u>*An Explanatory Memorandum: On the General Strategic Goal for the Group in North America*</u> (Explanatory Memorandum), presents its business model for how to accomplish settlement. Targeting education with pro-Muslim propaganda and using our religious freedoms against us are two tactical maneuvers in Islam's war against America that seeks to make America Muslim. The Memorandum should be required reading for every American. Here is its explicit mission statement:

> The process of settlement is a "Civilization-Jihadist Process" with all the word means. The Ikhwan [Muslim Brotherhood] must understand that their work in America is a kind of grand jihad in eliminating and destroying the Western civilization from within and "sabotaging" its miserable house by their own hands and the hands of the believers so that it is eliminated and God's religion is made victorious over all religions.

Islamization is a sinister plan that begins slowly through propagandized Pearson educational indoctrination in our schools (see *The Humanitarian Hoax of Pearson Education—Hoax 30*). It is promoted by the Muslim Brotherhood's propaganda organization, the Council on American-Islamic Relations (CAIR). It is CAIR that deceitfully screams "Islamophobia!" and brings lawsuits against any individual or institution that opposes special accommodations and privileges for Muslims.

Muslims who embrace Sharia law are free to live in any of the many Islamic countries in the world. Muslims who choose to live in America must assimilate, embrace the authority of the Constitution, and live within our laws, which are based on that Constitution.

The United States of America was founded on the principle of religious freedom. We fought the British for our freedom and established a country that deliberately separates church and state in order to ensure religious freedom. There is no separation of church and state in Islam.

Jihad goes far beyond the physical attacks of airplanes and suicide bombers—it is the insidious, stealthy Humanitarian Hoax of Five-Times-a-Day Islam demanding that America violate its own Constitution and make Islam the preferred religion of the country. That is the sinister plan to make America Muslim.

America-first President Donald J. Trump MUST designate the Muslim Brotherhood and every one of its seditious offshoots terrorist organizations. They are a clear and present danger to the freedom, security, and sovereignty of the United States.

The American people must oppose the Humanitarian Hoax of Five-Times-a-Day Islam with their voices and their votes. We must stand together against this egregious assault on our Constitution and protect the separation of church and state. If we fail to act, our constitutional foundation will collapse and our precious freedoms will be lost to the Islamic objective of settlement.

HOAX 32

The Humanitarian Hoax of Black-Only College Graduation Ceremonies

June 12, 2019

THE humanitarian hoax is the deliberate and deceitful tactic of presenting a destructive policy as altruistic. The humanitarian huckster presents himself as a compassionate advocate when in fact he is the disguised enemy.

The Humanitarian Hoax of Black-Only College Graduation Ceremonies is a classic example of destruction disguised as altruism. Let's examine how resegregation has become fashionable.

Martin Luther King Jr. was the icon of the civil rights movement in the United States from 1955 until his assassination in 1968. Dr. King advocated nonviolence and civil disobedience similar to Gandhi's nonviolent activism. At the legendary 1963 March on Washington, DC, Dr. King delivered his famous "I Have a Dream" speech, which exhorted Americans to judge each other by the content of their character, not the color of their skin. His impassioned speech facilitated the passage of the Civil Rights Act of 1964, which outlawed discrimination based on race, color, religion, sex, and national origin.

The Civil Rights Act, signed into law by President Lyndon Johnson, is considered the most comprehensive civil rights legislation since Congress passed the Thirteenth Amendment to the Constitution, which abolished slavery in 1865.

The Thirteenth Amendment and the Civil Rights Act were legislative remedies designed to achieve the constitutional principle that all persons are created equal. Black Americans, white Americans, brown Americans, red Americans, and yellow Americans are one united American family indivisible by color. Being American is the foundation and common denominator of equality.

A shocking May 16, 2019, article by San Diego State University student Drew Van Voorhis reported the findings of a National Association of Scholars (NAS) study of neo-segregation, the voluntary racial segregation of students.

Neo-segregation is the consequence of social scientists eliminating the merit system in favor of racial quotas. Racial quotas in the 1960s resulted in elite universities such as Yale admitting under-qualified minority students who were doomed to fail. Over a third of the students dropped out, and those who remained struggled academically and were often embittered.

It is important to remember that had an equal number of under-qualified white students been admitted, they would have suffered the same failure rate. This was always a qualification issue, not a racial issue, even though it was race-based.

Instead of learning from the failure rates and emotional misery that failure inevitably brings, the social scientists doubled down and provided remedial classes for under-qualified students in another ill-advised attempt to level the playing field.

The result, according to the NAS study, was that students turned to each other for emotional support and found inspiration in black nationalism. Radical and militant black groups on campus offered a new separatist ethic that rejected integration in favor of identity politics.

The NAS report states:

> On campus after campus, black separatists won concessions from administrators who were afraid of further alienating blacks. The pattern of college administrators rolling over to black separatists' demands came to dominate much of American higher education. The old integrationist ideal has been sacrificed almost entirely. Instead of offering opportunities for students to mix freely with students of dissimilar backgrounds, colleges promote ethnic enclaves, stoke racial resentment, and build organizational structures on the basis of group grievance.

More than 76 of the 173 universities studied by the National Association of Scholars, a whopping 44 percent, host black-only graduation ceremonies. Voorhis lists UC San Diego, UC Irvine, Stanford, UC Berkeley, UCLA, Yale, and Arizona State University among the notable universities participating.

Even <u>Harvard University</u> hosted its first black-only graduation ceremony on May 23, 2017.

What would possess university administrators to surrender to black separatists' demands and implement black-only study lounges, black-only clubs, black-only housing, black-only classes, black-only scholarships, black-only student associations, and black-only graduation ceremonies? Why has segregation become desirable again?

If you want to know the motive, look at the result. Race-based distinctions foment racial divisiveness and are antithetical to racial harmony. Leftism preaches unity while its policies foment racial tension. Can anyone imagine what would happen if these same universities held white-only graduation ceremonies or had white-only study lounges and housing?

Reverse discrimination is the wrong answer to racial tension, and is as egregious as the original discrimination. Harvard disingenuously describes its segregated graduation ceremony in lofty terms as being "designed to celebrate their unique struggles and achievements at the elite institution that has been grappling with its historical ties to slavery."

If the nation's goal is racial inclusion and harmony, then graduation ceremonies would be expected to celebrate the shared value of student achievement regardless of the color of skin. Graduations would honor white students, black students, Asian students, Indian students, and Latino students experiencing student life together. It would recognize the social value of studying together, and the commonality of learning together, achieving together, and graduating together.

Young children on playgrounds fulfill Martin Luther King's dream effortlessly because they naturally focus on character and not on race. Students at leftist colleges, on the other hand, unnaturally focus on race instead of character.

What happened? Why has resegregation become fashionable? Because the Left realized that racism is a useful and powerful political tool to create divisiveness and social chaos in America.

Not only are race-based policies an admissions debacle, they are a threat to the productivity of America as well. Lowering academic standards and course requirements collapses the integrity of universities and results in many useless degrees. Caps and gowns become costumes of competence that do not reflect actual competence.

Under-qualified students who cannot compete in the classroom cannot compete in the workplace either. This failure creates more anger and bitterness and simultaneously makes America less productive. It is the merit system that drives the engine of a fair, successful, competent, independent, thriving America.

It is the acquisition of skills that actually makes students proud of themselves—not the social engineering of leftist sociologists disingenuously insisting that performance, achievement, and merit are oppressive constructs of the white man. The blame game is a destructive, regressive, deceitful strategy calculated to foment racial discord because the leftist leadership understands that anger fuels the socialist revolution in America.

Social chaos is the prerequisite for seismic social change. In its quest to make America socialist, the regressive Left is inciting divisiveness, discord, and violence to make America ungovernable. Leftism has a lot of help these days from Islamists and globalists, who have common cause to join the "resistance" and destroy America from within.

Neo-segregation is a deliberate and alarming return to the fractious, divisive, hateful era of racial conflict before Martin Luther King Jr. arrived on the scene.

The racism and black separatism that has torn college campuses apart is now embraced by New York City public schools K-12.

Consider the "white-supremacy culture" training program for school administrators being promoted by the chancellor of the New York City Department of Education and Schools, <u>Richard Carranza</u>. His shockingly racist slide show presentation is derived from "Dismantling Racism: A Workbook for Social Change Groups," by Kenneth Jones and Tema Okun.

These are the dirty dozen hallmarks of "white-supremacy culture" that school administrators are directed to avoid:

1. Perfectionism
2. Sense of Urgency
3. Defensiveness
4. Quantity over Quality
5. Worship of the Written Word
6. Only One Right Way
7. Paternalism

8. Either/Or Thinking

9. Power Hoarding

10. Fear of Open Conflict

11. Individualism

12. Progress Is Bigger, More

13. Objectivity

14. Right to Comfort

Chancellor Carranza's openly race-based perspective is explosive. His fourteen-point mandatory training program assumes "implicit bias" and "white privilege." His directive creates reverse discrimination and supports a doctrine of "toxic whiteness." Instead of embracing the dream of Martin Luther King Jr., Carranza has chosen to emulate Nation of Islam leader Malcolm X, a black separatist and black supremacist who advocated against racial integration. Instead of supporting an American family of equality, integration, and equal opportunity, Malcolm X indicted the white community and blamed "whitey" for the failures of the black community.

Elijah Muhammad, leader of the Nation of Islam (NOI) from 1934 until his death in 1975, appointed Malcolm X as minister and spokesman for the NOI. Louis Farrakhan succeeded Malcolm X after his assassination in 1965 and continues to promote the Nation of Islam's black separatist beliefs:

- that black people are the original people of the world,
- that white people are "devils,"
- that blacks are superior to whites, and
- that the demise of the white race is imminent.

In a letter addressed to Dr. King on July 31, 1963, Malcolm X described the power of racial tensions, saying, "A racial explosion is more destructive than a nuclear explosion." Minister of Elijah Muhammad's New York Mosque at the time, Malcolm X sarcastically acknowledged the "minor" differences between his own approach and that of Dr. King.

Failed university policies of racial divisiveness are being repeated in New York City public schools by Chancellor Carranza and are supported by his leftist boss, Mayor Bill de Blasio. De Blasio, a radical socialist/communist, supports the long game of social chaos that racial divisiveness necessarily generates.

Race-based policies will fail in K-12 just as they are failing in universities. Instead of Dr. King's dream of harmony and respect, Carranza's racist policies encourage the nightmare of racial divisiveness and social chaos.

America is based on equal *opportunity*—not equal *outcome*. Competence is the mother of self-esteem. If administrators want to develop students who become citizens with self-esteem, they must abandon the failed strategy of artificially leveling the playing field and insist upon equal opportunity for all students, black, white, brown, red, or yellow. Only then will America reunite and Americans judge each other by the content of our character and not the color of our skin.

Resegregation is not a humanitarian effort that respects the black experience. It is a sinister exploitation of black students that fuels their anger and makes them useful to the revolution. Social chaos is the prelude to tyranny. The Humanitarian Hoax of Black-Only College Graduation Ceremonies is the intentional fomenting of racism designed to tear America apart and make it ungovernable.

Neo-segregation is a humanitarian hoax designed to ignite racial tensions that will trigger the nuclear explosion of anarchy that Malcolm X predicted. Anarchy is the leftist strategy for seismic social change designed to make America socialist—the necessary precursor to a one-world government. Game over.

HOAX 33

The Humanitarian Hoax of 'Neutral' Google Searches

June 19, 2019

THE humanitarian hoax is the deliberate and deceitful tactic of presenting a destructive policy as altruistic. The humanitarian huckster
presents himself as a compassionate advocate when in fact he is the disguised enemy.

The Humanitarian Hoax of "Neutral" Google Searches is a dangerous
example of destruction presented as altruism.

Google is an American multinational technology company that special-
izes in Internet-related services and products including online advertising
technologies, a search engine, cloud computing, software, and hardware.
Google's revenues in 2018 were a whopping $75 billion and its market
capitalization a staggering $791 billion—just behind Amazon's market
capitalization of $802 billion.

Google is currently the nation's premier Web-based information outlet,
with 63,000 searches per second, 3.8 million per minute, and 5.8 *billion*
searches a day. So, what is the problem?

Google has reversed its lofty 1998 foundational mission, "to organize
the world's information and make it universally accessible and useful."
Making information universally accessible and useful describes a free
and open Internet that is diametrically opposed to censorship, curation
of content, and algorithms for social engineering of the masses.

Google searches today are not neutral, free, unbiased, or random.
Here is how it works.

Form and content are two distinctly different aspects of technology.
Google's form is an astonishing accomplishment of user-friendly acces-
sibility—just type in your question or concern and immediately receive

multiple answers and source materials. But Google's content is astonishing in a very different way.

In a shocking two-minute video produced and filmed by Hay Festival for BBC Arts Digital 2019 at the annual festival, Carole Cadwalladr relates how she inadvertently exposed the alarming content issues involved in a simple Google search. Cadwalladr, an investigative journalist, became famous in 2018 when she exposed the Facebook Cambridge Analytica data scandal.

The video begins with Cadwalladr relating a humorous exchange between herself and a friend, who remarked, "I didn't know you were fifty!" Carole responded, "I am not fifty! I am forty-seven—there is a big difference." He insisted, "But Google says you are fifty!" She decided to explore why there was factual misinformation about her on the Internet.

Her investigation began when she decided to type in a controversial single word—Jew. She started to format the search word into a question, "Are Jews . . ." and Google auto-completed the question to "Are Jews evil?" Before Carole could even press the Enter key, the screen filled with an entire page of results, every single one answering, "Yes, Jews are evil." At the bottom of the page were suggested search terms. The first one was "Did the Holocaust happen?" Carole clicked on it and the screen populated with articles that deny the Holocaust in every single case. The top result was the Nazi Website Stormfront. Top results are determined by page rank—we will get to that later.

According to a Google spokesperson, "We took action within hours of being notified on Friday of the autocomplete results." Google responded to its anti-Semitic search results by altering the algorithm, which removed the anti-Semitic search results. So, why am I writing about it?

What caught my attention beyond the staggering anti-Semitism in the search results was Carole's comment on the video that Google searches are machine learning. The machine reads the Websites and then makes deductions. WHAT???

This essentially means that if enough misinformation and disinformation is put online in the databases, the Google search engine will indoctrinate itself and then propagandize the public with its machine learning. That is beyond frightening, because it means that whoever has the resources to upload the most information controls the information results for Google searches.

Machine learning is artificial intelligence—like the human brain, the machine processes the information it is programmed with. Whoever controls the information controls the society. *The Humanitarian Hoax of Pearson Education—Hoax 30* describes the propagandized textbooks and programs that indoctrinate American students to be anti-American, pro-globalist, anti-Christian, anti-Semitic, pro-Muslim collectivists. Google searches are exponentially worse because the resulting information and misinformation are disseminated worldwide in 63,000 searches per second, 3.8 million per minute, and 5.8 billion searches a day.

Google is a multibillion-dollar globalist enterprise and the potential medium for social engineering in the twenty-first century.

Google searches are designed to easily manipulate the public with Google's globalist narrative. How does that work?

Consider the seriousness of Carole Cadwalladr's experience. Anytime before Google reportedly changed its algorithm for the search, anyone who Googled the word "Jew" was inundated with anti-Semitic propaganda validating the most vicious, politically motivated lies about Israel and Jews. In an earlier article of mine, "The Political Purpose of Anti-Semitism," I discussed how the political purpose of anti-Semitism is to galvanize support for a political movement during times of social and political upheaval. The political movement that Google supports is globalism.

I discussed globalism at length in my article "Connecting the Dots: Islamism . . . Socialism . . . Globalism," In that article I explained how "the word globalism is often used in its narrowest context to mean global trade, which obscures its broader political intention to internationalize nation-states and ultimately impose a one-world government."

The globalist elite unapologetically envision a New World Order that restructures the world into a one-world community with a one-world currency, a one-world flag, and a one-world language imposed under the auspices of the United Nations—and ruled by the globalists themselves, of course. United Nations initiatives like its Agenda 2030 promote this restructuring with glorious promises of a better life for all. The 17 Sustainable Development Goals articulated in UN documents expose the plan to loot industrial countries, particularly the United States, and redistribute

U.S. wealth to non-industrialized countries to make the world a more "just and fair place."

The globalist vision of a one-world government offers global businesses like Google and Amazon an unfettered marketplace for their goods and services. Globalism is very good for global businesses. America-first policies are not good for global businesses—they are good for America and American workers. That explains why giant global businesses are uniformly hostile to America-first President Trump and his America-first policies.

The algorithms that control Google searches are easily altered to manipulate Americans with disinformation and misinformation designed to achieve Google's globalist goal of one-world government. The possibility exposes the mass social engineering potential of Google and why its content must be monitored. The anti-Semitic search results are a case in point that demonstrates the frightening ease with which disinformation can be distributed and how easily any information can be changed, with just the tap of a computer key.

To understand the simplicity of content manipulation, it is helpful to understand how Google's search engine works.

An eight-minute YouTube video presentation explains the basics. When the search engine is asked a question (Google search) it reviews (crawls) the available sites and databases on the Internet. It indexes the information, analyzes the data, ranks the information, and then provides an answer to the search in a matter of microseconds. Very impressive. How is this even possible?

Page rank (the number of people who link to you) + reputability (legitimacy of the Website) = page rank order. Page rank order determines what site appears as the first answer to a Google search. That is how the longest-running Nazi Website Stormfront appeared first in Carole Cadwalladr's Google search.

Blogger Neil Patel provides an easy-to-understand overview of Google's search engine information retrieval system. Patel explains the basics and tells us that Google co-founders Larry Page and Sergey Brin were concerned about content legitimacy, authoritativeness, and relevance from the very beginning. He provides the link to their January 29, 1998, abstract, "The PageRank Citation Ranking: Bringing Order to the Web." This abstract proposed the use of PageRank, "a method for computing a ranking for every web page based on the graph of the web." Google was actually built as a platform to demonstrate the value of PageRank.

So, twenty years ago, young Page and Brin developed a search engine model to crawl the Internet and provide search answers that would be legitimate and authoritative. So far, so good. What happened?

The Google startup business that Page and Brin founded in a Menlo Park garage in 1998 is now a $791 billion behemoth and the primary information provider to Internet users worldwide. The problem, of course, is the platform content. Google is curating content based on its globalist-elite objective of a one-world government. Its blatant political bias is evident in every search.

A simple Google search of Hillary Clinton is a laughable portrayal of her as an exceptional politician, diplomat, lawyer, writer, and public speaker—no mention of her political malfeasance in the Benghazi affair, her illegal basement email server, or the corrupt and now defunct Clinton Global Initiative. Why does this matter? It matters because people still believe that Google searches are factual, unbiased, and authoritative.

Google's ability to manipulate public opinion through its curated content makes Google capable of influencing elections and world events. It is a truly staggering level of social control concentrated in the hands of a few corporate globalists. Just imagine the difference in Google content if it embraced an America-first mentality determined to protect American interests, American sovereignty, and American independence.

Instead, Google provides its biased globalist support of the Leftist/Islamist/Globalist axis in support of illegal immigration, open borders, educational indoctrination, and anti-conservative, pro-liberal, anti-Christian, pro-Muslim views to facilitate its long-term objective of a one-world government.

Daniel Greenfield discussed the recent challenge to the First Amendment in his June 18, 2019, article, "16 Biggest Advertisers Ally to Censor 'Hate Speech' on Social Media." In an Orwellian gambit to "challenge hate speech and disinformation," these globalist behemoths formed the Global Alliance for Responsible Media, and plan to define hate speech and disinformation for us. Leftists and Islamists have already defined hate speech as anything they disagree with; the globalist advertisers will no doubt follow suit.

The Humanitarian Hoax of "Neutral" Google Searches is an end run around free speech. It seeks to indoctrinate and propagandize Americans into accepting the fiction that one-world government will bring peace and justice to the world. Any system of governance that can stand on merit does not require the sins of omission, commission, censorship, advertising cartel alliances, or the curated content that Google delivers daily with 63,000 searches per second, 3.8 million per minute, and 5.8 billion searches a day—7 days a week, 365 days a year.

Establishing a New World Order of one-world government is a long-term strategy, and time is on Google's side. Americans who want a free, sovereign, independent America must understand the globalist goals of biased Google content and always consider the source of its search results. It is time for Americans to become concerned about Google's content legitimacy, authoritativeness, and relevance. It is time for Americans to choose alternative search engines like Bing, DuckDuckGo, or Yahoo. Google's curated globalist content is not neutral—it is the enemy of American sovereignty and independence.

America-first President Donald Trump has defined his priority as Americanism. Google supports leftist Democrats and has defined its priority as globalism. Be skeptical of Google search results. Election 2020 will define the future of America. Be very careful who you vote for.

HOAX 34

The Humanitarian Hoax of Planned Parenthood

June 25, 2019

THE humanitarian hoax is the deliberate and deceitful tactic of presenting a destructive policy as altruistic. The humanitarian huckster presents himself as a compassionate advocate when in fact he is the disguised enemy.

Planned Parenthood began in 1916 as the American Birth Control League when Margaret Sanger and her two sisters opened the first birth control clinic in Brooklyn, New York. They distributed contraceptive devices, birth control advice, and birth control information. Abortion was illegal, and throughout her incumbency Sanger maintained that abortion would not be necessary if women had knowledge about contraception and access to birth control. In 1942 the name American Birth Control League was changed to Planned Parenthood Federation of America.

Planned Parenthood began advocating for abortion law reform in the early 1950s. At first it focused on therapeutic abortions—medically necessary abortions in the first trimester before the fetus is viable outside the womb. By the 1960s, the organization was advocating liberalizing abortion laws to include non-therapeutic abortions.

The first birth control pill was commissioned by Margaret Sanger and funded in 1953 by friend and fellow suffragist Katharine McCormick, a biologist and heir to the International Harvester fortune. On May 9, 1960, the FDA approved the pill, and women's reproductive freedom became foundational to the women's liberation movement, the sexual revolution, and the anti-establishment counterculture movement, which supported Planned Parenthood's rejection of any limits on abortion.

By 1969 Planned Parenthood was demanding total repeal of all abortion laws.

In January 1973, the Supreme Court issued its landmark decision in

Roe v. Wade, and abortion was legalized in America. Women had the right to choose whether to have an abortion, but the right was not absolute because of the competing interests of protecting prenatal life and also the government's interest in protecting women's health. The Court issued restrictions that addressed the complexity of the issue in what is known as a balancing test. Legal scholar Erwin Chemerinsky clarified this term in *Constitutional Law: Principles and Policies*:

> The Court resolved this balancing test by tying state regulation of abortion to the three trimesters of pregnancy: during the first trimester, governments could not prohibit abortions at all; during the second trimester, governments could require reasonable health regulations; during the third trimester, abortions could be prohibited entirely so long as the laws contained exceptions for cases when they were necessary to save the life or health of the mother.

In January 2019, New York lifted every restriction and legalized all abortions, including late-term abortions. Seven states and Washington, DC, followed New York's horrifying example:

- Alaska
- Colorado
- New Hampshire
- New Jersey
- New Mexico
- Oregon
- Vermont
- Washington, DC

This unnerving decision means it is legal to abort a viable baby up to birth—and even after birth in cases where the baby survives the abortion. The Reproductive Health Act, S.240, passed by the New York Senate and signed into law by Governor Andrew Cuomo, repealed section 4164 of New York's Public Health Law, which mandated medical care for any baby born alive during an abortion. New York's new law allows licensed health care practitioners other than physicians to perform abortions, legalizes late-term abortions to protect the patient's health, and revokes mandated medical care for babies born alive during the abortion procedure, effectively legalizing infanticide.

Late-term and after-birth abortions are NO ONE'S RIGHT TO

CHOOSE—they are legalized murder. A baby just before birth is not a cluster of undifferentiated cells; it is a fully formed, viable human being. How did murder become legal in the United States of America?

Planned Parenthood began as Margaret Sanger's women's health initiative to provide necessary contraceptive devices, birth control advice, and birth control information. It has become radicalized along with the radicalization of the Democrat party, which sponsors its initiatives including radicalized leftist sex education in schools.

One of these initiatives is <u>SIECUS</u>, the Sexuality Information and Education Council of the United States.

SIECUS was started in 1964 by Dr. Mary Calderone, who was medical director for the Planned Parenthood Federation. SIECUS publishes books and journals on sexuality and sex education that are used by professionals, parents, and the general public. It has developed curricula for medical schools and college students. SIECUS is responsible for the <u>Guidelines for Comprehensive Education: Kindergarten-12th Grade</u> that are part of the Common Core curriculum taught in public schools throughout America.

So, Planned Parenthood is in the <u>education business</u> and is actively indoctrinating American children with its radical views on sex, sexuality, and gender. SIECUS interim president Christine Soyong Harley unapologetically announced the group's conviction that "<u>Sex ed is a vehicle for social change</u>."

I will repeat: The SIECUS interim president stated that sex education is a vehicle for social change and promotes her activism, saying:

> While sex education is a necessary sexual health tool, it can (and should) be so much more than that. With sex education, we have a golden opportunity to create a culture shift—tackling the misinformation, shame, and stigma that create the basis for many of today's sexual and reproductive health and rights issues, like:

- Reproductive justice
- LGBTQ equality
- Sexual violence prevention
- Gender equity
- Dismantling white supremacy

Harley goes on to say that SIECUS already has the way to do this—through its <u>Comprehensive Sexuality Education</u> (CSE) that is currently indoctrinating your children from kindergarten through high school!

It gets worse. Planned Parenthood is no longer the Sanger sisters' birth control clinic in Brooklyn. Planned Parenthood is now a global health provider and the single biggest provider of reproductive health services, including abortion, in the United States. Planned Parenthood is an activist political organization disguised as a women's health initiative. According to <u>Wikipedia</u>,

> Planned Parenthood consists of 159 medical and non-medical affiliates, which operate over 600 health clinics in the United States. It partners with organizations in 12 countries globally. The organization directly provides a variety of reproductive health services and sexual education, contributes to research in reproductive technology and advocates for the protection and expansion of reproductive rights.

Planned Parenthood's international outreach is conducted by Planned Parenthood Global and by the International Planned Parenthood Federation (IPPF), which has 149 Member Associations in over 189 countries.

Planned Parenthood has a globalist agenda; it is an active participant in UN Agenda 2030 and its globalized educational programs designed to create a New World Order.

Using sex education to indoctrinate children into radical leftist/globalist ideology is a colossal abuse of power and exploitation of young children. What Planned Parenthood considers appropriate sex education is very different from what most parents worldwide consider appropriate, especially for young children. Let's take a look.

Planned Parenthood presents itself as a humanitarian organization dedicated to advancing women's health while it targets your children using perverse sex education as the vehicle to effect seismic social change.

Dr. Duke Pesta, FreedomProject Education's Academic Director and Professor of English at the University of Wisconsin–Oshkosh, has given public testimony against Common Core State Standards. Capt. Joseph John, USN/FBI (Ret.), has written an affirming assessment of Pesta's scathing testimony in his article "<u>Dr. Duke Pesta on the Shocking K-12 Common Core Sexual Education Standards</u>":

> Common Core is not only the development of national standards for math, English, biology, and science it also includes teaching shocking sexual education courses for students in grades kindergarten thru 12.

What is taught includes teaching inappropriate sexuality skills that shouldn't even be taught in college. According to child psychologists, the children are not mentally equipped to understand the detailed sexual indoctrination starting in kindergarten; they are indoctrinated in sexual practices that they should never be exposed to. Students are tested on their understanding of sex issues every year for the 12 years they are in school, and the views for each student on sex issues are being tested, recorded, and retained by Washington bureaucrats.

There is a heavy sociopolitical content of sex throughout Common Core curriculum being taught in every grade and in every subject. The student is taught that there is a sameness of gender; there is no longer simply boys and girls, according to Common Core. . . . Sexual activities and content are included in every subject taught. Sex is taught in the English curriculum, is included in the language curriculum, sex is woven into the science curriculum, in the math curriculum, in the social studies curriculum, and of course in biology.

Since sex practices are included in every subject taught, parents will no longer be able to opt out of sex education being taught to their children in city schools. . . . Children are taught holding hands, hugging, kissing are the same as every other deviant sex act—they are taught there is a sameness to "all" sex—there is no such thing as normal sex in Common Core; wide-open sex of every weird type is taught to be acceptable in Common Core.

Pornography is no longer looked down upon in the Common Core curriculum. . . . The Core Curriculum states the students must be taught cooperative and active sex, working together in lab sessions with each other. . . . Every imaginable inappropriate sexual skill is being taught to students in kindergarten thru grade 12. These inappropriate sexual skills are being driven into the Common Core curriculum and are being tested by the Department of Health Education and Welfare.

Now let's look at the misleading marketing campaign used by Planned Parenthood's SIECUS to sell its destructive sexual indoctrination to American children.

The <u>National Sexuality Education Standards: Core Content and Skills, K-12</u> provides the rationale, standards, and goal for sexuality education in public schools:

> The goal of the National Sexuality Education Standards: Core Content and Skills, K-12 is to provide clear, consistent and straightforward guidance on the essential minimum, core content for sexuality education that is age-appropriate for students in grades K-12.

Sounds great—but then humanitarian hoaxes always do.

The stated goals do not reflect Sayong Harley's "golden opportunity to create a culture shift" that is the actual goal of the leftist/globalist sexual education program. Sexual identity is the first thing announced in any language anywhere in the world when a baby is born: "It's a boy!" "It's a girl!" Only a minuscule fraction of the world's population has ambiguous sex organs that would leave the baby's sexual identity unclear.

The perverse movement to confuse children about their primary identity is a sinister attempt to destabilize society and create social chaos. Social chaos is the prerequisite for imposing the New World Order envisioned by the globalist elite. The concept is not new. Bertrand Russell wrote about it in his 1952 classic, *The Impact of Science on Society*. The New World Order is an internationalized world with one language, one currency, one flag, one educational system, one culture: one country ruled by the globalist elite under the auspices of the United Nations.

Dr. John Coleman describes the nexus of the conspiratorial elite seeking world domination in his book _Conspirators' Hierarchy: The Story of The Committee of 300_.

The attack on sexuality was articulated decades ago by Tavistock Institute as an effective tactic to break down the psychological strength of the individual and render that individual helpless to oppose the rulers of the New World Order. The strategy of the Culture War is to attack the infrastructure of American life—family, religion, patriotism, and sexual behavior. Why sexual behavior?

Sexual behavior reflects social norms in a society. Monogamous sex in marriage is a commitment that values loyalty to the spouse and family unit. It is also a reflection of the Judeo-Christian moral prohibition against infidelity. Not all couples manage fidelity, but it is still considered immoral. The breakdown of the family and rejection of the moral teachings of religion invite detachment and promiscuous sex. Destruction of traditional morality and normalization of deviance are deliberate strategies in the Culture War on America.

The Humanitarian Hoax of Planned Parenthood is a sinister attack designed to destroy America from within that has gone global with the help of the United Nations and its Agenda 2030. The New World Order is impossible without the breakdown of American society. Planned Parenthood and SIECUS are soldiers in the leftist Culture War on America.

Accusations of white supremacy are foundational to the leftist narrative. They are even part of the destructive sexual education program designed to create chaos in America. This is how it works.

The leftist narrative is designed to collapse America and create catastrophic tensions that will erupt in a race war—the goal of the white-supremacy narrative. The race war will lead to social chaos and the country will become ungovernable. At that point martial law will be declared and the leftist objective of socialism will be imposed.

The problem, of course, is that the leftists are just useful idiots for the globalists. Leftist leaders such as Christine Soyong Harley will no longer be useful to the revolution and will be "collateral damage." The globalists will then impose a one-world government, which was their goal all along: no more leftists, no more Islamists, no more Planned Parenthood. Just a catastrophic return to feudalism, with a very small ruling elite and the mass population who serve them. There is no middle class in feudalism, no private property, no upward mobility, no freedom of any kind. Only masters and slaves, just as the globalist elite desire.

Planned Parenthood is doing the dirty work of the globalist elite—its soldiers are just too arrogant and angry to notice that they are participating in their own destruction. The noisy leftist Democrats who support Planned Parenthood and promote its destructive agenda are also useful idiots of the globalist elite who fund their pricey political campaigns. The duped Democrats are mercenaries who haven't figured out that when this war is over they also will be expendable.

The winner in the fight for the soul of America will be determined by the 2020 elections. America-first President Donald Trump is the existential enemy of the Leftist/Islamist/Globalist axis that is trying to collapse our country and establish the New World Order. Do not let them. Do not be fooled by the Humanitarian Hoax of Planned Parenthood. Vote straight Republican and take back the House so that President Trump can keep America great.

HOAX 35

The Humanitarian Hoax of Ballot Harvesting

June 30, 2019

THE humanitarian hoax is the deliberate and deceitful tactic of presenting a destructive policy as altruistic. The humanitarian huckster presents himself as a compassionate advocate when in fact he is the disguised enemy.

Harvesting is defined as collecting or obtaining a resource for future use. We commonly equate harvesting with agricultural crops—but in the twenty-first century, harvesting has far more to do with political crops. The resource is votes.

Ballot harvesting is like the Greek hydra, the many-headed snake whose heads not only grew back but also multiplied as they were cut off. So, let's examine the heads of this ballot-harvesting Democrat hydra.

Ballot harvesting is political jargon for a practice in which organized workers or volunteers collect absentee ballots from certain voters and drop them off at a polling place or election office. WHAT?

Let's review. In ballot harvesting, someone picks up other people's ballots and drops them off somewhere else. Any voter who has ever voted in person knows that great care is taken to secure the confidentiality of voters, the security of their ballots, and the legitimacy of their votes. Ballots are filled out in the privacy of a voting booth, placed inside a secrecy sleeve, and then hand-delivered by the voter to a machine that automatically pulls the ballot into itself. No one besides the voter touches the ballot—the ballot chain is unbroken.

Absentee voting allows voting by mail. A vote-by-mail ballot is mailed to the registered voter, the voter marks the ballot, inserts the ballot in the secrecy sleeve, places the secrecy sleeve inside the envelope provided, seals the envelope, and then must sign the back of the envelope across the sealed closure. For the mailed ballot to be valid and counted, the signature must match the voter's signature on file.

In this case the ballot chain includes handling and transportation by the United States Postal Service (USPS). It is a federal crime to tamper with the mail. Absentee ballots may also be returned by a relative or legally authorized person to a polling place or election office.

Unlike mail-in ballots using the USPS, ballot harvesting uses organized workers or volunteers to collect absentee ballots from voters and drop them off at a polling place or election office. Ballot harvesting is an invitation for voter fraud because the ballot chain is broken by partisan political workers who can choose which ballots to collect or submit.

An article published in *The Federalist* on December 14, 2018, "How Ballot-Harvesting Became the New Way to Steal an Election," reports how a 2016 law legalizing ballot harvesting was responsible for the sweep of House seats in the former Republican stronghold of California's Orange County in the 2018 midterm election. Previously, California allowed only relatives or people living in the same house to drop off absentee ballots for another person. The article describes how the new law signed by Governor Jerry Brown allows anyone, even a paid political campaign worker, to collect and return ballots:

> In Orange County, an estimated 250,000 harvested ballots were reportedly dropped off on Election Day alone. County Republican Chairman Fred Whitaker claimed the 2016 law "directly caused the switch from being ahead on election night to losing two weeks later."

Voting is the most sacred of rights guaranteed by our Constitution and is protected at every point in the voting process. The idea that paid political campaign workers can pick up ballots and drop them off at a polling place or election office is equivalent to a broken chain of evidence in a criminal trial. When the chain is broken, the evidence is inadmissible because it may have been tampered with.

Ballot harvesting is the first head of the hydra. Next are unclean voting rolls. Tom Fitton, executive president of the watchdog organization Judicial Watch, has demonstrated that under President Obama's watch the voter rolls were not updated or accurate, so dead people were still listed, people who had moved away were still listed, and illegal immigrants were listed. This is the second head on the hydra of voter fraud.

In 2012, *PJ Media* reported that Obama's corrupt attorney general,

Eric Holder, actually sued Florida "to block its efforts to purge its voter rolls of dead people and non–U.S. citizens and to stop further attempts before the November 2012 presidential election."

In 2019 Judicial Watch won a huge case in California that required Los Angeles County to send notices to 1.5 million inactive voters. This is the first step toward removing ineligible voters from the voter rolls. Los Angeles County, with over 10 million residents, had allowed more than 20 percent of its registered voters to remain inactive without removing them from the voter list as required by law. California had not cleaned up its voter rolls in twenty years!

Purging inactive voters is critical to the integrity of elections because maintaining accurate voter registration lists insures that only eligible voters cast their ballots in their proper jurisdictions.

The National Voter Registration Act allows states to remove voters who have not voted in two consecutive federal general elections and have failed to respond to a confirmation notice from an election office. Voters are also removed from the list who are convicted felons, have died or moved to a different jurisdiction, are mentally incompetent, or have requested removal themselves.

The National Voter Registration Act is often called the "motor voter" law because it provides for voter registration at the Department of Motor Vehicles. That brings us to the third head on the hydra of voter fraud.

New York recently made it lawful for illegal aliens to receive driver's licenses. This makes it extremely easy to implement the next incremental step for Democrats to harvest votes—allowing illegal immigrants to legally vote. EXCUSE ME? Yes, the leftist Democrats leading the party want illegal aliens to vote. Of course they do—illegal immigrants will vote for Democrats and keep them in power for the foreseeable future.

A June 19, 2019, _Breitbart_ article explains, "In New York, U.S. citizens only need a driver's license to register to vote and though applicants are required to swear that they are eligible to vote, state election officials told the Post that 'it's basically an honor system.'" HONOR SYSTEM? Illegals are in this country illegally! How can an honor system possibly apply to people who are breaking our immigration laws every day they are in our country?

The Humanitarian Hoax of Ballot Harvesting is an assault on our

Constitution because its objective is to make citizenship irrelevant by giving illegal immigrants the same rights as legal citizens. This is how it works.

From January 2009 to November 2010 the Democrats held both houses of Congress and the presidency. For almost two years the Obama administration chose to ignore the growing border crisis and its humanitarian consequences. In fact, it was Barack Obama, not Donald Trump, who put illegal alien children in cages.

Now, with the upcoming elections in 2020, Democrats are wailing about inhumane conditions at our southern border. They deliberately ignore the fact that illegal alien parents are responsible for putting their children at risk by attempting to illegally enter the United States.

The Democrats find it politically expedient to weep about housing and medical care for illegals. Housing for illegals? Medical care for illegals? What about housing and medical care for legal citizens of the United States who are struggling financially? No matter—the Democrats do not care about legal citizens, because their goal is harvesting ballots through illegal immigration.

Remember, harvesting is the practice of collecting or obtaining a resource for future use. Illegal aliens are a bonanza for Democrats because they are the biggest resource imaginable for future votes. Democrats do not care if the massive invasion at the border collapses the welfare system—they *want* to collapse the system. Open borders are an expansion of the Cloward and Piven strategy described in *The Humanitarian Hoax of Community Organizing—Hoax12* that will create social chaos, economic collapse, and lead to socialism. This is how it works.

President Trump's America-first presidency and economic policies have been so successful that the Democrats cannot possibly collapse the economy any other way. The mass invasion of illegals into our country serves a dual purpose—harvesting votes for Democrats while collapsing our booming economy.

In case anyone actually believes that having illegal aliens overrun and collapse the U.S. economy is a good thing, let's talk about what will happen if this invasion is not stopped.

If Democrats are not stopped and they succeed in ballot harvesting to win the 2020 elections, the invasion on our southern border will continue. The massive influx of illegal immigrants will overwhelm and necessarily collapse the social welfare system, with social chaos and riots to follow. When the country becomes ungovernable, martial law will be declared. At that point socialism will be imposed in preparation for the final objective—a one-world government.

The leftist Democrats demanding open borders and socialism are the useful idiots for the globalist elite who finance their leftist political campaigns and anti-American policies. Globalists have their own, singular objective: a one-world government—ruled by themselves, of course. The Democrats have not figured out that there will be no place for them in the globalist elite's New World Order—the noisy Democrats are entirely expendable.

Before any voter is foolish enough to buy into the con of leftist Democrats promoting socialism and open borders, let's examine socialism. First, free stuff is never free. You pay with your freedom. So, let's discuss freedom.

In socialist countries the government owns all means of production and is in charge of distributing whatever is produced. There is no private ownership. There is no middle class or upward mobility in socialism because there is no private property. The Democrat candidates hawking socialism never mention these critical details.

Socialism is just a variation on the feudal structure of a very small ruling elite at the top of the social pyramid and a very large population of slaves at the bottom who service them. There is no middle class in feudalism. There is no private property. There is no upward mobility. There is no freedom. There are only masters and slaves.

Leftism is the path to socialism, and socialism is the path to feudalism. So, be very careful who you vote for in 2020. The Humanitarian Hoax of Ballot Harvesting is an insidious power grab by leftist Democrats intent on exploiting illegal aliens for votes. If the leftist Democrats succeed in their power grab and win the 2020 elections, the United States of America will cease to be a free country. We will become part of the globalists' supranational feudal New World Order.

Choose freedom and vote for America-first President Donald Trump. Choose freedom to protect our sovereignty and our precious Constitution that guarantees our liberties—including our property rights. In a free country we own ourselves and are not vassals of the state.

HOAX 36

The Humanitarian Hoax of the United Nations

July 3, 2019

THE humanitarian hoax is the deliberate and deceitful tactic of presenting a destructive policy as altruistic. The humanitarian huckster presents himself as a compassionate advocate when in fact he is the disguised enemy.

The United Nations is both an institutional humanitarian hoax and an international humanitarian huckster promoting its destructive Agenda 2030 infrastructure for one-world government as the altruistic advancement of world peace. This is how it works.

First, a little history. The United Nations began as a wartime alliance between the Allies against Nazi Germany in World War II. President Franklin D. Roosevelt suggested using the name United Nations to refer to the allies. In 1942, the declaration of the allied United Nations articulated its purpose and was signed by twenty-six sovereign governments:

A JOINT DECLARATION BY THE UNITED STATES OF AMERICA, THE UNITED KINGDOM OF GREAT BRITAIN AND NORTHERN IRELAND, THE UNION OF SOVIET SOCIALIST REPUBLICS, CHINA, AUSTRALIA, BELGIUM, CANADA, COSTA RICA, CUBA, CZECHO-SLOVAKIA, DOMINICAN REPUBLIC, EL SALVADOR, GREECE, GUATEMALA, HAITI, HONDURAS, INDIA, LUXEMBOURG, NETH-ERLANDS, NEW ZEALAND, NICARAGUA, NORWAY, PANAMA, POLAND, SOUTH AFRICA, YUGOSLAVIA

The Governments signatory hereto,

Having subscribed to a common program of purposes and principles embodied by the Joint Declaration of the President of the United States of America and the Prime Minister of Great Britain dated August 14, 1941, known as the Atlantic Charter,

Being convinced that complete victory over their enemies is essential to defend life, liberty, independence and religious freedom, and to preserve human rights and justice in their own lands as well as in other lands, and that they are now engaged in common struggle against savage and brutal forces seeking to subjugate the world,

DECLARE:

(1) Each Government pledges itself to employ its full resources, military or economic, against those members of the Tripartite Pact [Germany, Italy, Japan] and its adherents with which such government is at war.

(2) Each Government pledges itself to cooperate with the Governments signatory hereto and not to make a separate armistice or peace with the enemies. The forgoing declaration may be adhered to by other nations which are, or which may be, rendering material assistance and contributions in the struggle for victory over Hitlerism.

By late October 1945, twenty-five more sovereign nations had joined the alliance by signing the Declaration. The United Nations replaced the failed League of Nations and became a permanent international organization with the constructive mission to provide peace among sovereign nations through cooperation and communication.

The structure of the original United Nations was <u>fifty-one sovereign nations</u> organized by regions, including the five permanent members of the Security Council:

- United States
- Britain
- China
- Russia
- France

The Security Council originally consisted of eleven members—five permanent and six non-permanent members. The six non-permanent seats are elected by all the members of the United Nations, serve two-year terms on the <u>Security Council</u>, and are organized and apportioned by regions. Initially, there were two Latin American seats, one Commonwealth seat, one Eastern European & Asian seat, one Middle Eastern seat, and one Western seat. The presidency of the Security Council is held by each of the members for one month. The rotation is based on the English alphabetical order of member state names.

An amendment to the UN Charter in 1965 increased the Security Council to fifteen members—five permanent members plus ten non-permanent member seats—and adjusted the <u>regions</u> to include African nations and the Caribbean Group. Now there are five seats for the African and Asia-Pacific Group, including Arab nations; two Latin American and Caribbean Group seats; two Western European and Other Groups seats; and one Eastern European Group seat.

The structure of the United Nations is as significant as its policies, because its structure defines the power awarded to implement UN policies through its principal organs and related specialized agencies and organizations.

The United Nations System is structured with six principal organs:

- General Assembly
- Security Council
- Economic and Social Council
- Trusteeship Council (currently inactive)
- International Court of Justice
- UN Secretariat

The UN provides a helpful *Directory* of its complex system organizations. There are currently fifteen UN Specialized Agencies, five Related Organizations, and thirteen Funds and Programs, including the World Bank Group; the International Monetary Fund; the World Health Organization; the World Food Program; United Nations Education, Scientific, and Cultural Organization; and United Nations Children's Fund. The United Nations has become a comprehensive global organization influencing public policy worldwide. So, what is the problem?

The United Nations has abandoned its initial mission to encourage world peace for sovereign nations through cooperation and communication. It has redefined itself as a globalized body promoting peace through one internationalized world without borders. The reorganization features one government, one flag, one culture, one currency, one language, one educational curriculum, and one ruling elite. This rejection of the sovereignty of nations, including the unique cultures and traditions of individual countries, is an egregious power grab by the globalist elite who plan to return the world to the feudal structure of masters and slaves—a New World Order.

English aristocrat Bertrand Russell described the imperious power grab of the globalist elite in his unapologetic 1952 book, *The Impact of Science on Society.* Russell argued that the solution to the Malthusian dilemma of not enough natural resources to support the growing world population is imposition of the elitist New World Order. Russell's imagined New World Order is being implemented by the comprehensive UN Agenda 2030 through its system agencies, including:

- UN Paris Agreement: Redistribution of wealth disguised as combating Climate Change.
- UN Global Compact for Safe, Orderly, and Regular Migration: Mass immigration of populations with hostile norms designed to collapse the traditional Judeo-Christian infrastructure of sovereign Western countries, including the United States.
- UN Global Education Initiative: Educational indoctrination provided by propagandized textbooks, delivered through Google's Chromebooks and augmented with curated globalist Google searches on the Internet. (See *The Humanitarian Hoax of Pearson Education—Hoax 30*, *The Humanitarian Hoax of 'Convenient' Google Chromebook Education—Hoax 27*, and *The Humanitarian Hoax of 'Neutral' Google Searches—Hoax 33*.)
- Anti-Christian indoctrination included in Common Core and distributed through UN globalized educational initiatives (see *The Humanitarian Hoax of Common Core—Hoax 19*).
- Anti-Semitic indoctrination included in Common Core and distributed through UN globalized educational initiatives.
- Pro-Muslim indoctrination included in Common Core and distributed through UN globalized educational initiatives.

The announced and demonstrated goal of today's United Nations is to collapse the sovereignty of nations and to reform the nation-states into a globalized world order under a one-world government implemented by the United Nations itself. It is a long-term project. Globalized educational indoctrination prepares the world's young people for citizenship in the New World Order. The propagandized curriculum is designed to produce voters who will embrace and eventually vote to implement a supranational one-world government. Complete world domination, no bullets required.

Wealth redistribution, massive immigration, and educational indoctrination are the three main tactics in the UN's war on the sovereign nation-states of the world.

Consider the UN Agenda 2030 and its 17 Sustainable Development

Goals. All of the goals promote the globalist elite's New World Order—for our own good, of course. The globalist elite have just repackaged feudalism and are busy putting lipstick on a pig and selling it worldwide through the United Nation's principal organs and globalized integrated system agencies and organizations.

There are 193 member states in the United Nations today, and according to Freedom House, only 87 are full-fledged democracies. This means that the majority of UN member states are not democracies. Whether democratic or undemocratic, one state equals one vote in the UN. The Organization of Islamic Cooperation (OIC), which works to promote Islamic solidarity and the interests of Muslims worldwide, includes 56 UN member states. This means that theocracies ruled by Sharia law exert enormous influence at the United Nations. The effort to criminalize criticism of Muhammad as hate speech worldwide is a prime objective of the OIC.

The United Nations has launched a massive new anti-hate-speech campaign introduced by former socialist Prime Minister of Portugal, now UN Secretary-General Antonio Guterres on June 18, 2019. The campaign sounds humanitarian—political hoaxes always do. The reality is that socialists at the United Nations, in the United States, and around the world have a politically specific idea of what hate speech is: anything that disagrees with their socialist narrative. That concept poses a problem for nation-states and citizens who prefer their national sovereignty, property rights, free markets, and individual liberties including freedom of speech.

Free speech is universally the first liberty eliminated by every oppressive government in the world. The United Nations, in trying to drive the world toward one-world government, considers any opposition to its objective to be hate speech. The once extraordinary voice of sovereignty and freedom is now the tyrannical promoter of a one-world government implemented through its own globalized infrastructure.

The original mission of the United Nations was to protect the peace and sovereignty of the nation-states against Hitlerism. The United Nations is now the enemy of the sovereignty of nation-states and is diametrically opposed to traditional American values. Globalism rejects national sovereignty, defensible borders, independence, personal liberty, meritocracy, and the authority of the U.S. Constitution, which guarantees American citizens free speech and separation of church and state, and provides the mechanisms for legal immigration into the country.

The United Nations cannot be allowed to restrict free speech in the name of humanitarian altruism. It is a humanitarian hoax of colossal proportions. Free speech is the foundation of all freedoms—without free speech there is no freedom. We cannot allow anyone or any organization, including the United Nations, to dictate American policy and supersede the U.S. Constitution. The United Nations and its like-minded organizations, including the Muslim Brotherhood, the socialists leading the U.S. Democrat party, Google, Facebook, and Twitter, cannot be permitted to determine what is and what is not allowable speech in America.

The Islamists in the African and Asia-Pacific Group, including Arab nations, claim that Islam is peaceful. Peace for an Islamist means when the entire world is Muslim and ruled by Sharia law. The globalists at the United Nations claim their Agenda 2030, including its latest anti-hate-speech campaign, is peaceful. Peace for the UN's globalists means when the entire world is internationalized and united under a one-world government ruled by UN elite themselves.

If we allow the United Nations, the Muslim Brotherhood, or their quislings to restrict our free speech, then we are collapsing the foundation of our constitutional republic. We can never allow an international organization like the UN to dictate policy to the United States of America. If we do, we have surrendered our constitutional freedoms and become part of their feudal one-world government.

The fifteen-member UN Security Council is charged with maintaining peace and security among nations. The Security Council has the power to make binding decisions called resolutions that member states are required to carry out under the terms of the United Nations Charter of 1945, the foundational treaty of the United Nations. Each of the five permanent members has the power to veto any resolution. Even if fourteen members of the Security Council support a resolution, one permanent member can veto it.

This means that the vote of the United States is crucial. The U.S. vote on the Security Council can intervene and halt the egregious movement of the United Nations to deny national sovereignty and create a one-world government. Or the U.S. vote can help install a one-world government ruled by the globalist elite under the auspices of the United Nations.

The president of the United States appoints our ambassador to the United Nations, so the 2020 American presidential election is pivotal in determining the future of America and the future of the world. A vote for any of the Democrat party's candidates facilitates the United Nations' objective of a one-world government. A vote for America-first President Donald Trump ensures a free, sovereign, powerful America. I hope that in his second term, President Trump will consider withdrawing the United States from the institutional humanitarian hoax and international humanitarian huckster that is the United Nations.

I am an American citizen who rejects Islamic efforts to establish a worldwide Muslim caliphate ruled by Islamic Sharia law. I am an American citizen who rejects the UN's efforts to establish an internationalized world ruled by a one-world government. I am an American citizen who believes in the U.S. Constitution, the American flag, and the republic for which it stands. I am an American citizen who will exercise my precious right to vote and cast my 2020 ballot for America-first President Donald Trump and his efforts to keep America great, free, and sovereign. God bless America!

The Humanitarian Hoax of Leftism

July 7, 2019

THE humanitarian hoax is the deliberate and deceitful tactic of presenting a destructive policy as altruistic. The humanitarian huckster presents himself as a compassionate advocate when in fact he is the disguised enemy.

War makes strange bedfellows, and the current Leftist/Islamist alliance against America-first President Donald Trump is worth examining.

Islamic Sharia law—which endorses misogyny, homophobia, anti-Semitism, pedophilia, female genital mutilation, and wife beating—is diametrically opposed to leftist Democrats' proclaimed principles of women's rights, LGBTQ rights, children's rights, and anti-bullying. How, then, can leftists partner with Islamists?

The answer is that leftists are staggeringly hypocritical when it comes to their principles. Leftist metrics of inclusion are myopic; they consider only what a person thinks and ignore what a person does. The Left embraces every color, every sexual orientation, every religion, every deviant behavior as long as its members THINK alike. Leftist anti-American, anti-Trump groupthink is completely intolerant of any individual divergence of thought.

The demand for conformity among leftists is no different from any religious orthodoxy. Orthodoxy requires conformity for membership in the group. Leftists consider their tenets of political correctness, moral relativism, and historical revisionism to be incontrovertible.

The barbaric tenets of Islam are ignored as long as these Sharia-compliant Muslims are anti-American anti-Trumpers. Any anti-American, anti-Trump Islamist is welcomed into the leftist tribe because they are all warriors in the Culture War on America. America-first President Donald Trump is the existential enemy of the Culture War and therefore the target of the Leftist/Islamist alliance.

Islamists unapologetically tell the world that their goal is world domination and the establishment of an Islamist caliphate. Their condescending attitude asserts they are doing the West a favor by freeing us from our secular freedoms and imposing their supremacist religious Sharia law (see *The Humanitarian Hoax of the Muslim Brotherhood—Hoax 26*). Islamists do not recognize the authority of the secular U.S. Constitution, upon which all of our laws are based.

Leftists are equally condescending in their arrogant insistence that socialism, which they consider superior to capitalism and the free market, will bring social justice and income equality. Socialism has never kept these promises anywhere in the world that it has ever been imposed. Regardless, leftists insist they are doing us a favor by freeing us from our discriminatory constitutional freedoms and replacing them with equitable socialism. Just like Islamists, leftists do not recognize the authority of the U.S. Constitution.

In America, freedom of religion and the separation of church and state mean that the government is prohibited from establishing a state religion. But what happens when a political ideology is practiced with religious zealotry?

Red is the color of communism and Marxist socialism. Green is the color of Islam. When you combine red and green in the presence of light, <u>the mixture is yellow</u>—the color of cowardice. The Leftist/Islamist alliance is a cowardly consortium that rejects the U.S. Constitution and the meritocracy, with its free and open debate of ideas. The anti-American Leftist/Islamist alliance requires force, violence, propaganda, and indoctrination—the classic tools of tyranny.

The Leftist/Islamist alliance has the singular strategic goal of shattering the U.S. Constitution. The longer that leftists remain aligned with Islamists, the more their strategic tactics resemble those of Islamic jihad. The Culture War on America has multiple fronts. Let's take a closer look.

Political jihad. There is no tolerance for competing ideas in either Islamism or leftism; both systems require absolute conformity to their ideological tenets. The tyranny of both insists upon elimination of the opposition, the difference between them being the punishment for dissent. Islamist Sharia law demands the killing of infidels and apostates. Leftists in

America use social shunning, verbal abuse, litigation and corporate pressure to shut down speakers voicing opposing opinions, and even violence.

Physical jihad. Imams, mullahs, and leftist Democrat political leaders encourage violence because their systems cannot survive rational scrutiny and must be imposed on populations through fear and coercion. Political violence is normative in Islamic theocracies. Leftists in America are making political violence normative by abandoning America's civilized competitive free market of ideas in favor of lawlessness and the physical threat of Antifa violence. Antifa, an abbreviation for anti-fascists, is the biggest fraud of all, since they actually are today's fascists. Like many Muslim jihadis, Antifa thugs wear face masks to hide their identities.

Education jihad. Targeting education with political indoctrination to propagandize students is a powerful stealth war tactic of both Islamists and leftists (see *The Humanitarian Hoax of Pearson Education—Hoax 30*).

Taqiyya, lying in the service of Islam. Radical socialist Saul Alinsky introduced the concept to America in his 1971 book, *Rules for Radicals*, when he instructed his students to cut their hair, put on business suits, and blend in so that no one would suspect they were trying to overthrow both the American government and capitalism, and impose socialism—Alinskiyya, lying in the service of socialism.

Lawfare. Activist judges trying to stop or at least stall President Trump's America-first policies is the current tactic of both Islamists and leftists. Disingenuous accusations of Islamophobia, along with activist judges countermanding lawful executive orders, have become routine in America.

Victim identity. Islamists and leftists self-identify as victims so they can deceitfully engage the compassion of humanitarian citizens and divert attention from their underlying goal of shattering the Constitution.

Economic jihad. The Islamist Boycott Divestment and Sanctions (BDS) movement against Israel is embraced by leftists in a coordinated effort to demonize and destroy the economy of the only Democratic nation-state in the Middle East. The Leftist/Islamist alliance also targets conservative media outlets by pressuring sponsors to drop their ads from conservative radio and television programs in an effort to silence voices that support President Trump and his America-first policies.

Media jihad. Islamists and leftists are supported by the mainstream media, Hollywood celebrities, and Internet behemoths that censor and curate content in order to manipulate public opinion. It is coordinated social engineering on a massive scale. Media content is deliberately anti-American, anti-Trump, anti-Semitic, anti-Christian, and pro-Islamic. Political correctness, moral relativism, and historical revisionism are primary tactics used to deliver the content designed to destabilize and destroy America.

Islamists have a 1400-year history of destruction and conquest. An essential element of Islamic conquest is the complete destruction of any adversary's history and culture, including religious and historical icons. Churches are destroyed and replaced with mosques. Historical statues are smashed and paintings defaced. Leftists in America are now destroying American history and its representations by toppling historical statues and defacing paintings.

San Francisco is scheduled to spend up to $600,000 to paint over George Washington High School's historic wall mural, "The Life of Washington," painted by muralist Victor Arnautoff during the Great Depression of the 1930s. The San Francisco School Board's outrageous decision denies the historical fact of worldwide slavery. It also diminishes the historical facts that the United States abolished slavery while the Islamic nations continue its horrific practice.

President Trump hosted the first annual Salute to America in celebration of our nation's 243rd birthday on July 4, 2019, in Washington, DC. In violent protest, members of the Revolutionary Communist Party lit an American flag and threw the burning flag on a Uniformed Division Secret Service officer. Burning a flag was deemed constitutional in the 1989 landmark Supreme Court case *Texas v. Johnson*. Burning American flags is commonplace in Islamic theocracies—but throwing a lit flag at another human being has taken leftists beyond the savagery of their Islamic mentors.

Be careful of the company you keep.

As society becomes increasingly intolerant, it becomes increasingly violent. The Leftist/Islamist alliance rejects the authority of the U.S. Constitution and the constitutional legitimacy of our duly elected president, Donald Trump. The objective of the alliance to unseat POTUS has included all tactics of the Culture War and ranged from stealth jihad and

Antifa violence to repeated coup attempts against the sitting president of the United States.

Americans who value their freedom must seriously consider the danger of coups and culture wars. What has distinguished the United States of America for 243 years is our peaceful transfer of power. Patriotic, law-abiding Americans do not resort to coups or culture wars—we vote and then we accept election outcomes. We debate the merits of ideas, abide by our Constitution, and pass laws that reflect our changing norms when merited. Any American, regardless of his or her political views, must seriously consider the tyranny of the Leftist/Islamist axis, because without the Constitution we are just another lawless Third World banana republic enslaved by the conceit of autocratic rulers.

The Humanitarian Hoax of Leftism is its dishonest promises of social justice and income equality. Free stuff is never free—you pay with your freedom. What leftism and Islamism are selling is a medieval return to feudalism, where the middle class is destroyed and the masses are ruled by a very few rulers. Just ask the Venezuelans. They know.

HOAX 38

The Humanitarian Hoax of Tolerism

July 10, 2019

T HE humanitarian hoax is the deliberate and deceitful tactic of presenting a destructive policy as altruistic. The humanitarian huckster presents himself as a compassionate advocate when in fact he is the disguised enemy.

The conviction of journalist Tommy Robinson is a humanitarian hoax that has destroyed free speech in Britain and threatens free speech worldwide.

Tommy Robinson is a British journalist who has been reporting on Muslim rape gangs in England that have been raping little English schoolgirls with impunity for decades. The savagery of their acts, and the fact that British authorities are covering up this atrocity, is extremely destabilizing to British society. Civilized people reject protecting perpetrators at the expense of their victims, and for civilized people, Tommy Robinson is a heroic whistleblower.

British authorities protect Muslim rape gangs and embolden them by prohibiting the reporting of their heinous acts of savagery. Why is this happening? Let's sort this out by examining the reasons.

Tolerism

Tolerism is defined by Howard Rotberg in his 2014 book, *Tolerism: The Ideology Revealed*, as "excessive leniency to opinions of certain groups, and excessive intolerance to the opinions of other groups." Rotberg explains that the breakdown of Western society is a direct result of leftist tolerists, who insist that tolerance is more valuable than justice.

The word *dhimmi* is a transliterated Arabic word meaning a non-Muslim living in a Muslim state ruled by Islamic Sharia law. Dhimmis are second-class citizens required to pay *jizya*—a special tax. The word dhimmi is often used disparagingly in the West to describe non-Muslims or non-Muslim nations behaving in a conciliatory manner toward Islam. Once a free society, Great Britain has reduced itself to a dhimmi nation by tolerating its Sharia-compliant Muslim population at the expense of its native Christian population.

Make no mistake—an Islamic religious war is being waged worldwide that seeks to eliminate competing religions and establish a global Islamic caliphate ruled by supremacist religious Sharia law. Britain's leaders are tolerists, insisting that tolerating Muslim rape gangs in the name of cultural diversity is more important than justice for the gangs' victims. Tolerism is Britain's fatally flawed political ideology that is providing victory to the Muslim Brotherhood, the multinational organization that has declared Islamic religious war on the West.

Anyone who still questions the global intentions of the Muslim Brotherhood should read its 1991 mission statement, _An Explanatory Memorandum: On the General Strategic Goal for the Group in North America_.

Populism rejects the twisted logic of tolerism and embraces the commonsense warning of Austrian/British twentieth-century philosopher Sir Karl Popper:

> If we extend unlimited tolerance even to those who are intolerant, if we are not prepared to defend a tolerant society against the onslaught of the intolerant, then the tolerant will be destroyed, and tolerance with them. . . . We should therefore claim, in the name of tolerance, the right not to tolerate the intolerant.

The British court's conviction of Tommy Robinson valued tolerance over justice. Why would it do that?

Leftist/Islamist Alliance

In America the Leftist/Islamist alliance (see _The Humanitarian Hoax of Leftism—Hoax 37_) is trying to destabilize and overthrow duly elected populist president Donald Trump. President Trump is the consummate whistleblower in America, exposing the staggering malfeasance of the Washington swamp and the leftists, Islamists, and globalists who live there.

In Britain, the Labour Party is equivalent to the leftist Democrat party in America; both prefer globalism to national sovereignty. In Britain, the Labour/Islamist alliance is trying to destabilize Britain and create chaos in order to subvert the will of the people and stop the implementation of the British exit from the European Union known as BREXIT.

So, what do President Trump and Tommy Robinson have in common? President Trump is the existential enemy of the Culture War and the target of the Leftist/Islamist alliance, and Tommy Robinson is the existential enemy of the leftist Labour Party, which prefers tolerism to justice. Why are these two men targeted? Because both are claiming, in the name of tolerance, the right not to tolerate the intolerant.

Tolerism vs. Justice

What is the goal of tolerism in Britain and America? Why do leftists in America and the Labour Party in Britain ignore the obvious violations of the laws and norms in their Judeo-Christian countries and surrender their cultures to the savagery and barbarism of Islamic Sharia norms?

Tolerism is a paradox because tolerists selectively decide what to tolerate. Telling the truth about Muslim rape gangs is not tolerated, it is criminalized. So, a two-tier system of justice is established that prohibits anti-Muslim speech yet protects anti-Christian and anti-Semitic speech.

If you want to know the motive, look at the result. The effect of this egregious double standard is that anti-Christian burning of churches and anti-Semitism including defacing synagogues is rampant and unpunished in Britain. If the British courts continue to protect Sharia-compliant Muslim perpetrators and their criminal acts at the expense of native Britons, social chaos will result. Remember, seismic social change requires social chaos.

Sir Karl Popper warned us about tolerism. George Orwell warned us that "During times of universal deceit, telling the truth becomes a revolutionary act." Both Tommy Robinson and President Trump, each in his own way, are exposing the truth of tolerism and its global anti-American, anti-British attacks on our sovereignty and shared Judeo-Christian norms. Their separate efforts continue to unravel the ongoing deceitful multinational efforts fomenting the social chaos necessary to impose a globalized New World Order.

Freedom of Speech

Every tyrannical regime the world has ever known begins its reign of terror by eliminating freedom of speech. Lenin did it, Trotsky did it, Hitler did it, and now leftists in Britain and America are doing it by disingenuously relabeling free speech as hate speech. There is no freedom without freedom of speech, which is why speech is universally the first freedom eliminated by despots.

The same tolerist Culture War being waged against America by the Leftist/Islamist alliance is also attacking Britain. Leftism and Islamism have common cause to destroy the status quo even though their ultimate objectives will make them inevitable enemies. Islamists are fighting for a global religious Islamic caliphate. The Left and Labour are fighting to destroy the national sovereignty and cultural identities of their respective countries in preparation for socialism in America and a unified European State in Britain.

The irony, of course, is that members of the Leftist/Labour/Islamist alliance are all useful idiots for the globalist elite, who finance and foment their lawlessness. The alliance members are just too arrogant to realize that they are participating in their own destruction.

The Leftist/Labour/Islamic alliances in the United States and Britain are providing the necessary social chaos for the globalists, who fully intend to impose a New World Order—a supranational internationalized world ruled by themselves under the corrupt auspices of the United Nations (see *The Humanitarian Hoax of the United Nations—Hoax 36*). There is no humanitarianism in the conviction of Tommy Robinson. His conviction is part of the coordinated attack on free speech and a free and sovereign Britain imposed by the globalist elite using tolerism and the unholy Labour/Islamist alliance.

July 8, 2019, the day Tommy Robinson was convicted of reporting the crime of Muslim rape gangs in England, will be recorded as the day free speech died in Great Britain. The only law that Tommy Robinson broke was the Islamic supremacist Sharia law forbidding criticism of Islam. Islamic Sharia law does not consider the raping of little English girls to be a crime—the prohibition is against criticizing Islam and reporting it. Britain's Leftist/Labour alliance has transformed Britain into a grotesque dhimmi nation willing to sacrifice its own little girls to a globalist power grab.

The Humanitarian Hoax of Tolerism that convicted Tommy Robinson must not be allowed to silence him permanently. Hopefully, populist President Donald Trump will grant Tommy Robinson humanitarian asylum in the United States, where he can continue to expose the realities of an Islamized Great Britain.

The Humanitarian Hoax of the 2020 Democrat Party Platform

July 13, 2019

THE humanitarian hoax is the deliberate and deceitful tactic of presenting a destructive policy as altruistic. The humanitarian huckster presents himself as a compassionate advocate when in fact he is the disguised enemy.

The Democrat party platform for 2020 is a staggering political humanitarian hoax that disguises anti-Americanism as altruism. The Democratic National Committee presents itself as "working hard to advance issues like immigration reform, education reform, health care reform, and alternative energy." Sounds great—all humanitarian hoaxes do. So, let's see how this works.

Countries are defined by four basic elements, and the Democrat party has taken aim at all four. We will examine these elements—territory, population, culture, and government—one at a time.

Territory

Territory refers to the demarcation of a country's physical borders that define its earthly space and separate it from other countries, each with its own government. Without borders there is no country.

The open-borders platform embraced by the Democrat party is its signature anti-American immigration reform. Open borders deliberately threaten the sovereign territorial borders of the United States by rejecting any attempts to defend the borders against the current mass invasion of illegal immigrants. While disingenuously insisting that open borders are a humanitarian issue, Democrat candidates oppose border wall funding and propose abolishing ICE (Immigration and Customs Enforcement) so that nothing and no one can stop the flow of this massive invasion.

Open borders are an anti-American power grab by Democrats with twin benefits to themselves. First, mass immigration will overwhelm the country with illegals who will vote for the Democrats who let them in, creating a one-party system for the foreseeable future. Second, uncontrolled immigration will collapse the economy by overloading the welfare system—it is the destructive socialists' Cloward-Piven strategy on steroids.

In the 1970s, Columbia sociologists Richard Cloward and Frances Piven proposed poverty as the weapon of destruction that would collapse America and replace its government with their idealized totalitarian Marxist model. Cloward and Piven thought locally—the politicians of today think globally. The globalist elite fully support the Left's expanded Cloward-Piven strategy using mass uncontrolled immigration to destroy American democracy and replace it with socialism (see *The Humanitarian Hoax of Socialism—Hoax 12*).

In a <u>stunning interview</u> published on YouTube July 11, 2019, Speaker of the House Nancy Pelosi tutors illegal aliens on how to avoid deportation and actually says that the United States is part of a global community and illegals have rights! Excuse me? Illegals are illegal by definition and are most definitely NOT entitled to the rights of citizens of the United States, according to the U.S. Constitution. Yet, anti-American globalist Nancy Pelosi, voicing the 2020 Democrat party platform, declares that the United States is not a sovereign country with defensible borders, and that U.S. politicians have no right to stop this illegal immigration.

Former Florida congressman and retired U.S. Army lieutenant colonel <u>Allen West</u> responded, saying that Pelosi's actions border on treason: "Unless I am grossly mistaken, Ms. Pelosi just violated her oath of office and has committed a high crime and misdemeanor."

Globalism and American sovereignty are mutually exclusive. American sovereignty depends upon defensible territorial borders and a sovereign American government that upholds the U.S. Constitution. The 2020 Democrat party platform is a globalist, no-borders, anti-American assault on the Constitution that advances the doctrine of a one-world government.

Population

<u>Population</u> refers to the people living in a country. The <u>United States</u> is

the third-most-populous country in the world, with almost 329 million people as of May 2019. The U.S. Census Bureau is the primary source of information about our nation's people. The Census Bureau counts the entire U.S. population every ten years, and the results are used politically for apportionment. Apportionment determines the proportional number of members each U.S. state sends to the House of Representatives, and also establishes the number of eligible voters in that state. The question of citizenship has been part of the U.S. Census since its inception until Barack Obama deviously eliminated it.

In 1970 the Census Bureau started distributing two different question-naires: a short form sent to most households and a long form sent to one in six households. Only the long form asked about citizenship. The 2010 Census differed from previous censuses because every residence received a short form, billed as 10 Questions in 10 Minutes. The Obama admin-istration discontinued use of the long form, using only the ten-question short-form questionnaire that did not ask about citizenship. This sleight of hand allowed the Democrat party to disingenuously claim that Obama did not remove the citizenship question. He simply removed the form that asked it!

The Democrat party platform rejects restoring the census citizenship question because when illegals are not counted, the census results will reduce both Democrats' apportionment in Congress and the number of eligible Democrat voters.

Demography is the study of the characteristics of a population, and it is often said that *demography is destiny*. What does this mean?

Demography studies the size, structure, and distribution of different groups of people defined by age, sex, religion, education, nationality, ethnicity, etc. Social demography examines the relationship between eco-nomic, social, cultural, and biological processes influencing a population. As the demographics of a population change, public policy adapts to meet the changing requirements. So, flooding America with an immigrant population, particularly those with globalist and/or Sharia-compliant or otherwise hostile norms, changes the demographics and eventually changes public policy. This is the essence of the open-borders immigra-tion reform embraced by the Democrat humanitarian hucksters led by huckster-in-chief Obama.

Under Barack Obama, according to Department of Homeland Security data, the United States issued 680,000 green cards to migrants from Muslim-majority countries in the five-year period from 2009 to 2013. During Obama's eight years, 43,000 Sharia-compliant Somali refugees were resettled in the United States, many of whom settled in Minnesota. Ilhan Omar, a Sharia-compliant Muslim congresswoman, was elected by her constituency and protects their hostile norms in the name of diversity, using the tactic of labeling anyone who opposes her as being Islamophobic or racist. The same thing that is happening in Minnesota happened in Luton, England, because demography is destiny.

The small English town of Luton had only one mosque. Following the European Union demand for mass immigration of Sharia-compliant Muslims into England, the number of mosques swelled to thirty. This changed the demographics of Luton. The hostile social and cultural norms of Sharia-compliant Muslim immigrants created crime and social chaos in Luton. As discussed in *The Humanitarian Hoax of Tolerism— Hoax 38*, British journalist Tommy Robinson began reporting on Luton's Muslim sex grooming and rape gangs that were raping little English girls according to Sharia law, which views non-Muslims as inferior dhimmis.

Sex grooming is the horrific practice of cultivating schoolgirls for sex and turning them into bodies for sale. An exposé by Leo Hohmann published on *World Net Daily* April 24, 2016, explains: "They [gangs] hang around schools and malls and use an attractive young man to convince them [girls] he wants to be their boyfriend and he gets them to drink and do drugs and then she has sex with him and later his 'brothers' and his 'uncles' and whomever else he pimps her out to."

Author Peter McLoughlin published an exhaustive study on the subject in his 2016 book, *Easy Meat: Inside Britain's Grooming Gang Scandal*. McLoughlin reported that the organized seduction of English schoolgirls by Muslim rape gangs has been going on since 1988.

In the case of Tommy Robinson, British authorities protected the Muslim perpetrators in the name of cultural diversity and imprisoned Robinson for exposing the crimes and the British cover-up. Demography is destiny.

Sonia Bailley's article published in *American Thinker* on December 4, 2013, "Grooming Gangs and Sharia," explains why this horrific crime is a phenomenon that occurs mainly amongst Muslim immigrants from Islamic countries:

As it turns out this crime is religiously and politically motivated by Islamic doctrine, which calls for the capturing, raping, and prostituting of non-Muslim women and children after battle, as well as keeping or selling them as sex slaves.

Bailley's December 1, 2015, *American Thinker* article, "The Danger in Islamic Prayer," exposes the supremacist doctrine inherent in Islamic mandatory prayers:

> A deep hatred and rejection of Judaism and Christianity are hardwired into Islamic doctrine, including the Koran. Many of its chapters are incorporated into mandatory daily Islamic prayer. The very first Koranic chapter, considered the most exalted of all chapters, is a prayer directed to Allah asking him to keep Muslims away from the misguided path of Jews and Christians. This chapter is a necessary part of the five mandatory daily prayers, and is recited not once, but anywhere from 17 to 100 times a day by devout Muslims (or in a broader sense, 6200 to 36,500 times a year).
>
> Fifty-seven Islamic states united in the highly influential (UN) Organization of Islamic Cooperation rejected the [original UN] Universal Declaration of Human Rights that views all people as equal and free, and replaced it with the Cairo Declaration of Human Rights in Islam (CDHRI) that views people as neither equal nor free.
>
> Islam considers itself the mother religion of both Judaism and Christianity, that it existed prior to those two false religions that veered away from the path of strict monotheism. They became corrupt and ignorant until Mohammed was sent by Allah as a gift to set things straight and convert all back to Islam or "the religion of true unspoiled nature," as per the CDHRI.

Culture

Culture refers to the pattern of human activity and the symbols that give significance to humans. Culture manifests itself in the forms of art, literature, clothing, customs, language, and religion. The way people live and what they believe constitute their culture. Their principles and moral values also form an important part of their culture. People from different parts of the world have different cultural values. Cultural differences contribute to the diversity in people's thinking and styles of living.

Culture is not innate. It is learned. Culture is passed down from generation to generation at home and in school. American Judeo-Christian values were traditionally taught at home and reinforced in schools. Not anymore. Since Barack Obama forced Common Core education into American public schools, American education has become globalized instruction that reflects its anti-American, anti-Semitic, anti-Christian, pro-Muslim, pro-globalist agenda (see *The Humanitarian Hoax of Common Core—Hoax 19*). Common Core comports with UN Agenda 2030 and its 17 Sustainable Development Goals that are designed to internationalize the world under a one-world government. Common Core rejects American sovereignty, American exceptionalism, American Judeo-Christian traditions, and American meritocracy. Common Core's educational goal is to prepare the world's children for membership in the globalized New World Order of a one-world government.

Common Core has had a calamitous effect on America, American children, and American families. Joy Pullman's recent book, *The Education Invasion: How Common Core Fights Parents for Control of American Kids*, describes this catastrophe and exposes the federalized education scheme and the globalist funding that promoted it. Parents and teachers are finally recognizing the crippling anti-American nature of Common Core and are fighting to have it removed. Parents and Educators Against Common Core maintain a Facebook page that anyone interested can join.

Common Core is the globalized anti-American education reform embraced by the Democrat party platform in 2020. Its anti-American curriculum content provided by Pearson Education (see *The Humanitarian Hoax of Pearson Education—Hoax 30*) is Obama's dream of a globalized, internationalized, pro-Muslim education, facilitated courtesy of the Qatari government, Qatar Foundation International, and the Libyan Investment Authority's major Islam-promoting donors.

Common Core teaches American history as white racist oppression. Our American children are being indoctrinated to be self-loathing Americans who will reject all of our American values and eventually vote for collectivism and a one-world government. Common Core is part of the anti-American information revolution that will be won at the ballot box— no bullets required.

The current Democrat party platform presents slavery reparations as the remedy for white racist oppression. Leftist apostate David Horowitz, a multi-talented political analyst, author, and publisher, wrote an excellent analysis of the current Democrat "Reparations Shakedown" published in *Frontpage Magazine* April 8, 2019:

> The reparations demand is pure racism: Recipients will be paid on the basis of their skin color even if, like Kamala Harris, their ancestors were actually slave owners. It will be paid by people who had no historical connection whatsoever to slavery, and it will be paid by the very government that sacrificed 350,000 mainly white (and Christian) lives to abolish slavery and lead the world in doing so.
>
> The reparations campaign is a campaign to bury the fact that white Americans freed Black slaves who were originally put in chains by Black Africans and Muslims, and that the white Christian males who created this country are responsible for ending slavery and creating the most inclusive, tolerant and equal society on earth. It is a campaign to make Americans ashamed of their country, so that its enemies can more easily destroy it.

Any student of history knows that slavery was a heinous historical reality in every part of the world, including the United States. Any student of history also knows that Americans went to war in 1861 to free the slaves in this country. Slavery is still legal in fifteen countries, including China, Democratic Republic of the Congo, Dominican Republic, Guatemala, India, Indonesia, Iraq, Nigeria, North Korea, Pakistan, Philippines, Russia, Sudan, Uzbekistan, and Yemen. Almost half of those countries are dominated by Muslims.

Racism in America began as the consequence of slavery. Slavery was outlawed in America with the Thirteenth Amendment on December 6, 1865, eight months after the end of the Civil War, and the racist attitudes that supported it dwindled over time. America is not a racist country today—we elected a black president. Enough talk about reparations.

Race hustlers in the Democrat party disingenuously focus on historical slavery and intentionally ignore the ongoing slavery integral to Islamic Sharia law. In Sharia law, women are the property of their husbands—owning a human being is slavery. Young infidel girls are groomed to be sex slaves—rape and sex grooming are slavery. In the name of diversity, the Democrat party has surrendered its Judeo-Christian culture to the barbarism of Islamic Sharia law.

Government

The <u>United States of America</u> was formed as a constitutional representative republic designed to provide minimum government and maximum freedom for its citizens. The Democrat party's 2020 platform offers maximum government and minimum freedom for the American people. This is how the reversal operates.

Barack Obama's post-presidency "resistance" movement has mobilized his loyal soldiers embedded in the government and unleashed a cadre of anti-American activists, politicians, and community organizers bound together by identity politics and an anti-American ideology seeking to overthrow duly elected President Donald Trump. Obama's "hope and change" agenda is the Democrat party 2020 platform, featuring:

- Open borders
- Illegal immigration
- Educational indoctrination
- Anti-traditional norms in place of our Judeo-Christian culture
- Economy-killing, suicidal Green New Deal
- Centralized government offering one-payer health insurance
- Dissolution of the Constitution and our representative republic in favor of socialism and a one-world government

Obama's "resistance" movement poured the foundation for this twenty-first-century anti-American revolution. He subverted the liberal Democrat party, launching its transformation into the extreme leftist, anti-American, anti-Christian, anti-Semitic, pro-socialist, pro-Muslim, pro-globalist debacle that it is today.

Radical newcomers in Congress—Reps. Alexandria Ocasio-Cortez (D-NY), Ilhan Omar (D-MN), Ayanna Pressley (D-MA), and Rashida Tlaib (D-MI)—have cracked the once unified Democrat party and radicalized it to staggering levels. Obama's sycophants and embedded operatives have targeted the pillars of American society, including the meritocracy, the family, Judeo-Christian norms, and the Protestant work ethic. The 2020 Democrat party is an anti-American, anti-Semitic, anti-Christian, pro-communist, pro-Muslim, pro-globalist consortium of bad actors with common cause to shatter the United States of America from within.

If the Democrat party prevails in 2020 and manages to destroy the four elements that make a country a country, America will cease to exist as a sovereign nation. What then?

Historically, to the victor go the spoils—but not this time. The Leftist/Socialist/Islamist alliance and its 2020 Democrat party platform will splinter and the infighting will begin. The leftist/socialist Democrats foolishly presume they will impose their socialist fantasy of collectivism upon America. The Sharia-compliant Democrats foolishly presume they will settle America and make it Muslim. Both alliance partners are too arrogant to realize that they are the useful idiots of the globalists, who will exploit both groups and their common cause in order to create the social chaos required for globalist ambitions to rule the world under a one-world government.

Leftists and Islamists brought a knife to a gunfight. English aristocrat Sir Bertrand Russell described the planned globalist takeover in his classic 1952 book, *The Impact of Science on Society*. The fight for world domination is not new—it just has new scripts, new actors, new costumes, and new billing.

Barack Obama won the starring role of U.S. president in the 2008 Washington, DC, theatrical hit "Hope and Change" and then renewed his contract for the 2012–2016 season. As with so many long-running shows, "Hope and Change" flopped at the box office in 2016. The audience rejected Hillary Clinton, the actress hired to replace Obama, and stopped buying tickets to the play. A new script titled "Resistance" was created for Obama, and Alexandria Ocasio-Cortez auditioned for the supporting role of New York congresswoman and won the part. She performs her scripted lines well and will continue to do so until she is replaced by another auditioned actress.

The Democrat party is currently auditioning parts for the 2020–2024 season of "Resistance." Its plot disguises anti-Americanism as altruism, which explains why its globalist authors have requested anonymity. "Resistance" poses a clear and present danger to the world order of sovereign nations. Americans must recognize the humanitarian hoax being performed in "Resistance" and stop buying tickets at the box office.

Voters are being urged to invest in "Resistance," and millions of dollars are being spent to promote it. This particular globalist extravaganza enjoys record levels of free publicity by the mainstream media and in social media.

The 2020 presidential election will determine the success or failure of "Resistance." Voting Americans will decide if art imitates life or if life imitates art.

HOAX 40

The Humanitarian Hoax of Department of Homeland 'Security'

July 21, 2019

THE humanitarian hoax is the deliberate and deceitful tactic of presenting a destructive policy as altruistic. The humanitarian huckster presents himself as a compassionate advocate when in fact he is the disguised enemy.

The Department of Homeland Security (DHS) was established November 25, 2002, by the Homeland Security Act of 2002. DHS is a cabinet department formed in response to the September 11, 2001, terrorist attacks on America. The DHS mission statement is clear: "With honor and integrity, we will safeguard the American people, our homeland, and our values."

The <u>DHS website</u> describes the department with clarity and lists its fourteen operational and support components:

> The Department of Homeland Security has a vital mission: to secure the nation from the many threats we face. This requires the dedication of more than 240,000 employees in jobs that range from aviation and border security to emergency response, from cybersecurity analyst to chemical facility inspector. Our duties are wide-ranging, and our goal is clear—keeping America safe.

United States Citizenship and Immigration Services (USCIS)

United States Customs and Border Protection (CBP)

Federal Emergency Management Agency (FEMA)

United States Immigration and Customs Enforcement (ICE)

Transportation Security Administration (TSA)

Science and Technology Directorate

Office of Intelligence and Analysis

United States Coast Guard (USCG)

Cybersecurity and Infrastructure Security Agency (CISA)

Federal Law Enforcement Training Center (FLETC)

United States Secret Service (USSS)

Management Directorate

Countering Weapons of Mass Destruction Office

Office of Operations Coordination

The enormity of the Department of Homeland Security reflects the seriousness and magnitude of the acknowledged security threats to America in the wake of the 9/11 attacks. The Department of Defense works in the military sphere, while the Department of Homeland Security works in the civilian sector to safeguard America. The mission to safeguard America is unequivocally and unapologetically America-first. There is no ambiguity regarding which priority to protect—America is the uncontested priority.

Let's review what Homeland Security is pledged to safeguard:

- American people
- American homeland
- American values

Has DHS fulfilled its pledge?

Immediately after 9/11 there was a period of enormous cohesion and patriotism in the country. We were all Americans united by the shock of a terrorist attack and by our shared loss. We grieved together for our country. Soon, the grieving subsided and partisan politics began dividing the nation. Barack Obama was elected and delivered his infamous "New Beginning" speech on June 4, 2009, in Cairo. Obama told the world that part of his responsibility as president of the United States was to fight against negative stereotypes of Islam wherever they appear. WHAT?

The responsibility of the president of the United States is to fight against negative stereotypes of **AMERICANS** wherever they appear!

Obama's Cairo speech declared that his personal political priority to protect Islam would become public policy—and it did. Barack Obama's entire presidency was a violation of the establishment clause of our Constitution separating church and state. Protecting Islam, not America, became the national priority under his watch. Unimaginable accommodations and religious preferences were awarded to Islam at the expense of America and America's founding Judeo-Christian principles. How did he do it?

The policies of every sphere of the government were politicized to reflect Obama's personal pro-Muslim stance, especially homeland security:

- Homeland Security
- Education
- Economy
- Immigration

Let's examine them one at a time.

Homeland Security

Under the Obama administration, Islam was deliberately separated from its political aspirations to establish a worldwide religious caliphate. Any mention of Islam's plans to make America Muslim was scrubbed from training for the military, first responders, police, and homeland security and prohibited as being offensive to Muslims.

Former FBI special agent John Guandolo's September 13, 2016, article, "Islamic Movement in U.S. Preparing for Battle," reveals the catastrophic consequences of Obama's anti-American policies, particularly our suicidal unpreparedness. Guandolo explained how the Islamic movement to establish a worldwide caliphate is preparing for battle in the United States. Separating Koranic Islamic religious doctrine and its supremacist religious Sharia law from terrorism is like separating Hitler's *Mein Kampf* from Nazism in World War II's German army. Motivational texts are essential to understanding and defeating the enemy.

The Muslim Brotherhood (see *The Humanitarian Hoax of the Muslim Brotherhood—Hoax 26*) is the twentieth-century multinational organization of Sharia-compliant Muslims entrusted with settling America (see *The Humanitarian Hoax of Five-Times-a-Day Islam—Hoax 31*) and making it Muslim in the twenty-first century. Obama kept his Cairo promise of a "new beginning" and facilitated the Muslim Brotherhood's infiltration into homeland security, education, the economy, the State Department, and immigration policies.

In a jaw-dropping breach of national security, food trucks at airports servicing Middle Eastern airlines are forbidden to be inspected.

A July 4, 2019, Fox News report revealed that "special exemptions" are awarded by TSA and airport police to food trucks servicing planes headed to the Middle East from Washington, DC's Dulles Airport. Former air marshal and whistleblower Robert MacLean says he was blocked from searching a food truck during a random search operation. He was told to stand down. In what stretches credulity, the explanation given was "specially blessed airline meals have already been searched by an off-site private security company." Further, "The reason we don't break these seals and do open-and-look checks is because the public has religious rights under the First Amendment."

First Amendment protections??? **I don't think so!** The First Amendment was not designed to protect a political movement disguised as a religion, particularly one that openly seeks to overthrow our constitutional government. The First Amendment was designed to protect Americans from our government's establishing a preferred religion.

In case there is anyone who does not understand the ongoing threats to America and the gravity of this breach in airport security, an Iranian businessman was just caught in a plot to sneak nuclear enrichment components out of the United States. According to the DOJ, between 2008 and 2015 Behzad Pourghannad and two other Iranian nationals, Ali Reza Shokri and Farzin Faridmanesh, worked together to obtain carbon fiber from the United States and surreptitiously export it to Iran via third countries. Shokri worked for procurement, Pourghannad was the financial guarantor, and Faridmanesh the trans-shipper. Only Pourghannad is in custody; the other two remain at large.

Robert MacLean describes the TSA pat-downs and searches as "security theater": "We are spending all this manpower and hours patting down children and elderly veterans in wheelchairs but the airport workers motivated by greed can smuggle whatever they need past security."

Obama's pro-Muslim policies violate the establishment clause by treating Islam as a preferred religion with the absurd justification that Islamic meals are "blessed" and cannot be searched for security reasons. Domestic airlines and their Judeo-Christian food trucks are regularly searched to insure passenger safety and homeland security.

Education

From Obama's Cairo speech:

The United States will partner with any Muslim-majority country to support expanded literacy for girls and to help young women pursue employment. . . . We will encourage more Americans to study in Muslim communities. And we will match promising Muslim students our internships in America, invest in online learning for teachers and children around the world and create a new, online network so a young person in Kansas can communicate instantly with a young person in Cairo.

Obama kept this particular Cairo promise by facilitating Common Core and its pro-Muslim curricula courtesy of Pearson Education's 60 percent controlling interest in American textbooks. The Sharia-compliant Qatari influence in Pearson products is discussed at length in *The Humanitarian Hoax of Pearson Education—Hoax 30.* Pearson is the premier global educational humanitarian huckster hawking its anti-American message of globalism to K-12 students and teachers in America. Its globalized curriculum comports to Obama's pet Common Core State Standards (CCSS). Globally, Common Core originated from the One World Education concept, a global goal orchestrated by the Connect All Schools program. Its origin is funded by the Qatar Foundation International (QFI) and supported by UN Agenda 2030.

Obama bullied school districts into accepting Common Core with federal grants. When the college admissions test, SAT, restructured itself as an extension of Common Core's controversial public-school reading and writing standards, Common Core became the accepted standard throughout the country.

So, Obama's Common Core pet project with its anti-American, anti-Christian, anti-Semitic, pro-Muslim indoctrination violates the establishment clause by teaching Islam as a preferred religion throughout its curricula.

Economy

Obama's Cairo speech promise on economic development reassured Muslims that "There need not be contradictions between development and tradition." Obama invited Middle East investment in America, insisting that those countries' economies could grow enormously while preserving their distinct Islamic culture. There he goes again—protecting Islam and Sharia law at the expense of America and our Judeo-Christian traditions.

Obama's regulation-killing policies drove manufacturing businesses out of America and invited Muslim investment into the country. Islam's educational investment in America through Common Core in K-12 also targeted higher education. Money talks. Islam established new Middle East Studies Centers and endowed chairs at universities across the country to influence curricula, knowing that graduates would influence public policy toward Islam. An April 5, 2004, article, "The Saudi Fifth Column on Our Nation's Campuses" by Lee Kaplan, warned, "The head of the Muslim American Society, W. Deen Muhammed, has stated that Saudi gifts require the receiver to prefer the Saudi 'school of thought.'"

The 2004 Kaplan article ended with this statement:

> Academic departments with political agendas are a new phenomenon on American campuses and directly violates the principles of Academic Freedom established by the American Association of University Professors and long recognized by accrediting institutions.

Eight years later, on April 27, 2012, the article was reprinted in its entirety with a different ending:

> Academic departments laden with political agendas directly violate the principles of Academic Freedom established by the American Association of University Professors. The one-sided nature of Middle Eastern Studies programs—funded by the Saudi royal family and favorable to their Wahhabi extremism—impedes education and fans the flames of violence on campus. Congress needs to take a hard look at the way it provides money to underwrite these programs. University trustees and administrators need to be held accountable for this anti-American indoctrination. Our students—and our nation—deserve better.

Saudi Arabia's "Wahhabi Lobby" continues to fund the goals of radical Islam and pours huge amounts of money into prestigious American universities to establish and promote their anti-American, pro-Muslim agenda. Their staggering multi-billion-dollar investment in American universities is molding the minds of future American leaders. The Islamic investment is not restricted to Saudi Arabia; Qatari influence is escalating as it joins Saudi Arabia and plows billions more dollars into American universities, American media, American politics, American banking, American real estate, and the ever increasing mosque building—all to increase Muslim influence in America.

Islam is busy buying influence in America through financial investment, including entertaining targeted Washington swampsters. The Investigative Project on Terrorism (IPT) reported on the Democrats' December

2018 trip, "Qatar Paid for Congressional Democrats' Doha Trip." Qatar is one of the biggest funders of the Muslim Brotherhood and is home to its spiritual leader, Sheikh Yusuf Qaradawi. Islam is buying influence with the protection of the mainstream media that refuses to report the encroaching influence of Islam and Islamic Sharia law in America. Obama kept his Cairo promise of expanding the economies of Muslim countries and preserving their Islamic identity at the expense of America and American economic and cultural interests.

Immigration

Perhaps Obama's most devastating domestic policy was the mass importation of Sharia-compliant refugees with hostile-to-America norms.

The biggest lie in Obama's Cairo speech was his declaration:

> We will, however, relentlessly confront violent extremists who pose a grave threat to our security because we reject the same thing that people of all faiths reject, the killing of innocent men, women, and children. And it is my first duty as president to protect the American people.

Obama violated his oath of office by establishing Islam as a preferred religion with religious exemptions that created a two-tier system of justice and a two-tier system of investigation that continues to threaten the security of the United States. Obama endangered the American people, the American homeland, and the American values that he swore to protect.

Humanitarian huckster-in-chief Barack Obama's anti-American, pro-Muslim policies in the Department of Homeland Security continue to protect Islam at the expense of America. Homeland Security and every one of its 240,000 employees working for its fourteen operational support components must be re-schooled on the threat of Islamic Sharia law, starting with the insanity of the "blessed" food trucks and focusing on the seditious Muslim Brotherhood.

It is imperative that President Trump designate the Muslim Brotherhood a terrorist organization. In its own words, the 1991 mission statement of the Muslim Brotherhood, *An Explanatory Memorandum: On the General Strategic Goal for the Group in North America*, defines itself as an enemy of the United States whose objective is settlement and making America Muslim.

HOAX 41

The Humanitarian Hoax of the 2019–2020 Equality Act

July 26, 2019

THE humanitarian hoax is the deliberate and deceitful tactic of presenting a destructive policy as altruistic. The humanitarian huckster presents himself as a compassionate advocate when in fact he is the disguised enemy.

The 116th Congress 2019–2020 <u>H.R. 5: Equality Act</u> is a Democrat bill prohibiting discrimination based on sex, sexual orientation, and gender identity in multiple areas including public accommodations and facilities, education, federal funding, employment, housing, bank loans, and the jury system. Sounds great, so what's the problem?

The Equality Act "updates" the definitions of three terms: sex, sexual orientation, and gender identity, and "expands" the categories of public accommodations. On May 17, 2019, H.R. 5: Equality Act passed the Democrat-controlled House with unanimous support from Democrats plus eight Republican votes. Next, it goes to the Republican-controlled Senate for consideration. Why the partisan split?

The Equality Act seeks to amend and expand the expressly recognized "non-discrimination" categories in the <u>1964 Civil Rights Act</u>. The Civil Rights Act was designed to provide equal protection under the law to African-Americans and women in twentieth-century America, making it illegal to discriminate against them based on race, ethnicity, or gender. In 1964 the word "gender" was specifically understood to mean male or female in the biological, chromosomal, rational sense of the word. In the twenty-first century the leftist Democrat party is selling sameness as equality and feelings as facts.

Even the name Equality Act is part of the deception. The name evokes compassion in the casual observer, but there is nothing equal about the Equality Act. It is a colossal humanitarian hoax that redefines maleness and femaleness with the words "gender identity." This is how it works.

No longer satisfied with laws prohibiting discrimination based on gender, the radical Left has taken aim at the biological definition of maleness and femaleness, making it a subjective matter of opinion rather than an objective matter of chromosomes. Gender identity is not the same as gender. Why is this important?

Facts are not feelings. Facts support the objective reality that is the foundation of biological science, laws, and ordered liberty. Feelings support the subjective reality of political science, the arts, and psychology. We can have feelings about facts, but feelings cannot change facts in a society of ordered liberty. The danger of confusing objective and subjective reality is discussed at length in *The Humanitarian Hoax of Multiple Realities—Hoax 23*.

Biologically, the sex of an individual is determined by a pair of sex chromosomes found in that individual's DNA. Females have two identical chromosomes, XX, and males have two different chromosomes, XY.

Chromosomal sex determination in humans is a natural function of mammalian development, with both a primary and a secondary component. Primary development is the determination of gonads, internal sex glands that make sex hormones and reproductive cells—testes in the male and ovaries in the female. Secondary sex determination is based on the external expression of maleness and femaleness outside the gonads. This means a male has a penis, seminal vesicles, and prostate glands. The female has a vagina, cervix, uterus, oviducts, and mammary glands.

For the vast majority of the world population, including the United States, sexual development is an uncomplicated natural function of human reproduction. Only a minuscule portion of the human population has chromosomal abnormalities or ambiguous secondary sex characteristics, and leftist Democrats are exploiting them for political gain.

The leftist Democrat party is attempting to alter the biological science of objective reality, facts, and chromosomes, and replace it with the subjective world of feelings, shattering the foundation of biological science and turning it into political science. This is the core of the Humanitarian Hoax of the 2019–2020 Equality Act; it functionally obliterates the differences between maleness and femaleness, making them the same rather than equal.

This distinction is extremely important because sameness has serious consequence in society, both legally and socially.

Let's examine the consequences of the Democrat "update" including "gender identity" as it relates to the provisions of the 1964 Civil Rights Act, particularly Titles II, III, IV, and V.

Title II prohibits discrimination on the basis of race, color, religion, or national origin in public accommodations such as lodging, restaurants, and theaters.

Title III explicitly prohibits state and local governments from discrimination based on race, religion, color, or national origin in public facilities.

Title IV provides for the federal enforcement of desegregating public schools.

Title V empowers the Civil Rights Commission to further investigate and act on allegations of discrimination.

According to <u>Wikipedia</u>,

> Gender identity is the personal sense of one's own gender. Gender identity can correlate with assigned sex at birth or can differ from it. All societies have a set of gender categories that can serve as the basis of the formation of a person's social identity in relation to other members of society. In most societies, there is a basic division between gender attributes assigned to males and females, a gender binary to which most people adhere and which includes expectations of masculinity and femininity in all aspects of sex and gender: biological sex, gender identity, and gender expression.

The first and most basic human identity is universally announced around the world at the moment of birth. "It's a boy!" "It's a girl!" What this means is that in most societies people accept the binary definitions of maleness and femaleness based on XX and XY chromosomes and their factual physical expression. The leftist Democrat attempt to redefine maleness and femaleness as non-binary and a matter of personal feelings is a political power grab by the Left. Why?

If the Senate passes the Equality Act, schools will be teaching the leftist non-binary definition of maleness and femaleness to America's children. The biological differences between boys and girls will be denied and the social norms of privacy obliterated. Titles II, III, IV, and V will force the implementation of joint bathrooms, joint locker rooms, joint showering facilities, joint sports teams, etc., etc., etc. The deceitful Equality Act targets America's children with Vladimir Lenin's prescient warning, "Give me just one generation of youth, and I'll transform the whole world."

The leftist Democrat motivation is to collapse America from within and replace our democracy with socialism and our capitalist system with communism. The Left did not originate dirty political tricks; they have just honed them to an art form.

In the middle of the twentieth century, when W. Cleon Skousen published *The Naked Communist* and the Civil Rights Act was passed, it was unimaginable that leftist radicals would attempt to destabilize and transform society by redefining maleness and femaleness. Skousen, an anti-Communist and former FBI special agent and field director for the American Security Council, served President Ronald Reagan on the Council for National Policy. He maintained that communism was waging a psychological war designed to soften America and change American thinking in preparation for the final Communist takeover, and he listed forty-five Communist goals.

The forty-five goals were read into the <u>Congressional Record on January 10, 1963</u>. Goals 17, 24, 25, 26, 39, 40, and 41, which seek to collapse accepted norms and the authority of the family, are of special interest to this discussion.

From *The Naked Communist*, by W. <u>Cleon</u> Skousen, Waking Lion Press, 1958, pp. 224–227:

CURRENT COMMUNIST GOALS

1. U.S. acceptance of coexistence as the only alternative to atomic war.

2. U.S. willingness to capitulate in preference to engaging in atomic war.

3. Develop the illusion that total disarmament [by] the United States would be a demonstration of moral strength.

4. Permit free trade between all nations regardless of Communist affiliation and regardless of whether or not items could be used for war.

5. Extension of long-term loans to Russia and Soviet satellites.

6. Provide American aid to all nations regardless of Communist domination.

7. Grant recognition of Red China. Admission of Red China to the U.N.

8. Set up East and West Germany as separate states in spite of Khrushchev's promise in 1955 to settle the German question by free elections under supervision of the U.N.

9. Prolong the conferences to ban atomic tests because the United States has agreed to suspend tests as long as negotiations are in progress.

10. Allow all Soviet satellites individual representation in the U.N.

11. Promote the U.N. as the only hope for mankind. If its charter is rewritten, demand that it be set up as a one-world government with its own independent armed forces. (Some Communist leaders believe the world can be taken over as easily by the U.N. as by Moscow. Sometimes these two centers compete with each other as they are now doing in the Congo.)

12. Resist any attempt to outlaw the Communist Party.

13. Do away with all loyalty oaths.

14. Continue giving Russia access to the U.S. Patent Office.

15. Capture one or both of the political parties in the United States.

16. Use technical decisions of the courts to weaken basic American institutions by claiming their activities violate civil rights.

17. Get control of the schools. Use them as transmission belts for socialism and current Communist propaganda. Soften the curriculum. Get control of teachers' associations. Put the party line in textbooks.

18. Gain control of all student newspapers.

19. Use student riots to foment public protests against programs or organizations which are under Communist attack.

20. Infiltrate the press. Get control of book-review assignments, editorial writing, policymaking positions.

21. Gain control of key positions in radio, TV, and motion pictures.

22. Continue discrediting American culture by degrading all forms

of artistic expression. An American Communist cell was told to "eliminate all good sculpture from parks and buildings, substitute shapeless, awkward and meaningless forms."

23. Control art critics and directors of art museums. "Our plan is to promote ugliness, repulsive, meaningless art."

24. Eliminate all laws governing obscenity by calling them "censorship" and a violation of free speech and free press.

25. Break down cultural standards of morality by promoting pornography and obscenity in books, magazines, motion pictures, radio, and TV.

26. Present homosexuality, degeneracy and promiscuity as "normal, natural, healthy."

27. Infiltrate the churches and replace revealed religion with "social" religion. Discredit the Bible and emphasize the need for intellectual maturity which does not need a "religious crutch."

28. Eliminate prayer or any phase of religious expression in the schools on the ground that it violates the principle of "separation of church and state."

29. Discredit the American Constitution by calling it inadequate, old-fashioned, out of step with modern needs, a hindrance to cooperation between nations on a worldwide basis.

30. Discredit the American Founding Fathers. Present them as selfish aristocrats who had no concern for the "common man."

31. Belittle all forms of American culture and discourage the teaching of American history on the ground that it was only a minor part of the "big picture." Give more emphasis to Russian history since the Communists took over.

32. Support any socialist movement to give centralized control over any part of the culture–education, social agencies, welfare programs, mental health clinics, etc.

33. Eliminate all laws or procedures which interfere with the operation of the Communist apparatus.

34. Eliminate the House Committee on Un-American Activities.

35. Discredit and eventually dismantle the FBI.

36. Infiltrate and gain control of more unions.

37. Infiltrate and gain control of big business.

38. Transfer some of the powers of arrest from the police to social agencies. Treat all behavioral problems as psychiatric disorders which no one but psychiatrists can understand [or treat].

39. Dominate the psychiatric profession and use mental health laws as a means of gaining coercive control over those who oppose Communist goals.

40. Discredit the family as an institution. Encourage promiscuity and easy divorce.

41. Emphasize the need to raise children away from the negative influence of parents. Attribute prejudices, mental blocks and retarding of children to suppressive influence of parents.

42. Create the impression that violence and insurrection are legitimate aspects of the American tradition; that students and special-interest groups should rise up and use ["]united force["] to solve economic, political or social problems.

43. Overthrow all colonial governments before native populations are ready for self-government.

44. Internationalize the Panama Canal.

45. Repeal the Connally Reservation so the United States cannot prevent the World Court.

Texas Senator Tom Connally authored the August 14, 1946, Connally Reservation, a *six-word* amendment to the U.S. ratification of the UN charter that qualified U.S. acceptance of the compulsory jurisdiction of the UN International Court of Justice (ICJ). The Connally Reservation is the ending clause that denies the ICJ jurisdiction over domestic matters by excluding: "disputes with regard to matters which are essentially within the domestic jurisdiction of the United States of America *as determined by the United States.*"

The importance of the Connally Reservation to American independence cannot be overstated. Tom Connally's six words are what stand between American sovereignty and World Government, as described by legal scholar Howard H. Boyle Jr. in his exceptional 1960 *Marquette Law Review* article, "Proposed Repeal of Connally Reservation—A Matter for Concern."

Boyle begins:

> Our Constitutional protections can most effectively and abruptly be lost by surrender of judicial authority to a supreme supranational juridical body which is neither bound nor in sympathy with concepts which underlie that Constitution. Although it is not generally publicized, such surrender is now being arranged. The supreme supra-national juridical body to which our Constitution would be subordinated has already been set up and is ready for business. It is the United Nation's International Court of Justice. The surrender device is Senate Resolution number 94 which would repeal the "Connally Reservation."

Boyle was referring to Minnesota Senator Hubert Humphrey's 1959 Senate S. Res. 94 to repeal the Connally Reservation. The initial efforts failed, but the Connally Reservation remains a primary target for those who understand that six words prevent the World Court from legally interfering in American internal affairs.

It is chilling how much the 2020 Democrat party platform comports to the forty-five Communist goals listed in the 1963 Congressional Record. The Democrat party has devolved from the America-first voice of John Fitzgerald Kennedy to the howling of leftist radicals who embrace communism disguised as equality. Alexandria Ocasio-Cortez, the young face of the New Democrat party, unapologetically seeks to make America communist. She and her handlers have usurped the authority of former party leaders and are leading the insurrection against the Old Guard to establish the subversive new Democrat in Name Only (DINO) party.

Communism has always had world domination as its goal. Joseph Stalin explained how socialism is the stepping-stone:

> World dictatorship can be established only when victory of socialism has been achieved in certain countries or groups of countries . . . and when these federation of republics have finally grown into a world union of Soviet Socialist Republics uniting the whole of mankind under the hegemony of the international proletariat organized as a state.

Stalin elaborated:

> Divide the world into regional groups as a transitional stage to world government. Populations will more readily abandon their national loyalty to a vague regional loyalty than they will for a world authority.

Later the regions can be brought together all the way into a single world dictatorship.

Since its inception, communism has been determined to eliminate all religions and their moral authority. Communism views religions as competing ideologies to the absolute authority of the state. Evangelical leader Franklin Graham reveals how the Equality Act legalizes reverse discrimination against the moral teachings and authority of our American Judeo-Christian tradition. Of special interest to his argument are Communist Goals 27 and 28, which seek to discredit religion and its moral authority. Franklin Graham warns that the disingenuously named Equality Act will lead to Christian persecution as never before:

Christian employers would lose all protections to hire people who adhere to their biblical statements of faith. Christians will be persecuted for their sincerely held beliefs as never before. The clear teachings of the Bible on the sins of homosexuality and abortion will no doubt be considered "hate speech." It will be a nightmare from which this nation may never recover.

Five chairmen of the U.S. Conference of Catholic Bishops (USCCB) made the following corroborating statement on May 17, 2019:

Rather than offering meaningful protections for individuals, the Equality Act would impose sweeping new norms that negatively impact the unborn, health care, charitable services, schools, personal privacy, athletics, free speech, religious liberties, and parental rights.

The Act's unsound definitions of "sex" and "gender identity" would erase women's distinct, hard-won recognition in federal laws. Its sex-based nondiscrimination terms would end women's shelters and many single-sex schools. It would close faith-based foster care and adoption agencies that honor children's rights to a mother and father. The bill would even act as an abortion mandate.

Beyond its confusing, destabilizing, psychological consequences to children in American schools K-12, the Equality Act would eliminate separate bathrooms, locker rooms, bathing facilities, etc., for adult men and women in public spaces nationwide. Our cultural norms and ordered liberty in America have always recognized the biological differences between male and female. Men and women are NOT the same—equal, yes; the same, NO.

The 2019–2020 Equality Act is part of the sinister attack that political analyst and writer David Horowitz describes in his new book, *Dark Agenda:*

The War to Destroy Christian America. Horowitz explains how the Culture War on Christianity is a war against America and its founding principles rooted in Judeo-Christian norms and Western civilization. He reveals how, after the communist empire fell, progressives did not abandon their fight; they simply rebranded communism as "social justice."

A June 10, 2019, article by Robert Curry titled "Hey, Hey, Ho, Ho, Western Civ Has Got to Go" recalls Jesse Jackson's 1987 protest march at Stanford University. The protest was against Stanford's required introductory humanities program, "Western Culture"—not enough diversity for the social justice warriors. The aftermath is clear. Radicalized professors abandoned teaching Western civilization in favor of teaching multiculturalism. Protesters led by politicians at Stanford thirty years ago successfully rid the university of a course in Western civilization.

Protesters led by politicians today are targeting Western civilization itself. Skousen's forty-five Communist Goals are the dark agenda of the current radical leftist Democrat party. If we allow leftist politicians to redefine maleness and femaleness, we will be facilitating their communist goals and promoting the social chaos that seismic social change requires.

The goal of subversion is to shatter the authority of the three pillars of American society—family, God, and government/patriotism—and replace them with loyalty to the state. The collectivist infrastructure of socialism/communism requires complete centralization of authority so that the exclusive and singular authority is the state. The leftist Democrats imagine that if they succeed, _they_ will be the final authority, with complete power for the foreseeable future. They are deluded.

In a stunning 1984 interview, former Soviet KGB informant, Soviet journalist, and defector Yuri Bezmenov discussed the Soviet subversion attempts in America after World War II. Most Americans would find it difficult to accept that Russian attempts to infiltrate and collapse America are ongoing and that today's communists have found allies in leftist Democrats. Some of the Democrat collaborators are ideologues, others are corrupt politicians, but all are useful idiots working against the interests of the United States. Useful idiots?

Yes. Bezmenov makes it crystal clear that if the communists ever prevail, there will be no place in society for the collaborating leftists. They will all be killed. End of story.

The humanitarian hoax of the leftist Democrat Equality Act attempting to sell sameness as equality must be rejected entirely. If America allows the Left to substitute subjective reality for objective reality, we will find ourselves living in the communist nightmare that Yuri Bezmenov described.

I am an American.

I am an American and I reject communism.

I am an American and I reject communism and Marxist socialism.

I am an American and I reject communism, Marxist socialism, and leftist Democrats.

I am an American and I reject communism, Marxist socialism, and leftist Democrats. I support the U.S. Constitution.

I am an American and I pledge allegiance to the Flag of the United States of America, and to the Republic for which it stands, one Nation under God, indivisible, with Liberty and Justice for all.

I am an American and I entirely reject the humanitarian hoax of the very unequal leftist Equality Act. Tell your senators to vote NO on the deceitful H.R. 5: Equality Act while you still can.

HOAX 42

The Humanitarian Hoax of Islamic Zakat

July 31, 2019

THE humanitarian hoax is the deliberate and deceitful tactic of presenting a destructive policy as altruistic. The humanitarian huckster presents himself as a compassionate advocate when in fact he is the disguised enemy.

Barack Obama's infamous "New Beginning" Cairo speech, discussed in *The Humanitarian Hoax of Department of Homeland 'Security'—Hoax 40,* laid the groundwork for eight years of pro-Islamic policies at the expense of Judeo-Christian America. One of Obama's least understood and most destructive promises made in Cairo involved Islamic terror financing disguised as charitable giving and humanitarian relief. This is how it works.

There are Five Pillars of Islam that govern Muslim life. They are acknowledged, obligatory, and practiced by Muslims worldwide:

1. *Shahada*—the profession of faith
2. *Salat*—five-times-a-day prayer
3. *Zakat*—charitable giving
4. *Sawm*—fasting
5. *Hajj*—pilgrimage to Mecca

Zakat, the Third Pillar of Islam, requires Muslims to deduct a portion of their income to support the Islamic community. It is a religious obligation, a mandatory charitable contribution or tax, usually about 2.5 percent of an individual's income. Zakat sounds familiar and unthreatening, like traditional tithing to churches, synagogues, and temples paid by Christians, Jews, and Buddhists around the world.

On June 4, 2009, in Cairo, Egypt, Obama exploited that familiarity and promised the Muslim world that he would make zakat easier for American

Muslims, saying, "Freedom of religion is central to the ability of peoples to live together. We must always examine the ways in which we protect it. For instance, in the United States, rules on charitable giving have made it harder for Muslims to fulfill their religious obligation. That's why I'm committed to working with American Muslims to ensure that they can fulfill zakat."

But zakat is not charitable giving, like tithing in other religions. In 2009 Obama knew that zakat was being used to finance Islamic terrorism. Let's examine the chronology to confirm what Obama knew and when he knew it.

In August of 2004, Robert Mueller's FBI had already discovered the explosive 1991 Muslim Brotherhood mission statement, _An Explanatory Memorandum: On the General Strategic Goal for the Group in North America_. The Muslim Brotherhood is a multinational organization and parent of the terrorist group Hamas. The _Explanatory Memorandum_ is the Brotherhood's manifesto to make America Muslim. The document was used as evidence in the 2007 Holy Land Foundation trial.

On July 23, 2007, the Holy Land Foundation for Relief and Development and seven principal individuals went on trial charged with:

- Twelve counts of providing material support and resources to a designated foreign terrorist organization, Hamas
- Thirteen counts of money laundering
- Thirteen counts of breaching the International Emergency Economic Powers Act (IEEPA), which prohibits transactions that threaten American national security

On October 22, 2007, a mistrial was declared because the jury had been unable to deliver unanimous verdicts on most of the counts. The government streamlined its presentation and retried the case, proving that the Holy Land Foundation was a Hamas funder fully controlled by Hamas, and that the principals knew the money they raised in the United States was being used to finance Hamas.

The FBI reported on the Holy Land Foundation Convictions November 25, 2008:

> The FBI's fight against terrorism funding paid a big dividend yesterday when five former leaders of a U.S.-based Muslim charity were convicted of funneling more than $12 million to the Palestinian terrorist group Hamas.

Guilty verdicts on all 108 counts against the Holy Land Foundation for Relief and Development were announced in federal court in Dallas, Texas, representing the largest victory against terrorist financing in the U.S. since the 9/11 attacks.

"For many years, the Holy Land Foundation used the guise of charity to raise and funnel millions of dollars to the infrastructure of the Hamas terror organization," said Patrick Rowan, Assistant Attorney General for National Security. "This prosecution demonstrates our resolve to ensure that humanitarian relief efforts are not used as a mechanism to disguise and enable support for terrorist groups."

In May 2009 Texas federal Judge Jorge A. Solis sentenced the Holy Land Foundation and its five leaders.

"Today's sentences mark the culmination of many years of painstaking investigative and prosecutorial work at the federal, state and local levels. All those involved in this landmark case deserve our thanks," said David Kris, Assistant Attorney General for National Security. "These sentences should serve as a strong warning to anyone who knowingly provides financial support to terrorists under the guise of humanitarian relief."

The Holy Land Foundation was a political organization disguised as a charitable one. It was the biggest Islamic "charity" in the United States and existed to help Hamas jihadis eliminate the State of Israel and replace it with an Islamic Palestinian state. The terror-funding Holy Land "charity" and its defendants provided approximately $12.4 million in illegal support for Hamas in the mid 1990s. Unless Obama was unconscious during the Holy Land Foundation trial in July 2007 and the convictions in November 2008, he knew when he gave his 2009 speech in Cairo that zakat was being used to fund terrorism.

The Holy Land Foundation was the largest terror-funding trial in U.S. history and was all over the news. The seven named defendants and 300 unindicted co-conspirators were listed in government documents. The Muslim Brotherhood's propaganda arm, the Council on American-Islamic Relations (CAIR), is one of the unindicted co-conspirators on the list. According to Justice Department records, "The Holy Land Foundation was the chief fundraising arm for the Palestine Committee in the U.S. created by the Muslim Brotherhood to support Hamas."

An August 22, 2007, *National Review* article titled "Coming Clean About CAIR" details CAIR's involvement with the Holy Land Foundation and how its executive director, Nihad Awad, attended the Muslim Brotherhood 1993 Palestine Committee meeting. The Palestine Committee, which is Hamas in the United States, created CAIR at that meeting to be its "public relations" organization.

Former FBI special agent John Guandolo exposes CAIR on his website, *Understanding the Threat*, stating, "While CAIR bills itself as a 'Muslim civil rights' organization, the evidence does not support this and, in fact, demonstrate it is a Hamas entity. Hamas is a terrorist organization."

Barack Obama was president-elect of the United States when the Holy Land Foundation and its principals were convicted. He had to know that the Holy Land Foundation was using zakat to fund terrorism and yet, according to FBI whistleblower Philip Haney, "Obama's Justice Department shut the Holy Land Foundation trial down in 2009 despite its success in rooting out an underground network of financial donors to Hamas under the cover of 'charity.'"

Knowing that the Holy Land Foundation "charity" was guilty of financing terrorists, Obama still promised to find ways to help Muslims in America fulfill zakat. That brings us to Leo Hohmann's stunning May 18, 2016, article, "Refugees Sending Suitcases of Welfare Cash Home to Somalis."

In a jaw-dropping exposé, Hohmann revealed that in 2015, "Men and women pulling 'suitcases full of cash' started showing up at Seattle's Sea-Tac Airport holding tickets for international flights bound for Africa." Law enforcement noticed. The suitcase haulers were Somali-Americans who had come to the United States as refugees. So far so good. The problem was that they were also cash couriers working for Islamic hawalas. *Hawala* is the Arabic word for "transfer."

The hawala system is an underground method of transferring money outside traditional banking or wire transfers. The hawala is a "trust" system used extensively by Sharia-compliant Muslim immigrants sending money back home to avoid fees, and by Islamic terrorists to avoid a paper trail. Al-Qaeda uses the hawala system and so do Somali suitcase haulers.

Glenn Kerns, a Seattle police officer and fourteen-year member of the FBI's Joint Terrorism Task Force, decided to investigate the suspicious hawala transactions. Most Somali refugees receive welfare payments, so American taxpayer money was being sent back to Somalia and Kerns wanted to determine how much of the money was going to Al-Shabaab, the Somali terrorist organization.

Hawalas are big business. <u>Kerns recounted</u>, "The first cash shipment discovered at Sea-Tac was a man carrying $750,000 in cash who told Customs officials he was transporting the money overseas. Over the next few months couriers carrying as much as $2 million boarded commercial flights at Sea-Tac. One Seattle hawala sent back $20 million in 2015."

Kerns analyzed financial records filed with the Washington State Department of Financial Institutions and confirmed that the ten hawala clients transferring the most money were all receiving welfare benefits. Kerns said that it was "Straight-up fraud—every one of them." Kerns suspected that if welfare fraud was being committed in Seattle, it was probably happening in other large Somali settlement communities in the United States as well.

Kerns and an agent from another federal agency took their case to the U.S. Attorney's Office in Seattle. Acting U.S. Attorney General Annette L. Hayes, an appointee of Obama's attorney general, Eric Holder, was in charge at the time and refused to prosecute the case! WHY NOT?

Philip Haney and Art Moore, co-authors of the book *See Something, Say Nothing: A Homeland Security Officer Exposes the Government's Submission to Jihad*, have the answers. Haney and Moore explain that Islamic supremacism is the problem. Islam is an expansionist replacement ideology. Obama attempted to separate jihad violence from religious Islam by renaming it violent extremism. His denial policy, known as Countering Violent Extremism, downplayed the threat of supremacist Islam and endangered the nation. The idea of countering "violent extremism" is completely absurd. Obama's pro-Islam policies were protecting Islamic terror financing that was disguised as charitable zakat, was derived from welfare fraud, and was being delivered by Islamic hawalas.

See Something, Say Nothing exposes how deeply the submission, denial, and deception run. Haney, an intelligence expert and founding member of the Department of Homeland Security, gives a chilling first-hand account of trying to say something about the individuals and organizations threatening the nation with the expectation that the information would be pursued. Instead, Homeland Security scrubbed the information and investigated Haney! Obama's policies protected the enemy and punished the patriot.

Haney explains how Obama's administration, including the FBI under directors Robert Mueller and James Comey, launched sweeping changes in the ability of federal agents to screen out radical Islamists from entering the United States. They accomplished this with a little-known policy change not processed through Congress.

According to U.S. Citizenship and Immigration Services (USCIS):

> Generally, any individual who is a member of a "terrorist organization" or who has engaged or engages in terrorism-related activities as defined by the Immigration and Nationality Act (INA) is "inadmissible" (not allowed to enter) the United States and is ineligible for most immigration benefits.

The "Terrorism-Related Inadmissibility Grounds" (TRIG) is a statutory exemption provision created by Congress through which the secretaries of Homeland Security and State have the authority to exempt individuals from the grounds of inadmissibility.

The USCIS website reports:

> On February 5, 2014 the Secretary of Homeland Security Jeh Johnson and the Secretary of State John Kerry (the "Secretaries"), following with the Attorney General Eric Holder, exercised their discretionary authority not to apply the material support inadmissibility ground to certain applicants who provided certain limited material support to an undesignated terrorist organization, or to a member of such an organization. Limited material support may include:
>
> - Certain routine commercial transactions;
> - Certain routine social transactions;
> - Certain humanitarian assistance; and
> - Material Support provided under substantial pressure that does not rise to the level of duress ("sub-duress pressure").

So, Barack Obama exercised his discretionary authority to ignore zakat infractions, institutionalize taqiyya (lying in the service of Islam), and sacrifice American security to Islamic supremacist Sharia law.

On June 28, 2016, Philip Haney gave explosive testimony during a Senate hearing on the threat of Islamic Terrorism that exposed the dangerous consequences of Obama's policies deemphasizing radical Islamic terrorism. Haney testified that Obama invited Muslim Brotherhood–linked leaders to help formulate national security policies, and imposed their Sharia-compliant demands on the Department of Homeland Security. Haney assailed Obama's policies that required stripping the intelligence and official communications of any mention of Islam or the Muslim Brotherhood in association with terrorism. Islamic terrorism was renamed violent extremism. Obama purged training materials that cast Islam in a negative light, erasing and altering vital intelligence on terrorists and terror threats.

Barack Obama was the most anti-American president in U.S. history. For eight years Obama protected Islam at the expense of America. Whistleblower Philip Haney tried to raise American awareness of the existential threat of Islam, which is not a religion like any other. Islam is a sociopolitical movement disguised as a religion that is determined to establish a global caliphate ruled under supremacist religious Sharia law. Islam's unapologetic goal is to convert the world into a global Islamic theocracy.

The globalist Bush administration and the pro-Muslim Obama administration both protected Islamic leaders and their supremacist beliefs at the expense of America, American citizens, and the Constitution of the United States. George W. Bush insisted that Islam is a religion of peace and Barack Obama insisted that Islam is a religion like any other. Islam is neither. Islam is an expansionist political ideology with a religious wing, seeking world dominion. Today, the security of the United States of America is still compromised by Bush/Obama political decisions to protect Islam at the expense of America.

The Culture War on America is being fought by the Leftist/Islamist/Globalist axis seeking to destabilize and overthrow our duly elected America-first President Donald Trump. The 2020 presidential election will determine the future course of America. Will she remain a sovereign, independent nation ruled by the U.S. Constitution? Will she devolve into a collectivist state ruled by leftists promoting socialism? Or will she collapse into an Islamic caliphate ruled by Sharia law?

The Holy Land Foundation breached the International Emergency Economic Powers Act prohibiting transactions that threaten the security of the United States. The Somali cash couriers did the same—their hawalas fund Al-Shabaab terrorists in Somalia, who are affiliated with al-Qaeda. Al-Shabaab's brutal persecution and genocide against Christians has depopulated Christian Somalis to only a few hundred in a nation of over 11 million. Islamic terrorism is murdering any opposition to its intended caliphate.

The Humanitarian Hoax of Islamic Zakat continues to endanger America. Obama knowingly facilitated the deceitful use of zakat to fund terrorism, and his policies have not been reversed. America-first President Donald Trump must nullify the Obama administration's deceitful TRIG exercise of authority that created the statutory exemptions for Islamic zakat. President Trump must protect America and restore Homeland Security's authority to prosecute those who exploit our welfare system in order to fund terrorism.

On 9/11 Islamists declared war on Judeo-Christian America. It is time to admit that Islamic terrorism is not "violent extremism," it is part of Islam's comprehensive religious war against non-believers. Islam has been fighting its religious war against the Judeo-Christian world since the seventh century, and Islam is on the march again. Judeo-Christian denial is not a survival strategy for Western civilization.

We must oppose Islamist expansionism and end the Humanitarian Hoax of Islamic Zakat if America is to remain a free and sovereign constitutional republic. We must stand firm and proudly preserve our Judeo-Christian culture and moral values. We must never apologize for being American and for our signature ethos of hard work, equal opportunity, and the meritocracy that made America the freest, fairest, greatest nation in the world.

Islamists insist the world belongs to Allah. Islamists believe that using their mandatory religious obligation for zakat to fund worldwide Islamic terrorism is their duty. Islamists wrote the Muslim Brotherhood's *Explanatory Memorandum* articulating its stealth civilization jihad to make America Muslim. The Muslim Brotherhood and every one of its seditious offshoots are dangerous enemies of the state and must be designated terrorist organizations.

HOAX 43

The Humanitarian Hoax of 'Assisted' Suicide

August 11, 2019

THE humanitarian hoax is the deliberate and deceitful tactic of presenting a destructive policy as altruistic. The humanitarian huckster presents himself as a compassionate advocate when in fact he is the disguised enemy.

Dr. Jack Kevorkian was a Michigan pathologist and euthanasia advocate who supported the right of terminally ill people to die by physician-assisted suicide. His famous remark, "Dying is not a crime," launched a public debate about the ethics of physician-assisted suicide.

Dr. Kevorkian was a pioneer in the controversial matter. Dubbed Dr. Death by the media, Kevorkian's career and trials were widely publicized, and discussions about the ethics of physician-assisted suicide went mainstream. Between 1994 and 1997 Kevorkian was tried four times for physician-assisted suicide.

In 1998, Dr. Kevorkian was arrested and convicted of second-degree murder for his role in the suicide of Thomas Youk, a fifty-two-year-old man in the final stages of Lou Gehrig's disease. Kevorkian was sentenced to ten to twenty-five years in prison and then granted parole after serving eight years. He devoted his last years to lecturing and changing the laws on physician-assisted suicide.

As individuals living in a free country, we embrace our constitutional rights to life, liberty, and the pursuit of happiness, but what about our right to die? Dr. Kevorkian raised public consciousness about terminally ill patients and their right to die. The problem, of course, is the opportunity for abuse in "assisting" suicides.

Legalizing assisted suicide is legalizing self-murder, so beyond any religious opposition to "playing God," there is the secular opposition based on the possibility of murder disguised as suicide. That brings us to "politically assisted" suicide and the suspicious deaths of people connected to Bill and Hillary Clinton.

It is impossible to ignore the <u>growing list of individuals</u> scheduled to testify against the Clintons who were found dead before their court dates. Some have been ruled murders and some ruled suicides—but all are suspicious. Let's take a look at a few.

February 19, 1986: <u>Barry Seal</u>, the Louisiana pilot who smuggled drugs in and out of the Mena airport for the Medellin Drug Cartel, was murdered. Seal was earning as much as $1.3 million per flight to transport cocaine from Colombia and Panama to the United States. In 1984 Seal was caught and made a deal to become an informant for the Drug Enforcement Administration. Seal testified against the Medellin Cartel and was murdered by contract killers hired by Pablo Escobar, head of the cartel.

One might assume that Escobar acted alone in ordering the hit on Seal if it were not for the pesky fact that the CIA was implicated in the drug-running operations centered around the Mena, Arkansas, airport while Bill Clinton was governor of the state from 1983 to 1992. We will come back to this.

August 10, 1991: Danny Casolaro, a journalist working on a book exposing government-sanctioned drug running, was found dead in his hotel bathtub. His death was ruled a suicide even though the slashes severed the tendons to his fingers, making it impossible for him to slash both wrists, as his were. Casolaro was investigating the curious case of the Justice Department's theft of a law enforcement database software system called Prosecutors Management Information System (PROMIS) from a company called Inslaw. In 1991 PROMIS was unique because it could be programmed to automatically access other databases. It was a powerful spying tool used during the time of the Iran-Contra affair, the CIA's clandestine gun- and drug-running operation that supplied the Nicaraguan Contras with untraceable weapons. Under then-governor Bill Clinton's watch, Nicaragua was at one end of the drug-smuggling pipeline and Mena, Arkansas, at the other. Politically assisted suicide?

July 20, 1993: Vince Foster, deputy White House counsel, had intimate knowledge of the Clintons' personal finances and had been called to testify about records that Hillary refused to turn over. Foster was found dead in Fort Marcy Park in Washington, DC. His death was reported as a self-inflicted gunshot wound to his mouth and ruled a suicide even though the suicide note was forged and the gunshot wound to the back of his neck went unreported. Politically assisted suicide?

March 2015: FBI Special Agent David Raynor was found stabbed and shot with his own gun the day before he was scheduled to testify before a federal grand jury. Raynor was expected to expose Secretary of State Hillary Clinton's illegal cover-up of Obama's Fast and Furious scandal, a Justice Department program that allowed assault weapons to be sold to Mexican drug cartels, allegedly as a way to track them.

CNSNews published an article on Secretary Clinton's previous October 27, 2011, testimony before the House Foreign Relations Committee, "Hillary Clinton: 'No Evidence' DOJ Sought Required License to Send Guns to Mexico in 'Fast and Furious'":

> The federal Arms Export Control Act requires State Department involvement in any decision to send weapons across an international border. Under the act, it is illegal to "conspire to export, import, re-export or cause to be exported . . . any defense article . . . for which a license or written approval is required . . . without first obtaining the required license or written approval from the Directorate of Defense Trade Controls."

Clinton testified under oath there was "no record" that the Justice Department had given the State Department a "heads-up" about Operation Fast and Furious. Here is the problem.

Fast and Furious was exposed by the 2010 fatal shooting of U.S. Border Patrol Agent Brian Terry with one of those guns. Raynor was leading the investigation into the murder of one of the main witnesses, homicide detective Sean Suiter, who Raynor believed had been killed before he could testify that the Obama administration ". . . was criminally complicit in allowing guns to flow into the hands of criminals on the Mexican border." Politically assisted suicide?

June 22, 2016: Who can forget John Ashe, the former United Nations General Assembly president who "accidentally" dropped a barbell on his throat the day he was supposed to testify about Hillary Clinton's ties to Ng Lap Seng, the Chinese businessman on trial for bribery. Ng Lap Seng had been implicated in the 1996 China-gate scandal for funneling illegal donations to Bill Clinton's re-election campaign. Politically assisted suicide?

July 10, 2016: Seth Rich, the DNC Voter Expansion data director, was found shot multiple times near his home in Bloomingdale, DC. His death was ruled a robbery gone bad, even though nothing was taken—his wallet, watch, and cell phone were still on him. One wonders just how stupid the media think the public really is. Seth Rich has been identified by many as the internal leak of the 20,000 DNC emails sent to Wikileaks proving the DNC was rigging primaries to favor Hillary. Seth Rich could prove that there was no Russian hack because he personally leaked the emails—and then he was dead. Wikileaks' Julian Assange refused to identify his source while Seth Rich was alive. It was confirmed in a July 2019 lawsuit that Seth and his brother Aaron were Assange's source. Politically assisted suicide?

July 2017: Klaus Eberwein, a former Haitian government official scheduled to testify against Clinton Foundation corruption and malpractice, was found dead in Miami with a gunshot wound to his head. The death was ruled a suicide. Eberwein was expected to expose that only 0.6 percent of international donations for Haitian aid were actually received by Haitian organizations, 9.6 percent went to the Haitian government, and 89.8 percent—a whopping $5.4 billion—went to non-Haitian organizations. The *Atlanta Black Star* identified the non-Haitian organizations as "including private contractors, international NGOs, and military and civilian agencies of donor countries, including the Pentagon, which charged the State Department hundreds of millions of dollars." Politically assisted suicide?

The list of suspicious deaths, derisively called the Clinton body count or Arkancide, continues to grow, but perhaps the most intriguing at this moment is the death of CIA drug pilot Barry Seal. Are we supposed to believe that CIA drug-running stopped with Barry Seal's death? Not likely. Enter Jeffrey Epstein.

August 10, 2019: Convicted sex offender Jeffrey Epstein was found dead in his Manhattan jail cell the day after 2,000 court documents were unsealed. The media remain focused on the names of the rich and famous who would have been outed if Epstein's case went to trial. I am far more interested in what else was on Jeffrey Epstein's plane besides underage girls. Is it possible that Epstein replaced Barry Seal? Is it possible that Jeffrey Epstein's extremely suspicious "suicide" was an attempt to stop him from making a deal with the DOJ that would have outed Hillary, Bill, and Obama's malfeasance in CIA covert drug-running operations? Politically motivated suicide?

Financier Jeffrey Epstein worked at the investment bank Bear Stearns before forming his own firm in 1982, J. Epstein & Co., in St. Thomas, Virgin Islands. Epstein's firm serviced exclusively wealthy clients, with $1 billion or more in assets. The dubious nature of Epstein's business was discussed in a July 22, 2009, *Business Insider* article by Jay Carney titled "Is Jeff Epstein Also Running a Ponzi Scheme?"

Carney asked if Epstein was running a Ponzi scheme. There were no analysts, portfolio managers, or traders. All the investment decisions were made by Epstein himself. Epstein had absolute control of the money, charged a flat fee of between $25 million and $100 million, and took no share of the profits. Even more curious, according to Carney, "There are no SEC filings disclosing Epstein's holdings. Not one. It's hard to see how he could be managing billions without ever tripping a disclosure trigger, unless he avoids the stock market altogether and only invests in private deals." Perhaps Jeffrey Epstein's private deals were with the CIA.

Doug Band, deputy assistant, legal counselor, and aide to Bill Clinton during his presidency, introduced Epstein to Clinton and arranged for the former president to travel to Africa on Epstein's 727 in 2002. Band traveled with Clinton to 125 countries and over 2,000 cities while he was president. During Clinton's post-presidency, Band helped set up the Clinton Global Initiative and the Clinton Foundation. Band negotiated with the Obama administration to nominate Hillary Clinton as secretary of state.

In 2005 Doug Band launched the global corporate consulting firm Teneo, where Bill Clinton served on the board and was a client. Huma Abedin, Hillary Clinton's top adviser, was hired by Teneo as a consultant while still working at the State Department for Hillary Clinton, and also serving as a consultant for the Clinton Foundation. This highly irregular arrangement resulted in an investigation by the State Department inspector general due to the obvious conflicts of interest involved. Leaked emails from the investigation revealed that Teneo helped Bill Clinton secure tens of millions of dollars in speaking fees and other financial arrangements with large institutions.

The leaked emails released by Wikileaks include a twelve-page memo that Band wrote describing Teneo's work on behalf of his client. On October 28, 2016, *The Atlantic* published "The Man at the Center of 'Bill Clinton Inc.,'" describing Band's "unique role" in an "unorthodox arrangement" with Bill Clinton that helped Clinton and the Clinton Foundation by soliciting donations from his Teneo clients. Band wrote with regard to himself and Justin Cooper, another Clinton aide:

> Independent of our fundraising and decision-making activities on behalf of the Foundation, we have dedicated ourselves to helping the President secure and engage in for-profit activities—including speeches, books, and advisory service engagements. In that context, we have in effect served as agents, lawyers, managers and implementers to secure speaking, business and advisory service deals. In support of the President's for-profit activity, we also have solicited and obtained, as appropriate, in-kind services for the President and his family—for personal travel, hospitality, vacation and the like. Neither Justin nor I are separately compensated for these activities (e.g., we do not receive a fee for, or percentage of, the more than $50 million in for-profit activity we have personally helped to secure for President Clinton to date or the $66 million in future contracts, should he choose to continue with those engagements).

> With respect to business deals for his advisory services, Justin and I found, developed and brought to President Clinton multiple arrangements for him to accept or reject. Of his current 4 arrangements, we secured all of them; and, we have helped manage and maintain all of his for-profit business relationships. Since 2001, President Clinton's business arrangements have yielded more than $30 million for him personally, with $66 million to be paid out over the next nine years should he choose to continue with the current engagements.

The *Atlantic* article closed with "the Wikileaks hack has exposed that the former president's philanthropy, his personal enrichment, and the business interests of perhaps his closest aide were too closely tied." Doug Band knows where all the Clinton corporate business skeletons are buried. Does he have the information to blackmail Bill Clinton?

Jeffrey Epstein was notorious for providing underage girls to prominent businessmen and politicians. Surely Band knew Epstein's reputation and that any association with Epstein exposed then-President Clinton to the possibility of being blackmailed.

Perhaps Epstein's Lolita Express was flying cargo besides the conspicuously underage young girls. Perhaps Epstein was flying drugs and money in and out of the Virgin Islands, known to be the South American cartel's drug-trafficking trans-shipment point. According to an April 10, 2015, article in *Virgin Island News*, "One of the FBI's 10 most wanted fugitives was captured (a Virgin Islander, 'Jimmy the Juice' Springette) and testified in 2008 about the massive drug-trafficking operation transporting tons of cocaine for South American Cartels through the Virgin Islands to the mainland United States via the airport, cruise-ships, and other means."

Perhaps during the twenty-seven times then-President Bill Clinton flew with Jeffrey Epstein aboard the Lolita Express, the teenage girls onboard were the main attraction that shielded the late-night show. If the smugglers were ever caught, the sex trafficking would be the focus of the investigation and the drug-running would remain concealed. Diversionary tactics are classic strategies of war—why would drug wars be any different?

It simply strains credibility to believe that the extremely suspicious death of Jeffrey Epstein was a suicide—unless, of course, it was a politically assisted suicide.

The Humanitarian Hoax of "Assisted" Suicide must be investigated as part of Attorney General William Barr's efforts to drain the corrupt Washington swamp and restore government credibility. Enough is enough! The country has had enough of the Clinton crime family. It is time to investigate prominent American political crime families for racketeering, starting with the odious Clintons.

HOAX 44

The Humanitarian Hoax of White Supremacy

August 14, 2019

THE humanitarian hoax is the deliberate and deceitful tactic of presenting a destructive policy as altruistic. The humanitarian huckster presents himself as a compassionate advocate when in fact he is the disguised enemy.

The radical leftist hucksters in the Democrat party have repeatedly accused President Trump of being a racist and a white supremacist. Is this true? Let's find out.

Racial unity has been the subject of political speeches since before the Civil War. The United States was founded in 1776 during an era of worldwide slavery when even black men owned black slaves. Supremacy is the corollary of enslavement—you have to be a supremacist to own a slave. Slavery was outlawed in the United States in 1865 with the passage of the Thirteenth Amendment. So, let's be clear: slavery has been illegal in the United States of America for 154 years.

Many countries and religions in the world continue to legally practice and embrace slavery—but not Judeo-Christian America. The United States has constitutionally rejected slavery and the attitude of supremacism that supports it. Our American national credo strives for racial equality that is made possible through upward mobility and a robust middle class.

Equality in America is a matter of equal *opportunity*, not a guarantee of equal *outcome*. This is a very important distinction because it is what separates President Trump's America-first ethos of individualism from the radical leftist Democrat party's ethos of collectivism. We will come back to this.

President Donald Trump is an unapologetic advocate of upward mobility and wealth creation for ALL Americans. His rallying cry is Jobs! Jobs! Jobs! Manufacturing is the heart of a thriving industrialized economy. In 2017, 171,000 manufacturing jobs were added. In 2018, <u>284,000 manufacturing jobs</u> were added; it was the largest manufacturing job increase in twenty-one years. Additionally, in 2017, President Trump signed an executive order for an apprenticeship program to fill 6 million open positions—half are manufacturing jobs. By contrast, in 2009 under Obama, the U.S. lost a staggering 1,375,000 manufacturing jobs.

President Trump's economic policies are both color-blind and responsible for the lowest unemployment in the black community in American history, as well as the lowest unemployment rate for Hispanics in America since records were kept. So, why do the hucksters call President Trump a racist and a white supremacist? Let's find out.

We begin with a discussion of supremacy as a concept. A supremacist advocates the superiority of a particular group. Black supremacists believe blacks are the superior group. White supremacists believe whites are the superior group. Islamic supremacists believe Muslims are the superior group. Leftist supremacists believe the radical Left is the superior group. Male chauvinists believe men are the superior group, and radical feminists believe women are the superior group. So, being a supremacist is an arrogant attitude of exclusion and superiority, not necessarily a racial issue.

Of all the possible divisions in society, racial divisions are the easiest to see and, therefore, the easiest to exploit. Why does this matter?

President Trump is unapologetically pro-American and demands American sovereignty and the protection and preservation of the U.S. Constitution, which is a document of inclusion and equality. President Trump is the existential enemy of the Leftist/Islamist/Globalist axis that seeks both his destruction and the destruction of the Constitution he protects. The tactical strategy of the axis is projection. The axis accuses President Trump of being what they themselves are—political, religious, philosophical supremacists.

Arrogant leftists seek to destroy the Constitution and replace it with the centralized government of socialism. Arrogant Islamists seek to destroy the Constitution and replace it with supremacist Islamic Sharia law. Arrogant globalists seek to destroy the Constitution and internationalize the world under a one-world government that they themselves will rule. America-first President Donald Trump opposes all three groups, and no axis member can succeed in its individual objective without first succeeding in the shared objective of toppling President Trump and shattering America from within. What is the axis action plan?

There are two separate entities adjudicating cases in the United States today, with two very different agendas. The first is the legitimate federal judiciary, one of three co-equal branches of government organized under the U.S. Constitution and federal laws. This judiciary has courthouses where cases are adjudicated according to rules of evidence designed to establish the truth with facts and a foundational presumption of innocence until proven guilty. The second "judiciary" is the illegitimate court of public opinion, where the humanitarian hucksters try their cases on the Internet and in the entertainment and news media without regard for truth, facts, or the constitutional presumption of innocence.

The goal of the court of public opinion is mass social engineering. What this means is that members of the Leftist/Islamist/Globalist axis are cooperating in their shared effort to topple President Trump by smearing him with false accusations of racism and white supremacy. The accusations are patently absurd, but the directors of the axis powers don't care. Their ends-justify-the-means tactic is the foundation of every dictatorship in the world.

The once independent, informational World Wide Web has been co-opted by the radical Leftist/Islamist/Globalist axis for political purposes. This is how it works.

The Leftist/Islamist/Globalist axis falsely and hypocritically claims that open borders are humanitarian and that President Trump's legally mandated attempts to secure the nation's southern border are racist, a result of his feelings of white supremacy. The axis powers are not interested in facts, truth, and a presumption of innocence—only in destroying President Donald Trump. The Leftist/Islamist/Globalist axis is deceitfully using the court of public opinion to smear the president in preparation for the 2020 election.

Now let's continue our discussion of individualism and collectivism to see how they fit into this deception. Socialism, communism, globalism, and Islamism are collectivist systems of centralized government where the group takes precedence over the individual. Capitalism is a system that prioritizes the individual and the opportunity for upward mobility. In capitalism there is private property and the individual rights that support it. Individual property rights ensure upward mobility. Upward mobility is the foundation of the American dream that has taken the United States from an era of worldwide slavery to the election of a black president.

In collectivism there is neither private property nor individual rights—the government owns and distributes the fruits of your labor. The disingenuous accusations of racism and white supremacy lodged against President Trump completely disguise the racism and supremacist ideals of the Leftist/Islamist/Globalist axis accusers.

The black supremacist Black Panthers do not represent the greater black community, the white supremacist KKK does not represent the greater white community, the Sharia-compliant Islamic supremacists do not represent the members of the Muslim community who embrace our Constitution. The axis accusers make no such distinctions. They insist that since President Trump is white, he is a racist and a white supremacist. Their argument has no basis in rationality, facts, or truth, but that does not matter in the court of public opinion.

The court of public opinion follows the twelve rules for social revolution articulated in Saul Alinsky's infamous manual, *Rules for Radicals.* According to Alinsky, "Before men can act, an issue must be polarized. Men will act when they are convinced their cause is 100 percent on the side of the angels, and that the opposition are 100 percent on the side of the devil. . . . This includes lying a hundred thousand times over, if necessary, and always with a straight face."

The Leftist/Islamist/Globalist axis liars are non-sectarian supremacists following the rules of revolution where the ends justify the means. The leftist and globalist liars are endorsed by Alinsky; the Islamist liars are endorsed by taqiyya (lying in the service of Islam). If we are to avoid violent revolution in America, we must turn off the noise of the divisive false accusations made in the illegitimate court of public opinion. We must examine the facts of President Trump's color-blind policies and accomplishments according to the rules of evidence defined by the Constitution.

The false accusations of racism and white supremacy made in the court of public opinion are designed to create the social chaos necessary to make the supremacist axis dreams come true. Personally, I prefer the ordered liberty and equality of the American Dream. I reject entirely the supremacism of leftism, Islamism, and globalism.

Do not be fooled by the illegitimate court of public opinion—it is deliberately facilitating the Humanitarian Hoax of White Supremacy designed to kill America with kindness. President Donald J. Trump represents equality, ordered liberty, and the color-blind upward mobility of the American Dream. In the legitimate federal judiciary, facts prove that POTUS is not a racist or a white supremacist. It is his enemies who are both.

HOAX 45

The Humanitarian Hoax of the New World Order

August 31, 2019

THE humanitarian hoax is the deliberate and deceitful tactic of presenting a destructive policy as altruistic. The humanitarian huckster presents himself as a compassionate advocate when in fact he is the disguised enemy.

Every natural force on Earth, from fire to nuclear energy, has the potential for construction or destruction. This inherent duality presents man with moral choices between the two. Traditional Judeo-Christian morality deems construction good and destruction bad. What happens when the accepted foundational morality of society is challenged by a competing narrative that insists construction is bad and destruction is good? Let's find out.

Societies as small as families and as large as nation-states are organized by accepted principles codified into written and unwritten laws accepted by member units. When societies abide by the accepted rules, they are considered to be in homeostasis—at peace and in balance. When a competing narrative intrudes, the society becomes destabilized and must either accept or reject the competing ideology in order to regain that peace and balance.

Traditionally, American culture derives its stability and moral authority from its Judeo-Christian tradition, constitutional law, and parental authority in the family unit. God, government, and family are the triptych of American culture and the foundations for America's extraordinary ordered liberty and our unparalleled freedom and prosperity.

Today's radical leftist Democrat party is challenging the foundational American triptych and attempting to repaint its panels with socialism. Here is the problem.

In politics it is essential that the public evaluate policies with rational objectivity. When they don't, the consequence is belief in the unbelievable. I call this political mysticism—belief in the politically impossible. "Democratic" socialism is the twenty-first century's political mysticism, seducing Americans with promises of Heaven on Earth. Millennials disenchanted with the religious teachings of their Judeo-Christian heritage are searching for answers to man's moral dilemma elsewhere. Some find it in supremacist religious Islamic Sharia law. Others are duped by leftist radical Democrats advocating the political mysticism of secular democratic socialism.

No successful humanitarian huckster sells socialism by promising enslavement; they promise utopian social justice and income equality instead. They promise "free stuff" to the hopeful masses and con them into voting for their "deliverance" at the voting booth.

Let's be clear: FREE STUFF IS NEVER FREE. People always pay with their freedom!

Collectivism, whether marketed directly as communism, indirectly as socialism, or deceitfully as democratic socialism, is a structure of centralized government control. America's radical leftist Democrat party and its allied Islamists and globalists, are selling the upside-down notions and inverted logic of "democratic" socialism to shatter America from within in 2020.

Collectivism is slavery marketed as freedom. British author George Orwell described the upside-down notions and inverted logic of collectivism in his dystopian novel about totalitarianism, *1984*: "War is peace. Freedom is slavery. Ignorance is strength." Orwell was a political analyst who understood that "All tyrannies rule through fraud and force, but once the fraud is exposed they must rely exclusively on force."

There is no private property in collectivism. Individual citizens do not reap what they sow; the government does. So, first comes the fraud—the promise of social justice and income equality. Then comes the force—a centralized ruling government that owns or controls all means of production and its distribution.

Winston Churchill described the reality of socialism in two separate speeches:

> Socialism is a philosophy of failure, the creed of ignorance, and the gospel of envy. —Perth, Scotland, 28 May 1948

> The inherent vice of capitalism is the unequal sharing of blessings. The inherent virtue of Socialism is the equal sharing of miseries. —House of Commons, 22 October 1945.

Churchill understood that socialism is a return to feudalism, where the ruling elite benefit at the expense of the shared misery of the masses. Yes, you read that correctly: socialism is the stepping-stone to a one-world government ruled by the globalist elite.

Failed cultural Marxism has been repackaged with the magic word "democratic" to overcome reflexive American resistance to communism and socialism, and to disguise collectivism's tyrannical core. It is a fraudulent marketing technique designed to sell political mysticism. The word "democratic" is being used to paint lipstick on this political pig. Democratic socialism is presented with mystical reverence as deliverance of social justice and income equality—millennial salvation.

Radical socialist Saul Alinsky, the father of community organizing and mentor to Barack Obama and Hillary Clinton, clarified the objective of the deceit on page 10 of his political manifesto, *Rules for Radicals*:

> A Marxist begins with his prime truth that all evils are caused by the exploitation of the proletariat by the capitalists. From this he logically proceeds to the revolution to end capitalism, then into the third stage of reorganization into a new social order of the dictatorship of the proletariat, and finally the last stage—the political paradise of communism.

Humanitarian huckster-in-chief Barack Obama tried selling Alinsky's political paradise of communism to America by disguising it as socialism and presenting it as "hope and change." Obama might have succeeded if Hillary Clinton, his legacy candidate and fellow radical socialist, had been elected in 2016. Instead, today's emboldened radical leftist Democrats and their "resistance" movement have repackaged their product, reverently relabeling it "democratic socialism."

In theater as in religion, there is the concept of suspension of disbelief. The audience does not examine the plot or characters with the same rational analysis required of objective scientific study. When political theory is presented as religion, the same suspension of disbelief is accepted. Why does this matter?

It matters because suspension of disbelief is the core of political mysticism. Duped millennials argue that old attempts at communism and socialism were not the "real" communism and socialism—democratic socialism is the real deal.

The aspiration for world domination simply will not go away. A sovereign United States of America is the existential enemy of any aspirational movement for a one-world government whether secular or religious. It was clear to anyone and everyone after World War II that if the United States of America were ever to be defeated, it would have to be shattered from the inside out—military defeat was out of the question. With this mindset, the enemies of American greatness resolved to destroy America from within. The Culture War on America took aim at the foundational trinity—God, family, and government. The hearts and minds of patriotic Americans would have to be turned against themselves. America would have to implode.

The Leftist/Islamist/Globalist axis is targeting the foundations of American greatness to destroy her from within. The immediate goal is to defeat America-first President Donald Trump in 2020. The leftists are selling voters the political mysticism of secular democratic socialism, and the Islamists are selling voters the political mysticism of supremacist Islamic Sharia law.

In *The Story of the Malakand Field Force* (1898) Winston Churchill described Islamism:

> But the Mahommedan religion increases, instead of lessening, the fury of intolerance. It was originally propagated by the sword, and ever since, its votaries have been subject, above the people of all other creeds, to this form of madness. . . . In each case civilisation is confronted with militant Mahommedanism. The forces of progress clash with those of reaction. The religion of blood and war is face to face with that of peace.

In *The River War* (1899) Churchill warned:

> Thousands become the brave and loyal soldiers of the faith: all know how to die but the influence of the religion paralyses the social development of those who follow it. No stronger retrograde force exists in the world. Far from being moribund, Mahommedanism is a militant and proselytizing faith.

Churchill understood that, to an Islamist, peace on Earth will occur only when the entire world is Muslim. He recognized the militant theocratic foundation of Islam and its sociopolitical requirement that no separation exist between mosque and state—in Islam, religion is the centralized controlling government.

Winston Churchill was reviled for saying the unsayable. He spoke the inconvenient truth about Islamist and globalist aspirations for world domination in his time, and was hated for it until he was needed to save England from the Nazis.

History is repeating itself. Today, Islamism and democratic socialism are twin enemies of American sovereignty.

The Leftist/Islamist/Globalist axis is the facilitator of the Humanitarian Hoax of the New World Order, but it is only a temporary alliance.

If the axis can defeat President Trump in 2020, axis members will necessarily battle each other for dominance afterward. The provisional alliance will remain only until it can destabilize America and make the country ungovernable. Social chaos is the prerequisite for seismic social change. Anarchy is the goal.

Anarchy will launch a globalist elite takeover and it will become manifest that globalists have been financing and fomenting the leftist/Islamist mischief and mayhem in the United States. The leftists and Islamists are just useful idiots ushering in the New World Order that will be ruled by the globalist elite.

Leftists and Islamists are playing checkers while the globalist elite are playing chess.

The United States of America is at a tipping point. The 2020 presidential election will decide the country's future. Will we re-elect President Donald Trump and remain a sovereign, free, independent nation? Or will we choose Democrat political mysticism and devolve into the globalist elite's New World Order of feudalism and become their slaves? Your vote decides.

HOAX 46

The Humanitarian Hoax of Climate Change II: Debunking the Bunk

September 11, 2019

THE humanitarian hoax is the deliberate and deceitful tactic of presenting a destructive policy as altruistic. The humanitarian huckster presents himself as a compassionate advocate when in fact he is the disguised enemy.

The Humanitarian Hoax of Climate Change is so enormous and far-reaching that one chapter on the subject is simply not enough.

My first chapter on the topic, *The Humanitarian Hoax of Climate Change—Hoax 4*, was originally published as an article on July 21, 2017. A second article, "The Riddle of Climate Change," published on February 27, 2019, continued the discussion. Now it is necessary to explore the ever-expanding climate change hoax and examine the progress the hucksters have made in advance of the pivotal 2020 presidential election.

Let's begin with huckster-in-chief Barack Obama and his recent staggeringly hypocritical purchase of a $15 million waterfront mansion on Martha's Vineyard. Why would Obama purchase a waterfront mansion doomed to sink underwater in twelve years? He wouldn't. Let's review.

In Obama's first inaugural address, on January 20, 2009, he pledged to "roll back the specter of a warming planet." In his second inaugural address, on January 21, 2013, he affirmed climate change, saying, "We will respond to the threat of climate change, knowing that the failure to do so would betray our children and future generations." He went on to shame anyone who disagreed with his assessment: "Some may still deny the overwhelming judgment of science, but none can avoid the devastating impact of raging fires and crippling drought and powerful storms."

"The overwhelming judgment of science"?? Why did Obama ignore the damning 2009 Climategate scandal, NASA climatologist Dr. Roy Spencer's 2010 book, *The Great Global Warming Blunder*, and the 2014 Senate testimony of Greenpeace co-founder Patrick Moore? Let's find out. Wikipedia explains Climategate:

> Climategate is the scandal that erupted on November 19, 2009, when a collection of email messages, data files, and data processing programs were leaked from the University of East Anglia Climatic Research Unit (CRU) located in the UK, revealing scientific fraud and data manipulation by scientists concerning the global warming theory. Climategate is said to have revealed the biggest scientific hoax in world history.

> Its findings revealed that corruption of climate science is a worldwide problem and not confined to just Britain's CRU climate research centre. For instance, it was discovered that the reported warming trend in New Zealand over the past 155 years (from 1853 to 2008) was created by manmade adjustments of the temperature data.

WHAT?

The Climategate emails showed how all the climate data centers worldwide, including the American National Oceanic and Atmospheric Administration (NOAA) and National Aeronautics and Space Administration (NASA), conspired in the manipulation of global temperature records to suggest that temperatures in the twentieth century rose faster than they actually did.

Climategate occurred in the first year of Obama's first term. Climategate's stunning revelations showed that the "settled science" of climate change was completely fraudulent and politically motivated. Yet the mainstream media attempted to bury the Climategate story for years and continued to push for passage of the Paris Agreement during Obama's second term.

Obama committed his second term to promoting the fiction of *manmade* climate change and implementing regulatory environmental policies through the Environmental Protection Agency. *New York Times* writers Richard W. Stevenson and John M. Broder compared Obama's environmental efforts in their January 21, 2013, article, "Speech Gives Climate Goals Center Stage": "The approach is a turnabout from the first term, when Mr. Obama's guiding principle in trying to pass the cap-and-trade bill was that a negotiated legislative solution was likely to be more politically palatable than regulation by executive fiat."

Executive fiat is an executive order—a directive issued by the president of the United States that manages operations of the federal government and has the force of law. The Paris Agreement, aka Paris Climate Accord, was created by the United Nations Framework Convention on Climate Change on December 12, 2015. The Paris Agreement was <u>enacted by Barack Obama</u> during his second term by executive order, <u>without Senate ratification</u>, on August 29, 2016, effective November 4, 2016. Remember the signing date—it answers the question of what Obama knew and when he knew it.

<u>Doomsday articles</u> warning of cataclysmic flooding and drought began appearing. The narrative of manmade climate change hysteria was launched to support Obama's executive order limiting emissions, and the echo chamber of the mainstream media repeated the narrative incessantly. The problem, of course, was that unbiased scientists continued challenging the narrative and climate "science" of the United Nations. Let's review.

The climate does change, but *manmade* climate change is the deliberately misleading narrative that human behavior is causing cataclysmic changes to the Earth's climate. The Climategate scandal exposed the fraudulent "research" that supported its politically motivated claims and exposed the hoax.

Former Soviet President Mikhail Gorbachev emphasized the importance of using climate alarmism to advance Marxist objectives, saying, "The threat of environmental crisis will be the international key to unlock the New World Order." Gorbachev was referring, of course, to the New World Order of an internationalized world community administered under the auspices of the United Nations.

Dr. Roy Spencer, climatologist, author, and former NASA senior scientist, helped debunk the bunk being foisted on an increasingly worried American voting population in 2010. Dr. Spencer explained that <u>climate sensitivity</u> is the critical issue in finding the truth of climatic changes. "Climate sensitivity is the temperature response of the Earth to a given amount of 'radiative forcing,' of which there are two kinds: a change in either the amount of sunlight absorbed by the Earth, or in the infrared energy the Earth emits to outer space."

Political science and climate change huckster extraordinaire Al Gore claimed climate sensitivity is very high. Dr. Spencer relied on satellite evidence that suggests climate sensitivity is very low. Spencer made the claim for natural climate change—that climate change happens regardless of what humans do.

Dr. Spencer's 2010 book, *The Great Global Warming Blunder*, presented stunning new evidence that global warming is not the fault of humans; it is the result of chaotic internal natural cycles that have been responsible for fluctuating periods of warming and cooling for millennia. The book reveals how climate researchers have mistaken cause and effect of cloud behavior and fallen prey to groupthink acceptance of misguided political global-warming policy proposals.

Dr. Spencer's analysis is atmospheric science, not political science. He completely discards the claims of the United Nations Intergovernmental Panel on Climate Change (IPCC) that greenhouse gases alone explain global warming. Spencer shows how a natural, internally generated climate variability called "climate chaos" that is generated by clouds is responsible.

In the Introduction & Background section of the 2012 edition of his book, Spencer exposes the political motivations of IPCC reports, saying, "The IPCC process for reviewing the science of global warming and climate change has been a peculiar perversion of the usual practice of scientific investigation. Science normally involves the testing of alternative hypotheses, not picking the first one that comes along and then religiously sticking to it. But that is exactly what the IPCC has done."

Of course it is. Dr. Spencer exposed the IPCC's politicization of science:

> As I wrote this book, I found myself increasingly criticizing the IPCC's leadership and the way it politicized my scientific discipline, atmospheric science, in order to promote specific policies. The truth is that the IPCC doesn't actually do scientific research. It is primarily a political advocacy group that cloaks itself in the aura of scientific respectability while it cherry-picks the science that best supports its desired policy outcomes, and marginalizes or ignores science that might contradict the party line. It claims to be policy-neutral, yet it will not entertain any science that might indicate there is no need for policy change on greenhouse gas emissions. Contrary to what the public has been led to believe, the IPCC's relatively brief Summary for Policymakers is not written by hundreds of scientists, but by about fifty handpicked true believers who spin the science of climate change to support specific policy goals.

The goals of the United Nations IPCC are unapologetically stated in <u>United Nations Agenda 2030</u>, the manifesto for imposing the New World Order of a one-world government. The 17 Sustainable Development Goals reaffirm the UN's globalist stance that planet Earth and its ecosystems are "our common home and that 'Mother Earth' is a common expression in a number of countries and regions." This is all Orwellian doublespeak to rationalize the imposition of a one-world government under the auspices of the corrupt United Nations.

Nazi propaganda minister Joseph Goebbels infamously remarked, "If you repeat a lie often enough, people believe it." That is exactly what has happened with manmade climate change. Let's recap.

Huckster-in-chief Barack Obama presented himself as your children's advocate, altruistically implementing policies for their safety. The presidential huckster issued executive orders that seriously restricted the emissions you are told are killing your children and the planet. The lie was told so often by so many that the general population started believing it and then began ostracizing and shaming anyone who didn't believe the lie.

Apostate Greenpeace co-founder and former president of Greenpeace Canada Patrick Moore told the U.S. Senate Environment and Public Works Committee, Subcommittee on Oversight unequivocally on February 25, 2014, "There is no scientific proof that human emissions of carbon dioxide are the dominant cause of the minor warming of the Earth's atmosphere over the past one hundred years."

Moore requested that the chapter on climate change from his book, *Confessions of a Greenpeace Dropout: The Making of a Sensible Environmentalist*, be made part of the Congressional Record.

His testimony exposed the lie of "settled science" to the Committee. Moore explained how environmental science has been completely co-opted by political science. There is not a shred of credible evidence that manmade climate change exists—but no matter. The truth never stops determined hucksters.

Patrick Moore's explosive testimony preceded both the December 2015 United Nations Climate Change Convention and Obama's executive order authorizing the Paris Agreement in August 2016. Obama knowingly deceived the American public with political science masquerading as environmental science.

Three years later, on March 7, 2019, *Breitbart* writer Robert Kraychik reported on an interview with Patrick Moore in his article, "Greenpeace Founder: Global Warming Hoax Pushed by Corrupt Scientists 'Hooked on Grants.'" During the interview Moore explained how fear and guilt are leveraged by proponents of climate change:

> When they talk about the 99 percent consensus [among scientists] on climate change, that's a completely ridiculous and false number. But most of the scientists—put it in quotes, "scientists"—who are pushing this catastrophic theory are getting paid by public money. They are not being paid by General Electric or Dupont or 3M to do this research, where private companies expect to get something useful from their research that might produce a better product and make them a profit in the end because people want it—build-a-better-mousetrap type of idea.

Moore described the details of the climate change hoax and the green movement:

> And so you've got the green movement creating stories that instill fear in the public. You've got the media echo chamber—fake news—repeating it over and over and over again to everybody that they're killing their children.

Shaming is a powerful tool used and abused by humanitarian hucksters to promote their manmade climate change narrative and to silence any opposition to their false claims of "settled" climate science.

The manmade climate change hucksters continue to perpetrate their monstrous hoax through fear and guilt. Fear is a powerful motivator for behavior change. If parents can be convinced that catastrophe will strike their children unless they change their own behavior, their guilt will motivate parents to change and the big lie of manmade climate change becomes generational.

Children are being indoctrinated to believe the lie by their parents and by the collaborating educational curriculum courtesy of Common Core and UN Agenda 2030. More on that later.

The Big Lie continues today. A recent bill proposed by <u>Democrat Senator Edward Markey</u> of Massachusetts would authorize the National Oceanic and Atmospheric Administration to establish a "Climate Change Education Program." This legislation deceitfully denies that manmade climate change is a disputed scientific theory and, instead, presents its disinformation as factually irrefutable.

Markey, like his fellow Democrats, ignores Patrick Moore's emphatic warning:

> The narrative of anthropogenic [manmade] global warming or "climate

change" is an existential threat to reason. It is the biggest lie since people thought the Earth was at the center of the universe. This is Galileo-type stuff. If you remember, Galileo discovered that the sun was at the center of the solar system and the Earth revolved around it. He was sentenced to death by the Catholic Church, and only because he recanted was he allowed to live in house arrest for the rest of his life.

So this was around the beginning of what we call the Enlightenment, when science became the way in which we gained knowledge. Instead of using superstition and instead of using invisible demons and whatever else, we started to understand that you have to have observation of actual events and then you have to repeat those observations over and over again, and that is basically the scientific method.

But this abomination that is occurring today in the climate issue is the biggest threat to the Enlightenment that has occurred since Galileo. Nothing else comes close to it. This is as bad a thing that has happened to science in the history of science.

Moore concluded: "It's taking over science with superstition and a kind of toxic combination of religion and political ideology. There is no truth to this. It is a complete hoax and scam."

Obama deceitfully ignored the 2009 Climategate scandal, Dr. Spencer's 2010 book, and Patrick Moore's stunning 2014 testimony when he signed the 2016 Paris Agreement that overrode our national sovereignty. The Paris Agreement required individual countries to comply with UN-determined standards of greenhouse gas emissions and UN-determined financial contributions starting in the year 2020. The contributions required of each participating country were labeled "nationally determined contributions."

But Donald Trump defeated Obama's legacy candidate and fellow manmade climate change huckster, Hillary Clinton. One of the first things President Trump did was withdraw the United States from the egregious Paris Agreement.

The climate change hoax is being perpetrated worldwide by globalists in charge of global education and United Nations Agenda 2030. The hucksters do not care about Climategate and that their "science" is demonstrably false. They continue to perpetrate the lie with the confidence that if you tell a lie big enough and often enough it will be believed. So it is with climate "science."

Manmade climate change hysteria has reached epic proportions in advance of the 2020 elections. America-first President Donald Trump recognizes the Humanitarian Hoax of Climate Change being perpetrated by the enemies of American sovereignty, and he stands firm on his decision to withdraw from the deceitful Paris Agreement in spite of being viciously attacked for that decision.

The Paris Agreement is an anti-America humanitarian hoax designed to transfer the wealth from industrialized countries, especially the United States, to non-industrialized countries. The purpose of the climate change hoax is to de-industrialize the United States of America and collapse her economy in preparation for a one-world government.

American democracy is the single greatest existential threat to a one-world government. The globalist elite are desperate to stop President Trump because if Obama is exposed as a con man it leaves them without their prime-time huckster to continue marching America toward anarchy and socialism with his "resistance" movement. The globalist elite who fund the leftist humanitarian hucksters are using them as useful idiots to facilitate climate alarmism and the great Humanitarian Hoax of Climate Change worldwide. It is a deliberate plan to create the overwhelming social chaos necessary to impose the globalist elite's totalitarian New World Order.

Debunking the Humanitarian Hoax of Climate Change exposes its sinister objective to return the world to the feudal system of a one-world government. Obama ignored Climategate, Dr. Spencer, and Patrick Moore when he signed the Paris Agreement in 2016. Huckster-in-chief Barack Obama, his $15 million waterfront mansion, and his family are all safe because the claims of manmade climate change are complete and utter bunk—and that is what Obama knew and when he knew it.

HOAX 47

The Humanitarian Hoax of Disinformation

September 22, 2019

THE humanitarian hoax is the deliberate and deceitful tactic of presenting a destructive policy as altruistic. The humanitarian huckster presents himself as a compassionate advocate when in fact he is the disguised enemy.

A friend of mine from high school, a well-intentioned and impassioned gallerist in Washington, DC, emailed the following invitation superimposed on an original oil painting depicting a pack of menacing rabid dogs:

> **We're inviting America's artists to help prevent the spread of Trump's dystopia and the contagious HATE it causes . . . and needs to survive.**

The invitation to participate in the juried show was followed by a red, white, and blue poster asking the following question:

> **When your grandchildren ask you what you did to rid the body politic of Trump's dystopia in 2019 and 2020 before it was too late: What will you tell them?**

I like and respect this very kind, intelligent, and considerate man even though our worldviews are diametrically opposed to one another. I simply could not ignore the radical leftist political assumption of his question, so I answered my friend:

I will tell them I write to fight.

I will tell them that I fought with every word on every page to ensure an informed electorate in 2020.

I will tell them that they and their parents were subjected to a most vile disinformation campaign that began with Jimmy Carter and the establishment of the Department of Education in 1979 run by leftist radicals intent on collapsing America and replacing our free-market capitalism with socialism.

I will tell them that the regressive pressure to ignore facts and focus on feelings was a deliberate effort to infantilize the nation and indoctrinate its children to accept collectivism and cradle-to-grave dependence on the government. A dependent society, unaware and compliant, is easy to control.

I will tell them that indoctrination is revolution without bullets because disinformed children grow up and vote for collectivism. The leftist propaganda machine was stunningly successful—just look at the 2020 Democrat candidates and how their anti-America platform bifurcated the country.

I will tell them that the 2009 Climategate scandal exposing the fraudulent science of manmade climate change was deliberately buried by the colluding mainstream media under Obama's watch.

I will tell them that the same fraudulent science continued to disinform the public with politically useful manmade climate change hysteria in advance of the 2020 election.

I will tell them that manmade climate change is the Big Lie of the twenty-first century, designed to redistribute wealth and collapse America's industrial economy in a sinister effort to bring the United States into the New World Order of a one-world government.

I will tell them that many intelligent, well-intentioned, good-hearted liberals were duped into participating in their own destruction.

I will tell them I fought the good fight for their freedom because free stuff is NEVER free—you pay with your freedom.

I will tell them that dystopia is and always was the globalist will to power and a regressive return to feudalism.

I will tell them that President Donald J. Trump was the existential enemy of globalism and that the leftist radicals in the Democrat party were the useful idiots of the globalist elite.

I will tell them that the United Nations was the vehicle for imposing a one-world government and that America's children were deliberately indoctrinated with the globalized education of Common Core in public school and dumbed down to accept its anti-American content.

I will tell them that failed educational policies of sight words and new math deliberately confused and frustrated children to the point of academic failure and negative behavior.

I will tell them that I tried to save our beloved country from the jackals at the door who fully intended to enslave them after ceding our national sovereignty to an international body politic.

I will tell them that no stranger ever seduced a child with spinach, and that the leftist Democrat offer of eternal childhood and free stuff was the candied invitation to get them inside the car.

I will tell them I love them and that freedom is the most important value. I will tell them that there is no freedom in the centralized governments of collectivism. No American has ever risked his life on a raft to get to Cuba—Cuban escapees always sail toward Miami and freedom.

I will tell them to listen to the dissidents who have lived the collectivist lives they are being promised, and to ignore the lies of the mainstream media's paid political pundits, who are lackeys to their globalist bosses.

I will tell them I love them and hope they understand that I write to fight for their future.

The Humanitarian Hoax of Zero Population Growth

September 25, 2019

THE humanitarian hoax is the deliberate and deceitful tactic of presenting a destructive policy as altruistic. The humanitarian huckster presents himself as a compassionate advocate when in fact he is the disguised enemy.

The Humanitarian Hoax series has discussed The Humanitarian Hoax of Globalism, The Humanitarian Hoax of Socialism, The Humanitarian Hoax of Climate Change, The Humanitarian Hoax of Climate Change II, and The Humanitarian Hoax of the United Nations. Now it is time to examine the Humanitarian Hoax of Zero Population Growth and see how all of these hoaxes are interconnected.

The humanitarian hoaxes are globalist cons designed to redistribute the world's wealth and population. Their unifying objective is to create an internationalized New World Order of a one-world government under the corrupt auspices of the United Nations. The 2020 American presidential election will be a domestic political contest between Americanism and globalism that reflects the worldwide political contest between national sovereignty and globalism.

President Donald J. Trump stunned the world on September 24, 2019, with his brilliant speech to the 74th United Nations General Assembly. It was a calm, measured, powerful statement of purpose and resolve highlighting the twenty-first-century conflict between the U.S. demand for national sovereignty under the Trump administration, and the UN's expanding efforts to globalize the world. President Trump presented his proud, America-first leadership unapologetically and with equal respect for the national sovereignty, cultures, and religions of the nations of the world represented in the General Assembly, saying:

> In America, the people govern, the people rule, and the people are sovereign. I was elected not to take power, but to give power to the American people, where it belongs. In foreign affairs, we are renewing this founding principle of sovereignty. Our government's first duty is to its people, to our citizens, to serve their needs, to ensure their safety, to preserve their rights, and to defend their values. As president of the United States, I will always put America first. Just like you, as the leaders of your countries, will always and should always put your countries first.

President Trump reminded the world that the United Nations was founded as an international body respectful of national differences and dedicated to mutual cooperation among sovereign nations to achieve international peace. The president criticized and warned the United Nations against its efforts to internationalize the world and impose a one-world government with his stunning admonition:

> The future does not belong to the globalists. The future belongs to the sovereign and independent nations, who protect their citizens, respect their neighbors, and honor the differences that make each country special and unique.

So, what do the UN's efforts to globalize the world have to do with Zero Population Growth?

Zero population growth is the condition of demographic balance in which the population is stable and neither grows nor declines.

In the late 1960s Zero Population Growth (ZPG) was a powerful political movement in the United States and Western Europe. ZPG marketed its message to an unsuspecting public as the altruistic humanitarian method for limiting the growing world population. ZPG was going to save the planet from the catastrophic Malthusian prophecy that population growth would outstrip agricultural production and result in too many people and not enough food. Sound familiar? It should—it is the basis of the United Nations' egregious Agenda 2030, its 17 Sustainable Development Goals, and the ruinous Democrat Green New Deal. Let's review.

English theologian and scholar Thomas Robert Malthus wrote his famous prediction in his 1798 book, _An Essay on the Principle of Population_. The Malthusian Theory is based on the assumption that populations increase geometrically (2, 4, 8, 16, 32, 64, etc.), but food supplies increase arithmetically (2, 4, 6, 8, 10, 12, etc.).

The obvious flaws in the assumption are twofold. First, Malthus's fatalistic prediction never materialized. Second, Malthus lived over two hundred years ago, when agricultural practices were limited by eighteenth-century technology. Malthus simply could not imagine a time of twenty-first-century science and agricultural technology. So, why is the United Nations resurrecting the dire predictions of an eighteenth-century Malthusian catastrophe with apocalyptic warnings of catastrophic manmade climate change? Let's find out.

Fear is a powerful force, one used by the globalist community to effect seismic sociopolitical change. Young people worldwide are indoctrinated in the globalized educational initiative of the United Nations. They are terrified that cataclysmic manmade climate change is ending the world and that they will surely drown or starve. Many indoctrinated millennials refuse to have children in order to protect their unborn from such catastrophic certainties. The problem, of course, is that their fears are manmade, designed to dupe them into becoming global citizens in a globalized world where accepting the radical leftist global environmental narrative will protect them and keep them safe.

The Zero Population Growth movement of the late 1960s succeeded in reducing the populations of Western countries but not the populations in countries most needing population reduction. What is the globalist solution? Massive uncontrolled immigration, marketed deceitfully as the replacement population that will bring economic stability and growth to the depleted workforce of Western nations.

What is the reality?

President Trump answered that question in his extraordinary speech:

> We have learned that over the long term, uncontrolled migration is deeply unfair to both the sending and the receiving countries. For the sending countries, it reduces domestic pressure to pursue needed political and economic reform and drains them of the human capital necessary to motivate and implement those reforms. For the receiving countries, the substantial costs of uncontrolled migration are borne overwhelmingly by low-income citizens whose concerns are often ignored by both media and government.

So, the Humanitarian Hoax of Zero Population Growth, the resurrected

Malthusian prophecy, the concept of manmade climate change, open borders, uncontrolled immigration, and globalized education are all efforts of the United Nations globalist elite to internationalize the world and impose one-world government.

All of these concepts function to blur ethnic, cultural, religious, and racial boundaries. The result is sameness—one people, one religion, one flag, one language, one currency, one globalized culture, all controlled by the globalist elite in a one-world government under the auspices of the United Nations.

President Trump understands that the globalist New World Order is a return to the old feudal system, where the very few enslave the many. President Trump rejects globalism and feudalism entirely, respects the sovereignty of all nations of the world, and is deeply committed to upholding the United States Constitution, which guarantees the self-rule of American citizens and the independence of the United States.

Globalism is socialism on a massive international scale where the assets of producing countries are confiscated and transferred to non-producing countries. President Trump is profoundly opposed to such an arrangement and has renegotiated unfair trade deals that penalize the United States and confiscate America's wealth.

The notion of manmade climate change is based on fraudulent science that was exposed in the staggering 2009 Climategate scandal, yet the United Nations continues to promote its false narrative with the Paris Agreement and apocalyptic warnings that the world will end in twelve years. The manmade climate change hysteria is the globalized political effort of the United Nations to unite the world's population in fear.

The environmental lobby that promoted ZPG has moved on to manmade climate hysteria in its global effort to con the world's population into accepting globalism as deliverance from the doomsday climate predictions. The problem, of course, is that globalism is just another name for the medieval feudal structure of centralized, internationalized one-world government that deprives individual nations of their national sovereignty.

The 2020 presidential election will be a pivotal election in our nation's history. A vote for President Trump will be a vote for national sovereignty, freedom, the U.S. Constitution, and individual rights. A vote for any of the Democrat candidates will be a vote for socialism, globalism, and a return to feudalism.

America-first President Donald J. Trump told the world at the 74th United Nations General Assembly:

> Socialism and communism are about one thing only: power for the ruling class. Today, I repeat a message for the world that I have delivered at home: America will never be a socialist country.

HOAX 49

The Humanitarian Hoax of Impeachment

September 28, 2019

THE humanitarian hoax is the deliberate and deceitful tactic of presenting a destructive policy as altruistic. The humanitarian huckster presents himself as a compassionate advocate when in fact he is the disguised enemy.

The entire 2020 lineup of leftist Democrats and their congressional sycophants have assured the nation that impeachment of President Donald Trump is necessary in order to protect the nation. It is an odd assertion considering that President Trump has been wildly successful by pro-America standards. Let's review.

In less than three years, under the administration of President Trump, 6 million jobs have been added to the workforce and unemployment is the lowest it has ever been for the black, Hispanic, and Asian communities. The United States is energy independent and we are now the leading exporter of energy in the world. So, what exactly do the Democrats mean when they say that YOU, the nation, will be safer without this particular POTUS? Let's find out.

It appears that there is pervasive pronoun confusion in the Democrat assertion! The corrupt pay-to-play Democrats would definitely be safer without America-first President Trump in charge, but YOU, the American taxpaying voter, will definitely not be safer.

In 1994, ice-skater Tonya Harding stunned the world with her participation in the unprecedented and shocking physical attack against competitor Nancy Kerrigan. Fans were familiar with the practice of anabolic steroid doping in athletics, but a physical assault intended to break a rival's leg?? The attack was simply beyond the threshold of public tolerance. Fans want a fair fight—a fair competition between athletes who perform and compete fairly for the competition prize, no cheating or dirty tricks allowed.

So it is with politics. The radical leftist Democrat party has pushed the public past the threshold of tolerance. Americans voters want a fair fight—a fair competition between politicians who present their positions and compete fairly for the election prize, no cheating or dirty tricks allowed.

The radical leftist Democrat party under Barack Obama fully expected his legacy candidate, Hillary Clinton, to win the 2016 election. Donald Trump's victory stupefied the Democrats. Instead of concentrating on finding an electable candidate in 2020, Obama's Democrat "resistance" movement was immediately launched to disable and destroy President Trump and his America-first agenda.

The Democrats have stunned the world with their shocking attacks against President Trump. We are witnessing repeated coup d'état attempts against the sitting president of the United States. Like the attack on ice-skating champion Nancy Kerrigan, the Democrat coup attempts have failed, leaving President Trump bruised but not destroyed.

The absurd accusation that the president is a Russian agent, whom the Kremlin helped elect, launched the first failed White House coup that morphed into the failed Mueller "investigation." Mueller's witch-hunt wasted millions of taxpayer dollars and two years trying to accomplish the overthrow of a duly elected sitting president while that president strengthened the economy and the military, both of which Obama had intentionally weakened. So, what happened next?

Yet another coup attempt was launched against President Trump in the form of the media made-for-television Ukraine affair. On cue, the desperate Democrats, starring Democrat chairman of the House Intelligence Committee Rep. Adam Schiff, began their hysterical, unsubstantiated, completely fraudulent calls for impeachment. Here is the problem. The Democrat bag of dirty political tricks is full of boomerangs that expose their own staggering malfeasance. Let's review.

The Democrats accused President Trump of extorting Ukrainian President Volodymyr Zelensky to "manufacture" dirt on Joe Biden, a potential rival in the 2020 presidential election. President Trump knew he was innocent and the White House released the transcript of the telephone conversation that completely exonerated him. No matter. Adam Schiff intentionally lied about the transcript and insisted that the President had committed an impeachable offense.

A powerful article by Jeffrey T. Kuhner, titled "Trump's Real Crime? 'He's Serious About Draining the Swamp'," appeared in the September 27, 2019, *World Tribune*. In the article, Kuhner explained how the call to President Zelensky was completely appropriate, since Zelensky was elected on a platform to crack down on graft and corruption in his country. We also have a treaty with Ukraine to help each other investigate crimes that include political corruption.

So, it should come as no surprise that President Trump asked President Zelensky to look into allegations of Russian meddling in the 2016 election. Kuhner quotes President Trump from the transcript:

> "I would like you to find out what happened with this whole situation with Ukraine, they say CrowdStrike," Trump says, referring to the private security firm that examined the hacking of the Democratic National Committee's emails. The DNC refused to hand their server over to be analyzed by FBI forensics experts. Instead, they had Crowdstrike do it. And the company's server is based in Ukraine—meaning it could shed light on whether Russian intelligence agents really did hack the DNC's emails.

CrowdStrike, founded in 2011, is an American cybersecurity technology company and FBI contractor. According to *Bloomberg News*, in 2017 tech giant Google and global private equity firm Warburg Pincus, among others, invested $256 million in CrowdStrike. Since CrowdStrike has top secret clearance, so do Google and the other investors, giving them access to FBI data, files, and surveillance information.

CrowdStrike's co-founder and CTO, Dmitri Alperovitch, is a senior fellow at the Atlantic Council, an anti-Russian, anti-Trump, globalist think tank supported by George Soros, in the $250,000–$499,000 donor class, and Ukrainian billionaire Victor Pinchuk. The Victor Pinchuk Foundation is listed on the $10 million–$25 million donor roster of the Clinton Foundation. Also serving on the International Advisory Board of the Atlantic Council is James Clapper. Are you surprised?

The Markets Work website offers some interesting background on the Atlantic Council:

> In addition to being a Clinton Foundation donor, Pinchuk is also on the International Advisory Board of the Atlantic Council—a NATO-aligned American think tank specializing in the field of international affairs.
> . . . In January 2017, the Atlantic Council announced partnership with

> Ukrainian natural gas company Burisma Group. . . . April 18, 2014, Hunter Biden was appointed to the Board of Directors for Burisma.

Kuhner is quite right in his assessment: Democrats are wildly upset because President Trump is draining the swamp. Consider the Biden boomerang. President Trump released the conversation transcript and Kuhner explained what it exposed:

> Trump asks Zelensky to look into the firing of the former top prosecutor, Viktor Shokin, who was investigating Burisma, the natural gas company in which Hunter Biden was on the board. He was collecting $83,000 a month (for doing nothing). In May 2018, Joe Biden publicly bragged that, when he was vice president, he deliberately withheld $1 billion in U.S. aid unless Shokin was pushed out, thereby ending the investigation into Burisma—and of course, shielding Hunter from any prosecution. It was Biden who engaged in sleazy, criminal behavior, using American taxpayer dollars to blackmail a foreign government into allowing his drug addict son to continue enriching himself. In all, Hunter amassed over $3 million in Ukraine (through China his equity firm would collect $1.5 billion—an obscene sum). In short, Biden is one of the most corrupt politicians in Washington. Trump did what he is supposed to do: Investigate Biden's illicit activity and demand the new Ukrainian government honor its commitment to tackle corruption.

Everything the swampsters have accused President Trump of doing is precisely what they have done themselves. In psychology that cognitive reversal is called projection. In everyday language, what the Democrats have done and continue to do is simply called lying. The Democrats are lying in the service of their political ideology, in which the ends justify the means. It is political cheating on a staggering scale.

The Humanitarian Hoax of Impeachment is that it usurps the will of the American people by pretending to protect America. The globalist elite and their Democrat hucksters are determined to overthrow duly elected President Donald J. Trump. The Democrats, funded by globalists like George Soros and supported by think tanks like the Atlantic Council, have an elitist operating principle that says, "We are superior to you, we are smarter than you, we know better than you, and we are going to remove the president you elected in 2016 and install our own puppet president against your will—for your own good, of course."

It is the same arrogant elitist operating principle that is subverting the will of the British people who voted to leave the European Union. The globalists and their political puppets in England are refusing to implement BREXIT (British exit). It is the same shocking deep-state challenge to the will of the people by globalist powers who fully intend to cheat the English voters and usurp the power of the British people.

The lesson of Tonya Harding is that the international world of figure skating is diminished by cheating. The sport is not better off with an arrogant, ends-justify-the-means attitude, and neither is America. President Donald J. Trump has proven that his America-first policies strengthen the United States both domestically and internationally. He is the voters' choice and the right choice for America.

President Trump insists on protecting Americans, preserving the American Constitution, our representative republic, free-market capitalism, our national sovereignty, and most of all, the will of the American people.

We must never allow the Humanitarian Hoax of Impeachment to succeed. It is the dirtiest of Democrat political tricks, designed to protect the corrupt Washington swamp and deny the will of the people who have elected President Trump to drain it.

HOAX 50

The Humanitarian Hoax of Eternal Childhood

October 3, 2019

THE humanitarian hoax is the deliberate and deceitful tactic of presenting a destructive policy as altruistic. The humanitarian huckster presents himself as a compassionate advocate when in fact he is the disguised enemy.

The Humanitarian Hoax of Eternal Childhood is a deliberate political strategy to destroy America from within by regressing its chronological adults to emotional children unable to think and behave as rational adults. It is a sinister strategy of psychological operations (PSYOPS) designed to invert the psychological growth process and deny Americans the emotional maturity required to support ordered liberty and a free society.

The United States of America is the greatest experiment in individual freedom the world has ever known. Our Founding Fathers drafted a constitution that rejected monarchy, oligarchy, theocracy, and any other form of statism that deprived citizens of their God-given individual rights. The United States of America celebrates individualism in a socioeconomic structure that demands the adult attributes of self-sufficiency, autonomy, and willingness to compete in a system of free-market capitalism.

Freedom is an adult enterprise, requiring adult rationality and responsibility. A society of emotional children cannot sustain a free society. This is the key to understanding the insidious scheme to destroy America from within.

The globalist elite have been trying to control America since the end of World War II. Eisenhower warned our nation about the military-industrial complex. The Deep State is the intelligence arm of the globalist elite, who are the industrial component of the military-industrial complex.

The globalist elite identified the essential difference between two political ideologies: free-market capitalism requires psychological growth and independence, while socialism requires eternal childhood and dependence. This realization was a political bonanza for the globalists and their tactical decision to collapse America from within using mass social engineering. The battle plan was to regress America's chronological adults to eternal childhood, where they could be easily manipulated and controlled. It is revolution without bullets.

Regressed Americans could be seduced to willingly surrender their individual freedoms for "free stuff," and the mighty United States would finally collapse under globalist control. The globalists and their conspirators took direct aim at the three supporting pillars of American greatness and our constitutional republic: faith, flag, and family.

It took seventy-five years to undermine our traditional American values and make collectivism/socialism/communism fashionable. The 2020 parade of Democrat presidential candidates demonstrates the stunning success of the globalist effort.

How did they do it?

The humanitarian hucksters promised the people the glories of eternal childhood dependence as liberation! They promised to "liberate" Americans from the burdensome adult responsibilities of freedom. The hoax weaponized narcissism and launched Civil War II, the War Between the Selves. What do I mean by this?

My philosophy book _Dear America: Who's Driving the Bus?_ discusses the infantilizing of America. The book describes the universal psychological growth process and is a reminder that we are each individually the sum of our parts and are collectively a society that interacts with each of those parts. A state of mind is not fixed. It constantly shifts along the growth continuum, from total, infantile narcissism to responsible adulthood. From _Dear America_:

> Civil War II is not a race war, an economic war, or a war between states. It is a psychological battle between states of mind that will determine who has the power in our society, who is in control. . . . We all begin as children: helpless, dependent, self-absorbed, and completely lacking boundaries. We exist in a state of fusion unable to distinguish self from other. The task of childhood is to emerge from this state of total narcissism. . . . The child learns to identify "self" by discovering the reality of "other."

Chronological age is an uncontested biological accomplishment. Psychological growth is another matter entirely. . . . Psychological growth is the universal challenge of childhood. Every society in the world needs its children to grow into physical and psychological adulthood in order to continue the cycle of life. Theoretically, if a society were to remain a nation of children it would necessarily collapse and extinguish itself. (*Dear America*, pp. 13–15)

> Narcissism is the natural and appropriate attitude of infancy and early childhood, but it is inappropriate when one advances into adulthood. . . . The responsible adult works for what she wants. The narcissistic adult either snatches it, or demands that someone provide it, usually her family, or the government via social programs funded by the taxpaying, responsible adult. The narcissistic adult is as demanding as the infant. (*Dear America*, p. 26)

> Civil War II begins as a personal, internal war and eventually finds its way into external society. First, the child battles "self" for control, and then she battles "other." The inner children of our minds are very egalitarian; they will struggle for control with any rational adult, our own or somebody else's. (*Dear America*, p. 18)

The natural and normal inner struggle to grow up psychologically has been deliberately interrupted and politicized to subvert the growth process. The globalist elite need an unaware and compliant citizenry—a population of infantilized adults who think like children and can be easily controlled. The swagger and adult confidence of Americans in the forties who made America great has been perversely subverted to achieve childish submission, fear, and fragility. Infantilized students on college campuses even require "safe spaces" in order to hide from opposing ideas.

Children who are indoctrinated in collectivism/socialism are not permitted to compete. They are pushed toward passivity and not allowed to strive for excellence. Sameness and uniformity are extolled. Participation rather than achievement is awarded: every child receives a trophy because awarding achievement might hurt someone's feelings. The meritocracy has been abandoned and replaced with a focus on feelings, participation, and groupthink. Individualism is deliberately rejected in the regressive leftist Democrat vision of America.

Thought precedes behavior. If the individual thinks like a child, that individual will vote like a child. If the individual thinks like an adult, that individual will vote like an adult. The 2020 election will be a referendum on American sovereignty, independence, and national identity. If our society has been infantilized to the point of collectivism, we will soon find our childish society run by the globalist elite, who have been intentionally regressing Americans for six decades through educational indoctrination and mainstream media programming.

All fifty humanitarian hoaxes in this book are connected thematically by the overarching globalist effort to destabilize America and reduce her people to a state of eternal childhood. This sinister PSYOPS (psychological operations) strategy has successfully divided America between rational adults demanding national sovereignty and infantilized adults demanding socialism.

Children believe what they are told. They do not require facts and they are easily exploited. A regressed population is as gullible as a child.

The humanitarian hoaxes expose Barack Obama's "hope and change" as an Orwellian attempt to turn America upside down and inside out. The humanitarian hoaxes are all deceitful political attempts to dupe Americans into accepting a socialist America and then, of course, the dystopian New World Order of global citizenship advanced by the United Nations.

The globalist elite and the corrupt radical leftist Democrats have revived collectivism and made dependence fashionable by using educational indoctrination and media programming to infantilize America, shatter traditional American values, and sell collectivism to narcissistic adults.

The November 2020 presidential election will determine the future of America. President Donald J. Trump represents adult independence, freedom, and national sovereignty. The Democrat candidates represent childish dependence and the globalists' unceasing efforts to replace our constitutional republic with socialism.

Here is the dirty little secret of the globalist elite humanitarian hucksters pulling the political strings: socialism is the prerequisite for the imposition of a one-world government. One-world government is a return to feudalism, where the globalist elite rule the world under the auspices of the corrupt United Nations.

The future will shock the infantilized voters who naively believed that their support for socialism would be liberation, social justice, and income equality. Free stuff is never free—the price for eternal childhood is eternal servitude. The cost of "free stuff" is your freedom.

Civil War II has been waged by the globalist elite to bring socialism to America. The transformation of America was well under way after eight years of Obama's deceit, and would have been complete if Hillary Clinton had been elected. When Donald Trump was elected president in 2016, the globalist elite and their Democrat/RINO (Republican in name only) conspirators went berserk; the inexorable Democrat march toward socialism was halted. What did they do?

The conspirators launched a coordinated campaign of character assassination against America-first President Trump, and attempted a series of coups d'état.

Civil War II, which began as a personal, internal war, has found its way into society. We have arrived at the tipping point of the war between emotional adulthood and eternal childhood—between national sovereignty and globalism. The decisive battle will be fought at the ballot box on November 3, 2020.

President Donald Trump understands the political threat that eternal childhood poses to American productivity and American sovereignty. He understands that American greatness depends on an adult population that embraces the responsibilities and attitudes of adulthood.

President Trump's promise to drain the swamp is exposing the sinister globalist plan to collapse America. POTUS has boldly taken on the Deep State, the corrupt Democrats, the colluding RINOs, and the "fake news" media.

In 1775, when America was still fighting for its independence, Paul Revere warned the colonists that the British were coming. The colonists understood the physical attack on their freedom and the need to repel the British.

Today, 245 years later, America is fighting for its independence once again. President Trump is warning America of a far more insidious attack on its sovereignty, one that began decades ago with the Humanitarian Hoax of Eternal Childhood. This battle is fought without bullets. It is a psychological battle between states of mind that must be won psychologically in order to defeat the sinister globalist challenge to our freedom.

Dear America, we must grow up psychologically. We must be rational adults. We must defeat narcissism. We must reject socialism. We must reject globalism. We must reject the Humanitarian Hoax of Eternal Childhood in order to keep America great, sovereign, and free. God bless America!

EPILOGUE

January 2020

HUMANITARIAN hoaxes are destructive policies deceitfully presented as altruistic by dishonest humanitarian hucksters disguised as public advocates. The obsessive Democrat party campaign to remove the sitting president of the United States is the consummate and most consequential humanitarian hoax in American history. It is an existential threat to our constitutional republic.

Democrat coup d'état attempts began hours after President Trump's inauguration on January 20, 2017. Partisan removal efforts expanded and metastasized into two articles of impeachment approved by the Democrat-controlled House of Representatives on December 18, 2019: Article 1 (Abuse of Power) and Article 2 (Obstruction of Congress).

Radical leftist Democrats House Speaker Nancy Pelosi, Senate Minority Leader Chuck Schumer, House Intelligence Chair Adam Schiff, and House Judiciary Chair Jerry Nadler were the lead hucksters in the December impeachment coup attempt.

Their effort was the culminating humanitarian hoax in the Democrats' desperation to remove President Trump from office and delegitimize the first three years of his spectacularly successful presidency. America-first President Donald Trump is the existential enemy of leftists, Islamists, globalists, and Deep State operatives seeking to shatter our nation from within. Trump is the great disruptor of the status quo and has made many enemies in his battle to drain the teeming Washington swamp and expose its hidden creatures.

THE HOUSE IMPEACHMENT

The 2019 Democrat articles of impeachment represent the apotheosis of tactical political projection. In psychology, projection means accusing someone else of doing what you yourself are doing. Projection has been the key to understanding the Democrat playbook since Donald Trump won the 2016 presidential election. Projection underlies the Democrats' demented and unprecedented political attacks against President Trump, and it explains their weaponized impeachment process in advance of the approaching 2020 election.

The first attack on President Trump accused him of colluding with the Russian government to meddle in the 2016 election in order to secure victory. That effort became the corruptly created and constitutionally abusive Mueller investigation, which found no evidence whatsoever to support its foundational political lie that the Trump campaign colluded with the Russians.

The second attack on President Trump accused him of exacting a *quid pro quo* from Ukraine's president, Volodymyr Zelensky. That effort became the basis for the Democrats' constitutionally illegitimate articles of impeachment.

Harvard Law School professor, legal scholar, and lifelong Democrat Alan Dershowitz, in his *Gatestone Institute* commentary of December 11, 2019, "How Should the Senate Deal with an Unconstitutional Impeachment by the House?" rejected the partisan Democrat impeachment process and stated unequivocally:

> These two grounds of impeachment—abuse of power and obstruction of Congress—are not among the criteria specified for impeachment. Neither one is a high crime and misdemeanor. Neither is mentioned in the Constitution. Both are the sort of vague, open-ended criteria rejected by the framers. They were rejected precisely to avoid the situation in which our nation currently finds itself.

Professor Dershowitz clarified the issue in an earlier article, "Impeachers Looking for New Crimes," published on October 24, 2019:

> So, the question remains: Did President Trump commit impeachable offenses when he spoke on the phone to the president of Ukraine and/ or when he directed members of the Executive Branch to refuse to cooperate, absent a court order, with congressional Democrats who are seeking his impeachment?

The answers are plainly no and no. There is a constitutionally significant difference between a political "sin," on the one hand, and a crime or impeachable offenses, on the other.

Even taking the worst-case scenario regarding Ukraine—a *quid pro quo* exchange of foreign aid for a political favor—that might be a political sin, but not a crime or impeachable offense.

In a classic example of projection, the Democrat political machine did precisely what it accused President Trump of doing; it abused its own power and obstructed Congress with its unprecedented, unconstitutional, partisan impeachment process. To begin with, the transcript of President Trump's July 2019 telephone call to the Ukrainian president is clear that there was no bribery and no *quid pro quo*. The "whistleblower" whose hearsay complaint launched the entire congressional impeachment process had no direct knowledge of the phone call. He simply "felt" that the president wanted a *quid pro quo*. So, the sitting president of the United States was charged with a thought crime by a "whistleblower" who was not in the room and had no first-hand knowledge of the call. THIS was what the Democrat-controlled House of Representatives accepted as a reliable witness and an impeachable offense!

By comparison, the evidence that Joe Biden did demand a *quid pro quo* while serving as vice president of the United States is incontrovertible. Biden is shown live on videotape at the January 23, 2018, meeting of the Council on Foreign Relations bragging about how he pressured then–President of Ukraine Pyotr Poroshenko to fire Prosecutor General Viktor Shokin. If he wasn't fired, Biden would withhold $1 billion in U.S. aid to the country. Shokin was investigating political corruption in the Ukrainian natural gas company Burisma Holdings. With no expertise or experience in the energy industry, Joe Biden's son Hunter served on Burisma's board of directors from 2014 to 2019 and received millions of dollars in compensation for his service.

In Joe Biden's own words:

> And I went over, I guess, the twelfth, thirteenth time to Kiev [Ukraine]. And I was supposed to announce that there was another billion-dollar loan guarantee. And I had gotten a commitment from [President] Poroshenko and from [Prime Minister] Yatsenyuk that they would take action against the state prosecutor. And they didn't.
>
> So they said they had—they were walking out to a press conference. I said, nah, I'm not going to—or, we're not going to give you a billion dollars. They said, you have no authority. You're not the president. The president said—I said, call him.
>
> (Laughter)

I said, I'm telling you, you're not getting the billion dollars. I said, you're not getting the billion. I'm going to be leaving here in, I think it was about six hours. I looked at them and said: I'm leaving in six hours. If the prosecutor is not fired, you're not getting the money. Well, son of a bitch. (Laughter). He got fired. And they put in place someone who was solid at the time.

Volodymyr Zelensky beat Pyotr Poroshenko in Ukraine's sixth presidential election and assumed office in May 2019.

On November 14, 2019, indictments were drawn up by Ukraine's Office of the Prosecutor General against Burisma owner Nikolai Zlochevsky, Hunter Biden and his partners, and Franklin Templeton Investments, an investment fund executing purchases of external government loan bonds totaling $7.4 billion. News website *ZeroHedge*, in an article published November 21, 2019, "Ukrainian MP Claims $7.4 Billion Obama-Linked Laundering, Puts Biden Group Take at $16.5 Million," quoted Ukrainian Members of Parliament Alexander Dubinsky and Andriy Derkach.

According to Dubinsky, Hunter Biden's income from Burisma is a "link that reveals how money is siphoned [from Ukraine]," and how Biden is just one link in the chain of Zlochevsky's money laundering operation which included politicians from the previous Yanukovich administration who continued their schemes under his successor, President Pyotr Poroshenko.

"The son of Vice President Joe Biden was receiving payment for his services, with money raised through criminal means and money laundering," he [Dubinsky] then said, adding, "Biden received money that did not come from the company's successful operation but rather from money stolen from citizens. . . .

Derkach added, "*The son of Templeton's founder, John Templeton Jr., was one of President Obama's major campaign donors.* Another [Franklin Templeton Investments] fund-related character is Thomas Donilon, Managing Director of BlackRock Investment Institute [and] shareholder [of] Franklin Templeton Investments, which has the largest share in the fund. *It is noteworthy that he previously was Obama's national security advisor.*"

Derkach then demanded, "*President Zelensky must pick up the phone, dial Trump, ask for help and cooperation in the fight against corruption and fly to Washington.* The issue of combating international corruption in Ukraine with the participation of citizens, businessmen and U.S. officials should become a key during the meeting of the two presidents."

Interestingly, Adam Schiff's <u>Financial Disclosure Report #10016142</u>, filed May 2017, shows significant personal investments in both Franklin Templeton and BlackRock.

House Speaker Nancy Pelosi has also been exposed as having a personal stake in the outcome of this scandal. Her son Paul Jr. served on the board of Viscoil Holdings, a now defunct gas industry company registered to a Russian national doing business in Ukraine. There is no denying Pelosi's involvement, since Pelosi herself is featured in one of the company's <u>2013 promotional videos</u>.

Patrick Howley's explosive December 23, 2019, *National File* article, "<u>EXPOSED: Pelosi Jr. Worked in Ukraine with Accused Fraudster Facing Prison</u>," included revelations about Speaker Pelosi's family business dealings in Ukraine. The article recounts Paul Jr.'s 2017 trip to Ukraine representing Asa Saint Clair and the World Sports Alliance.

> "Today we're here to talk about soccer," Paul Pelosi Jr. said in his television interview in Ukraine. "We recently got an endorsement from the World Sports Alliance and we've spoken with the Ukraine government about collaboration for soccer for young people. Ukraine has a great history in soccer and we hope to share in that tradition going forward."

> The World Sports Alliance is a front group run by Paul Pelosi Jr.'s good friend Asa Saint Clair, who served as president of the Alliance. Asa Saint Clair now faces 20 years in prison for allegedly running a fraudulent cryptocurrency scheme through the World Sports Alliance. Records reveal that Pelosi Jr. and Asa Saint Clair were directly working with one another during the period of Saint Clair's alleged criminality.

The Democrats' "one-two" Mueller-Ukraine punch was countered by President Trump's eloquent letter to Nancy Pelosi written on December 17, 2019, the day before the House voted to impeach him. The <u>president's letter</u> was written for posterity and closed with "One hundred years from now, when people look back at this affair, I want them to understand it, and learn from it, so that it can never happen to another President again." The letter is included in its entirety at the end of this epilogue.

Democrat hypocrisy throughout the impeachment affair was staggering. In another stunning abuse of power and challenge to the Constitution, Speaker Pelosi attempted to orchestrate the Senate's participation in the impeachment proceedings. She announced that she would not present the Democrat articles of impeachment to the Senate for trial until she could see "what the trial will look like."

The *Daily Caller* published an article by Rudy Takala on December 20, 2019, "<u>Dershowitz: Pelosi Doesn't Have the Impeachment Power She Believes</u>":

> "I can imagine nothing more unconstitutional than a House impeachment without sending it to the Senate," Dershowitz said. "It's just unheard of. The Constitution provides that it is a two-step process, not a one-step process. It doesn't say the president may be impeached, period, that's the end of the matter. It says the president may be impeached, and if he's impeached by the House, the Senate then gets to decide whether he should be removed.

> Whether the House wants it to be in the Senate or not, the matter is now properly before the Senate," Dershowitz said in a call with the Republican National Lawyers Association. "The presiding officer of the Senate can set a trial date, convene the chief justice and begin the trial. So I don't think that Pelosi has the power that she thinks she has, or that my colleague Larry Tribe thinks she has."

Dershowitz was referring to Harvard Law professor Laurence Tribe, who suggested withholding the articles of impeachment until the Senate changed its rules to be more favorable to the Democrats.

Pelosi's impeachment ploy did not succeed. Even leftist Harvard Law professor Noah Feldman, who testified for the Democrats during the House impeachment hearings, stated that "President Trump is NOT impeached until the House sends the articles of impeachment to the Senate."

Professor Feldman agreed with Professor Dershowitz's definition of a constitutional impeachment in Feldman's December 19, 2019, *Bloomberg Opinion* article, "<u>Trump Isn't Impeached Until the House Tells the Senate</u>." According to Feldman,

> Impeachment, as contemplated by the Constitution, does not consist merely of the vote by the House, but of the process of sending the articles to the Senate for trial. Both parts are necessary to make an impeachment under the Constitution: The House must actually send the articles and send managers to the Senate to prosecute the impeachment. And the Senate must actually hold a trial.

> If the House does not communicate its impeachment to the Senate, it hasn't actually impeached the president. If the articles are not transmitted, Trump could legitimately say that he wasn't truly impeached at all. . . .

For the House to vote "to impeach" without ever sending the articles of impeachment to the Senate for trial would also deviate from the constitutional protocol. It would mean that the president had not genuinely been impeached under the Constitution; and it would also deny the president the chance to defend himself in the Senate that the Constitution provides. . . .

Strictly speaking, "impeachment" occurred—and occurs—when the articles of impeachment are presented to the Senate for trial. And at that point, the Senate is obliged by the Constitution to hold a trial.

What would make that trial fair is a separate question, one that deserves its own discussion. But we can say with some confidence that only the Senate is empowered to judge the fairness of its own trial—that's what the "sole power to try all impeachments" means.

Of course, the colluding mainstream media ignored the constitutional illegitimacy of the Democrat impeachment process and helped the Democrat smear machine with their premature headlines screaming "TRUMP IMPEACHED." Noah Feldman soft-sold the damaging headlines in the same article:

As for the headlines we saw after the House vote saying, "TRUMP IMPEACHED," those are a media shorthand, not a technically correct legal statement. So far, the House has voted to impeach (future tense) Trump. He isn't impeached (past tense) until the articles go to the Senate and the House members deliver the message.

The entire partisan performance by the Democrat impeachment team would be laughable if it were not such an overt challenge to the Constitution of the United States. In an October 8, 2019, letter to House Democrat leaders, White House counsel Pat Cipollone wrote:

As you know, you have designed and implemented your [impeachment] inquiry in a manner that violates fundamental fairness and constitutionally mandated due process. For example, you have denied the President the right to cross-examine witnesses, to call witnesses, to receive transcripts of testimony, to have access to evidence, to have counsel present, and many other basic rights guaranteed to all Americans.

In summary, the deranged Democrats held one-sided, closed impeachment hearings denying the president due process rights or even the ability for his lawyers to participate in the hearings. They approved articles of impeachment that have no constitutional basis, and then Speaker Pelosi made the jaw-droppingly unconstitutional demand that the House determine the Senate trial rules.

THE SENATE TRIAL

On January 15, 2020, the House voted 228–193 to send the impeachment articles against President Trump to the Senate, and named seven Democrat "impeachment managers" to act as prosecutors for the trial:

> House Intelligence Chair Adam Schiff
>
> House Judiciary Chair Jerry Nadler
>
> House Caucus Chair Hakeem Jeffries
>
> Rep. Val Demings
>
> Rep. Zoe Lofgren
>
> Rep. Sylvia Garcia
>
> Rep. Jason Crow

In a statement of quintessential deceit, Speaker Pelosi explained why she broke precedent from the three prior impeachments by choosing managers from outside the House Judiciary Committee. Pelosi is quoted in the January 19, 2020, Olivia Beavers article in *The Hill*, "Meet Pelosi's 7 Impeachment Managers":

> She [Pelosi] said one factor has guided her decision-making: litigation experience. "The emphasis is on litigators. The emphasis is on comfort level in the courtroom. . . . The emphasis is on making the strongest possible case to protect and defend our Constitution."

The entire impeachment offensive against President Trump lacked constitutional legitimacy. In his brilliant remarks in defense of the Constitution, Alan Dershowitz excoriated the impeachment offensive against President Trump, saying the charges against him were "outside the range of impeachable offenses."

Contrary to the words of Speaker Pelosi's litigators, Professor Dershowitz's argument was an actual defense of our Constitution that provided truth for the American people. Dershowitz explained how using illegitimate impeachment as a political weapon shatters the Constitution and infrastructure of the constitutional republic established by our Founding Fathers. On January 27, 2020, Professor Dershowitz presented a moving speech in defense of the office of the president. He began:

> Mr. Chief Justice, distinguished members of the Senate, our friends, law-
> yers, fellow lawyers it's a great honor for me to stand before you today to
> present a constitutional argument against the impeachment and removal
> not only of this president, but of all and any future presidents who may
> be charged with the unconstitutional grounds of abuse of power and
> obstruction of Congress.

Dershowitz's entire argument was about the WHAT of impeachment, not
the WHO. He continued:

> I stand against the application and misapplication of the constitutional
> criteria in every case and against any president without regard to whether
> I support his or her parties or policies. I would be making the very same
> constitutional argument had Hillary Clinton, for whom I voted, been
> elected and had a Republican House voted to impeach her on these
> unconstitutional grounds.

The Humanitarian Hoax of Impeachment—Hoax 49 recalls figure skater
Tonya Harding's unprecedented 1994 attack on rival Nancy Kerrigan.
Harding's thugs used a metal baton to club Kerrigan's knee in order to
eliminate the competition. Speaker Pelosi's goons used an unprecedented,
illegitimate, unconstitutional impeachment to club President Trump.

In a three-day verbal attack led by Adam Schiff, Democrat House
managers clubbed the president with misinformation, disinformation,
and outright lies based on Democrats' *feelings* in their infantile world
of subjective reality. The following day the president's legal team began
presenting its case of constitutional law with *factual* evidence based on
the adult world of objective reality. The contrast was striking for anyone
who actually watched the proceedings or read the transcripts. Predictably,
mainstream media reporting was pure partisan propaganda.

FAKE NEWS MEDIA COLLUSION

On January 29, 2020, *Newsbusters.org* reported, "Evening News Spin:
100% Negative on Trump Defense, 95% Positive Dems." From that article:

> Between Wednesday, January 22, when Democratic House impeachment
> managers launched their opening arguments, and Tuesday, January 28,
> when the President's defense team rested, evening newscast reporters
> and anchors made a total of 34 evaluative statements about the merits
> and effectiveness of both sides.

> Democratic impeachment managers received a total of 21 evaluative
> statements from ABC, CBS, and NBC journalists. Of that total, 95 per-

cent of those (20) touted their efforts and presentations, which means only one of their evaluative comments was negative. ABC's *World News Tonight* had eight positive comments, *CBS Evening News* had five, and *NBC Nightly News* seven. NBC had the lone negative comment.

The extraordinary level of biased reporting against President Trump during the Senate trial was a crescendo of negative and partisan reporting. It began with Trump's announcement of his candidacy, intensified during his presidential campaign, expanded during his presidency, and exploded into unprecedented heights when House impeachment managers addressed the Senate.

In a January 13, 2020, article, "TV's Trump News: Three-fourths Impeachment and 93% Negative," *Newsbusters.org* reported:

> A Media Research Center analysis finds the Big Three [ABC, CBS, NBC] evening newscasts have battered the President with 93% negative coverage and promoted impeachment at the expense of nearly all other Trump news.

> At the same time, the broadcast networks donated at least 124 hours of wall-to-wall live coverage as they pre-empted regular programming in favor of House Democrat-led impeachment activities.

So, what is the biggest difference between the Harding and Pelosi attacks? Media reporting! In 1994 the media were still outraged by cheating. In 2020 the media are complicit in massive social engineering designed to influence presidential election outcomes, perpetrating sins of omission as well as sins of commission.

Beginning January 22, 2020, the mainstream media broadcast all three days of the House Democrat impeachment managers' speeches on the Senate floor attacking President Trump. The coverage was blatantly partisan and hyperbolic. CNN described Schiff's speech as "coherent," "decisive," "dazzling," "forceful," "inspiring," "powerful," and "remarkable."

The Trump team began its defense on January 25, 2020. In an astonishing display of bias and collusion, ABC, NBC, and CBS all participated in a sin of omission by blacking out former Florida Attorney General Pam Bondi's January 27, 2020, speech before the Senate defending President Trump. Bondi's speech included the incriminating videotape of Joe Biden bragging about his *quid pro quo* in Ukraine.

Why has media reporting changed so dramatically in the last twenty-six years?

In 1994 there were fifty media outlets; today there are six. According to Internet marketing firm *Webfx:*

> While independent media outlets still exist (and there are a lot of them), the major outlets are almost all owned by six media conglomerates. To be clear, "media" in this context does not just refer to news outlets—it refers to any medium that controls the distribution of information. So here, "media" includes 24-hour news stations, newspapers, publishing houses, Internet utilities, and even video game developers.

These six globalist media companies are known as the Big 6:

National Amusements

Disney

TimeWarner

Comcast

News Corp

Sony

The globalist takeover of the media threatens American national sovereignty. Media conglomerates are for-profit businesses that do not report stories detrimental to their business interests. Their self-interested pro-globalism bias explains why media reporting across the Big 6 is so similar in content and consistently promotes the removal of America-first President Donald J. Trump.

A particularly egregious example of fake news is reported by Sean Davis in his September 26, 2020, article, "Complaint From So-Called 'Whistleblower' Is Riddled With Gossip, Blatant Falsehoods":

> Contrary to news reports asserting that the complaint included volumes of information incriminating Trump, it is instead based entirely on the president's July 25 phone call with Ukrainian President Volodymyr Zelensky and various public media reports.

> "I was not a direct witness to most of the events" characterized in the document, the complainant confesses on the first page. Instead, the complainant notes, the document is based on conversations with "more than half a dozen U.S. officials." Those officials are not named, and their positions are not identified anywhere in the letter.

> The complainant begins by falsely characterizing a July 25 phone call between Trump and Zelensky, the transcript of which was released by the White House on Wednesday.

Americans can no longer trust the media to report the news fairly. The fake news media, like the deceitful Federal Reserve System (see *The Humanitarian Hoax of the Federal Reserve System—Hoax 25*), are for-profit companies presenting themselves as public advocates instead of what they actually are: self-serving business entities. The hoaxes they perpetrate on the public lack truthfulness and transparency, and they rely on the imbalance of Joseph Stiglitz's economic theory of asymmetric information to succeed (see *The Humanitarian Hoax of Globalism—Hoax 24*).

If the Federal Reserve System presented itself as a for-profit business, Americans could assess the Fed's economic decisions with profit in mind. Similarly, if the media presented themselves honestly, Americans would know that the Big 6 media function as propagandists for the Democrat party and serve globalist elites' interests. We could then assess information the media provide the same way we assess paid political advertisements and pharmaceutical commercials. But the media do not disclose their bias. This is the definition of asymmetric information.

Instead, the media, including the Internet behemoths, collude to misinform and disinform an uninformed public in a coordinated attempt to manipulate public opinion and advance their hidden globalist agenda. It is a sinister power grab designed to achieve global power over an inter-nationalized world that provides unrestricted access to the profitable global marketplace.

This brings us back to the coordinated attempts to delegitimize and remove our America-first president, Donald Trump. Remember, the pre-ferred Democrat tactical strategy is projection—accusing the president of what they themselves are doing. These are the Democrat accusations:

- *Quid pro quo*
- Abuse of power
- Lying
- Obstruction of Congress
- Election meddling

Let's examine the impeachment process and how partisan media coverage advanced each of these five Democrat accusations based on projection.

Projection 1: *Quid pro quo*. Joe Biden demanded a *quid pro quo* from Ukraine when he ordered the firing of the prosecutor investigating his son Hunter in exchange for $1 billion in U.S. foreign aid. The infamous

January 2018 CFR videotaped recording of Joe Biden bragging about his *quid pro quo* proves it; the media discounted and under-reported the videotape. No media outrage.

> In a bombshell development, on January 28, 2020, former Ukrainian Prosecutor General Viktor Shokin, fired by Biden's *quid pro quo*, filed a complaint with Ukraine's National Bureau of Investigation demanding that an investigation be opened into Democrat presidential candidate and former vice president Joe Biden. The <u>complaint</u> charges Biden with abuse of power in ousting Shokin.

> Shokin's complaint states that Biden's pressure represented interference in the internal affairs of Ukraine on the part of a foreign government in violation of one of the principles of international law. The complaint also states that the circumstances he describes are confirmed by an independent journalistic investigation named "<u>UkraineGate</u>," conducted and published by Les-Cruises.fr.

> Unsurprisingly, the mainstream media did not publish the story; the facts do not support their anti-Trump narrative.

Projection 2: Abuse of power. Democrats abused their power by willfully ignoring constitutional law that requires a full House vote in order to proceed with impeachment. Instead, Speaker Pelosi unlawfully empowered two partisan House committees headed by two partisan Democrat chairmen to pursue impeachment—House Intelligence Committee Chairman Adam Schiff and House Judiciary Committee Chairman Jerry Nadler. The politically motivated committees held secret meetings and denied the president due process. The media did not report these outrageous and unconstitutional breaches of protocol. No media outrage.

Projection 3: Lying. The Democrats and their media allies lied to the American public by a sin of omission when they colluded to black out Pam Bondi's explosive speech and CFR videotape that clearly shows Joe Biden bragging about his *quid pro quo* in Ukraine. Adam Schiff repeatedly lied to Congress and the American people by misrepresenting President Trump's July 25, 2019, telephone call to President Zelensky. No media outrage.

Projection 4: Obstruction of Congress. Democrats obstructed Congress by denying Republicans the opportunity to call *fact* <u>witnesses</u> during the House impeachment committee inquiry—only witnesses approved by Schiff were permitted. The singular Republican witness allowed to testify was George Washington University law professor Jonathan Turley. Eighteen witnesses were called by House Democrats and none were permitted to be questioned by Republicans. The House Democrats controlled the meetings and made the rules with no regard for impeachment precedent or protocol. Transcripts of seventeen witnesses were made public, but the testimony of Intelligence Community Inspector General Michael Atkinson, who had first-hand knowledge of the whistleblower complaint that led to impeachment, was withheld and has never been made public. No explanation, and no media outrage.

Projection 5: Election meddling. The entire Democrat impeachment movement was a partisan political scheme to meddle in the 2020 election and defeat President Donald Trump at the polls. No media outrage.

As in the Tonya Harding affair, Americans are shocked by the magnitude of the Democrats' dirty dealings, their flagrant disregard for constitutional law, and their unprecedented refusal to accept an election outcome.

We are the United States of America. We are a constitutional republic that respects election outcomes and transfers power peacefully from one president to the next. We are the land of the free and the home of the brave because adult citizens agree to compete fairly and accept competitive outcomes with grace. We do not cheat or try to game the system—we follow the rules and when we lose, we train harder for the next tournament. But not the leftist Democrats.

On January 31, 2020, the Senate voted 51–49 to defeat a motion to allow subpoenas for witnesses and documents that could prolong the impeachment trial indefinitely. Two Republican senators, Susan Collins of Maine and Mitt Romney of Utah, joined the Democrats.

Democrats were apoplectic over the loss. They knew they did not have the required two-thirds Senate majority for conviction; their strategy all along was to prolong the political theater of impeachment and its nonstop media negativity until November in hopes of irreparably damaging the president in the 2020 election.

Speaker Pelosi announced that if the Senate acquitted President Trump, she would not accept the acquittal! I must repeat this astounding development: Speaker of the House Nancy Pelosi announced that if the Senate acquitted President Trump, she would not accept the acquittal. And she was not alone!

An Associated Press news clip on January 31, 2020, "Schumer: Any acquittal of Trump 'has no value'," was recorded just hours before the Senate vote on the issue of new witnesses. Schumer said, "The acquittal of President Donald Trump in his impeachment trial is meaningless with no new evidence and witnesses and will have no value."

Sen. Mazie Hirono (D-HI) made a shockingly dismissive remark about the Constitution. In an interview with Brian Williams after the 51–49 Senate vote defeating the introduction of additional witnesses she said, "I don't care what kind of nice, little, legal, constitutional defenses that they came up with, all in my view in bad faith."

The entire impeachment campaign was a Democrat sin of commission designed to influence the 2020 presidential election.

In a very manipulative sin of omission, House impeachment managers spent three days before the Senate quoting testimony from seventeen witnesses interviewed during their House impeachment inquiry and conspicuously omitted the eighteenth—Intelligence Community Inspector General (ICIG) Michael Atkinson.

WHO IS MICHAEL ATKINSON?

The Conservative Treehouse article of September 27, 2019, "ICIG Whistleblower Form Recently Modified to Permit Complaint 'Heard from Others'. . . ," identified Michael Atkinson as the ICIG who created the new whistleblower complaint form that specifically allows for the filing of complaints heard from others—in other words, hearsay:

> Prior to the current "whistleblower complaint" the Intelligence Community Inspector General did not accept whistleblower claims without first-hand knowledge. However, the ICIG [Michael Atkinson] revised the protocol in August 2019 allowing for the EXACT type of complaint now registered from the CIA whistleblower.

Margot Cleveland's explosive September 30, 2019, article in *The Federalist* asked and answered the question, "Did the Inspector General's Office Help the 'Whistleblower' Try to Frame Trump?" Cleveland began:

> To fully grasp the depths of the deception and duplicity, however, requires a familiarity with the governing whistleblower laws. Once those laws are understood, the latest attempt by the Deep State to take down our duly elected president becomes even more obvious. It also becomes clear that the "whistleblower" was not acting alone, and members of the intelligence

community inspector general's office were likely providing an assist in the attempt to bury Trump.

The Intelligence Community Whistleblower Protection Act [ICWPA] of 1998 provides a path for the intelligence community to share classified information with congressional intelligence communities only when the complaint or information involves an urgent concern.

Cleveland explained the importance of using the term "urgent concern" legally:

> But without an "urgent concern," none of these provisions apply. Without an "urgent concern," the ICIG would reject the complaint. And without an "urgent concern," the IC operative could not legally provide the classified information to the congressional intelligence committees under the guise of a whistleblowing scandal—which of course was the sole reason for the complaint. . . .
>
> What matters is whether the ICIG changed its position on *accepting* complaints under the ICWPA. If, prior to this charge against Trump, the ICIG refused to accept complaints based on second-hand information, but altered its procedure to trigger the ICWPA for the president, that is a huge scandal and implicates many besides the so-called whistleblower.
>
> While the whistleblower's plot to manipulate the ICWPA is obvious from the complaint, and so is his inaccurate partial quote of the statutory definition of "urgent concern," the change in the form suggests complicity in the ICIG's office. The director of national intelligence, who oversees the ICIG, should immediately investigate the investigator and determine whether there was a change in policy, when it occurred, why it occurred, and who initiated the change.

Sean Davis's September 27, 2019, article in The Federalist, "Intel Community Secretly Gutted Requirement of First-Hand Whistleblower Knowledge," reported:

A previous version of the whistleblower complaint document, which the ICIG and DNI until recently provided to potential whistleblowers, declared that any complaint must contain only first-hand knowledge of alleged wrongdoing and that complaints that provide only hearsay, rumor, or gossip would be rejected.

"The [intelligence community inspector general] cannot transmit information via the ICPWA based on an employee's second-hand knowledge of wrongdoing," the previous form stated under the bolded heading "FIRST-HAND INFORMATION REQUIRED." "This includes information received from another person, such as when an employee informs you that he/she witnessed some type of wrongdoing."

"If you think that wrongdoing took place, but can provide nothing more than second-hand or unsubstantiated assertions, [the intelligence community inspector general] will not be able to process the complaint or information for submission as an ICWPA," the form concluded. . . .

The Ukraine call complaint against Trump is riddled not with evidence directly witnessed by the complainant, but with repeated references to what anonymous officials allegedly told the complainant: "I have received information from multiple U.S. Government officials," "officials have informed me," "officials with direct knowledge of the call informed me," "the White House officials who told me this information," "I was told by White House officials," "the officials I spoke with," "I was told that a State Department official," "I learned from multiple U.S. officials," "One White House official described this act," "Based on multiple readouts of these meetings recounted to me," "I also learned from multiple U.S. officials," "The U.S. officials characterized this meeting," "multiple U.S. officials told me," "I learned from U.S. officials," "I also learned from a U.S. official," "several U.S. officials told me," "I heard from multiple U.S. officials," and "multiple U.S. officials told me."

The whistleblower's complaint against the president failed to meet the standard of an "urgent concern." Pelosi and Schiff's legal deceit was exposed to the public when Pelosi withheld the obviously not-so-urgent articles of impeachment from the Senate for four weeks. But Democrats had more reasons than the illegitimate whistleblower complaint to omit the public testimony of ICIG Atkinson.

American Greatness reporter Julie Kelly explored the omission in her January 28, 2020, article, "It's Time to Question Michael Atkinson on FISA Abuses."

> The top lawyer at the National Security Division when all four FISA warrants on [Carter] Page were processed was Michael Atkinson, the intelligence community's inspector general who pushed the "whistleblower" complaint at the heart of the current impeachment effort. . . .
>
> Atkinson is the one figure tied to the Russian collusion hoax, the FISA abuse scandal and so-called Ukrainegate. Although Atkinson testified behind closed doors last year during the House's impeachment inquiry, Schiff won't release the inspector general's transcript to the public. . . .

In her January 9, 2020, article, "Intelligence Community's Inspector General is the Link Between FISAgate and Impeachment," Kelly reported:

> Atkinson, you may recall, launched the impeachment saga when he determined that the accusations by the "whistleblower" about Trump's phone call with the Ukrainian president last summer were so alarming as to deem the complaint a matter of "urgent concern." (It wasn't). . . .

> "Your disappointing testimony to the Senate Intelligence Committee on September 26 was evasive to the point of being insolent and obstructive," [Senator] Cotton [R-AR] wrote on October 6. Cotton was specifically concerned about Atkinson's unwillingness to disclose his knowledge of the "whistleblower's" political bias.

> Rep. Devin Nunes (R-CA), the ranking Republican member of the House Intelligence Committee, told Fox News this week that House Republicans are investigating Atkinson for his handling of the "whistleblower" complaint and possible coordination with Schiff's staff. More on that in a moment. . . .

> Republicans have many questions for Atkinson and since, astonishingly, he remains in public office, he should be forced to answer those queries. Last September, Nunes, along with Rep. James Jordan (R-OH) and House Minority Leader Kevin McCarthy (R-CA) sent a lengthy letter to Atkinson demanding to know when and why he changed the official form to allow hearsay on the complaint.

In a shocking October 7, 2019, article, "Intel Community IG Stonewalling Congress on Backdated Whistleblower Rule Changes," *The Federalist*'s Sean Davis reported:

> Michael Atkinson, the inspector general for U.S. intelligence agencies, acknowledged that his office secretly changed key whistleblower forms and rules in September, but refused to explain to lawmakers why those changes were backdated to August.

The whistleblower complaint was filed on August 12, 2019. Davis highlighted the importance of backdating the form in the contents of the Nunes/Jordan/McCarthy letter to Atkinson:

> "The timing of the removal of the first-hand information requirement raises questions about potential connections to this whistleblower's complaint," three House Republican lawmakers wrote in a letter to Atkinson on September 30. "This timing, along with numerous apparent leaks of classified information about the contents of this complaint, also raises questions about potential criminality in the handling of these matters. . . ."

Atkinson ignored legal guidance from both the director of national intelligence and the Department of Justice that the anti-Trump complaint was statutorily deficient and forwarded it to HPSCI [House Permanent Select Committee on Intelligence] even though it did not meet the legal definition of an "urgent concern" that is required to be given to Congress.

The embattled ICIG also admitted on Friday [October 4, 2019] that the anti-Trump complainant lied on his whistleblower complaint form by concealing the complainant's previous secret interactions with House Democratic staff prior to submitting the complaint. Atkinson never even bothered investigating potential coordination between the complainant, whom DOJ said showed evidence of partisan political bias, and House Democrats prior to the filing of the anti-Trump complaint.

Michael Atkinson's first-hand knowledge of the whistleblower complaint, his secret impeachment inquiry testimony, and his personal involvement in the political malfeasance of earlier Democrat coup attempts against President Trump make him a very serious threat to the Democrats. Adam Schiff has named Michael Atkinson *the one who will not be heard.* This brings us to Eric Ciaramella, *the one who will not be named.*

Eric Ciaramella, a CIA analyst, former Obama staffer, and former National Security Council staffer, has been cautiously identified as the whistleblower multiple times in the media. Republicans have serious concerns about Ciaramella, his partisan Democrat background, and his loyalty to the Obama administration. The controversy escalated when Chief Justice John Roberts improperly refused to read Senator Rand Paul's January 30, 2020, question mentioning Eric Ciaramella during the Senate impeachment trial. It was the only question submitted by senators during the impeachment trial that the chief justice refused to read.

The Whistleblower Protection Act of 1989 is a protection against reprisals; it is not a guarantee of anonymity. Sen. Paul's angry Twitter response was reported by *PJ Media* on January 30, 2020:

"My question today is about whether or not individuals who were holdovers from the Obama National Security Council and Democrat partisans conspired with Schiff staffers to plot impeaching the President before there were formal House impeachment proceedings," Rand tweeted.

"My exact question was: Are you aware that House intelligence committee staffer Shawn Misko had a close relationship with Eric Ciaramella while at the National Security Council together [. . .] and how do you respond to reports that Ciaramella and Misko may have worked together to plot impeaching the President before there were formal House impeachment proceedings."

"My question is not about a 'whistleblower' as I have no independent information on his identity," Senator Paul tweeted later. "My question is about the actions of known Obama partisans within the NSC and House staff and how they are reported to have conspired before impeachment proceedings had even begun."

Eric Ciaramella is at the center of the whistleblower complaint that launched the articles of impeachment against President Trump. Ciaramella's credibility is highly suspect, particularly when coupled with the irregular backdated rule changes that eliminated the established requirement of first-hand information and allowed hearsay to be accepted. It makes one wonder if Eric Ciaramella is the mysterious Democrat jihadi whistleblower who strapped on the impeachment complaint to blow up President Trump.

A *Gateway Pundit* article published on January 26, 2020, "Schiff, House Democrats Conceal Testimony of 18th Witness from Trump Team," justified suspicions of the underlying Democrat coverup. Michael Atkinson delivered 179 pages of testimony and had *direct first-hand* knowledge, not *second-hand hearsay* speculations, about the origins of the whistleblower complaint that launched the impeachment. Neither Schiff nor any of the other House impeachment managers mentioned ICIG Atkinson in any of their arguments, and his testimony remains sealed. The article stated:

"The reason it hasn't been released is it's not helpful to Adam Schiff. It is not helpful to the whistleblower," said Texas Rep. John Ratcliffe. And Ratcliffe knows: he is among the lawmakers who attended the October interview of Atkinson. "It raises credibility issues about both of them."

"Schiff," Ratcliffe said, "is trying to bury that transcript."

Mr. Schiff denies he had contact with the whistleblower, but it was later revealed that his staff met with the whistleblower before the complaint was filed with Mr. Atkinson. The whistleblower is said to be a CIA analyst assigned to the White House who has ties to the Democratic Party and Mr. Biden.

The Senate heard closing arguments from the House impeachment managers and the president's defense team on Monday, February 3, 2020. Senators had time to speak on Monday and Tuesday before the final Senate vote on Wednesday, February 5, 2020—one day *after* President Trump's State of the Union Address.

THE STATE OF THE UNION

On February 4, 2020, President Trump delivered a powerful <u>State of the Union Address</u> to Congress and the nation. He confidently compared and contrasted the stunning successes of his America-first policies to the destructive policies of previous administrations that crippled and diminished America. President Trump's unapologetic record of achievement was thematic throughout.

Speaking directly to the American people, the president proudly affirmed the extraordinary accomplishments of his administration's first three years, promising the nation, "The best is yet to come."

President Trump is the consummate businessman whose particular skill set is renovation, rehabilitation, and redevelopment. He was hired by the American people to reverse the trajectory of a failing nation. President Trump's State of the Union Address was the patriotic equivalent of a new CEO reporting the fantastic turnaround and profitability of the business he was tasked to revive.

The State of the Union Address is always high drama. Congress assembles, with Republicans and Democrats seated on opposite sides of the aisle, and the president stands facing the nation on the dais, the vice president and speaker of the house seated behind him. This year, a smiling Vice President Mike Pence stood proudly, applauding the administration's many successes, while a grimacing Nancy Pelosi could barely contain her animus.

President Trump's speech completely ignored the House impeachment proceedings and the pending Senate vote. It was a presidential statement on the illegitimacy and irrelevance of the entire politically motivated Democrat impeachment process.

In a moment that will go down in American history as the most inappropriate display of childish anger, at the conclusion of President Trump's State of the Union Address, Speaker Pelosi stood and tore up her copy of the president's speech before disdainfully tossing it on the desk in front of her. It was a defining moment—the president receiving a thunderous standing ovation for strengthening the nation, and a seething, embittered

Nancy Pelosi behind him having a deranged temper tantrum because her partisan impeachment ploy had clearly failed. It was astounding.

THE SENATE VOTES TO ACQUIT

On February 5, 2020, the Senate acquitted President Trump on both impeachment charges. Senators voted 52–48 in favor of the president on the charge of abuse of power and 53–47 on the charge of obstruction of Congress. The Senate vote required a two-thirds majority (67–33) for conviction. A lawful House of Representatives would accept the Senate vote and move on—but Speaker Pelosi's House is lawless. Deranged Democrats have already committed themselves to further investigations, future impeachment articles, and more squandering of American taxpayer money.

The only way to end continuous partisan Democrat congressional attempts to remove President Trump is for Republicans to take back the House in 2020. Otherwise, the Democrat party will continue paralyzing the government with unremitting impeachment attempts and investigations according to Saul Alinsky's leftist playbook, *Rules for Radicals*. Alinsky's tenth rule delineates the Democrat strategy of obsession:

> *The major premise for tactics is the development of operations that will maintain a constant pressure upon the opposition.* It is this unceasing pressure that results in the reactions from the opposition that are essential for the success of the campaign. It should be remembered not only that the action is in the reaction but that action is itself the consequence of reaction and of reaction to the reaction, ad infinitum. The pressure produces the reaction, and constant pressure sustains action.

The Democrats are at a strategic disadvantage because they do not understand that Saul Alinsky's tenth rule demands subjective reality and cannot work on a man like President Trump, who demands objective reality. Facts, not feelings, are President Trump's unyielding defense against the Democrats' political ploy of constant pressure—the echo chamber of Democrat lies has met its match.

Alinsky's tenth rule for radicals anticipates surrender in the face of unyielding pressure to demoralize, destabilize, and delegitimize the opponent. President Trump's reaction to the pressure of Alinsky's tenth rule is to harden his resolve. President Trump will never surrender to Democrat political pressure and dirty tricks. Instead, the president has turned the impeachment offensive into a boomerang that exposed the

Democrats' underlying deceit. By declassifying documents, as he did with the Zelensky transcript, President Trump spoke truth to Democrat lies. President Trump is an existential threat to the Democrat party's will to ermanent power because the president has nothing to hide. The facts are President Trump's best defense, and transparency is his favorite weapon.

ANALYSIS

Lawrence Sellin's December 28, 2019, *American Thinker* article, "Herbert Marcuse and the Democrats' Impeachment," is an extraordinary explanation of the illegitimate, biased impeachment of President Donald Trump and its singular political objective:

> The partisan impeachment of President Donald Trump, its shredding of the Constitution and disregard for due process, are just symptoms of the Democrat party's abandonment of both democracy and sanity in its ruthless pursuit of permanent political power at any cost.

> Although it may appear inexplicable, the behavior of the modern Democrat party is not without historical precedent. As Democrats continue their political march leftward, they have begun to adopt the non-democratic tactics of the extreme left. . . .

> The inevitable outcome of Democrat policies is a dystopia, characterized by a cataclysmic decline of a society, in which a totalitarian government enforces ruthless egalitarianism by suppressing or denouncing ability and accomplishment, or even competence, as forms of inequality. It creates compete dependency on the state and attempts to eradicate the family as a social institution.

> In his article "Why Americans Are Not Taught History," Christopher Hitchens identified the vulnerability of America's present-tense culture to the Democrat party's leftist utopian myth.

> For the true blissed-out and vacant servitude required by the Democrats' strategy, you need a society that lacks any sense of itself through an understanding of its own history and traditions. The low-information voter will submit to a combination of governmental coercion as in George Orwell's *Nineteen Eighty-Four* and the hedonist nihilism of a painless, amusement-sodden, and stress-free consensus managed by the nanny-state found in Aldous Huxley's *Brave New World*.

> No matter how idealistic are the foundations of the United States or how honorable its previous history, the accumulation of excessive power in the federal government transforms it into a dysfunctional super-state

dedicated to maintaining its own power irrespective of the well-being of its citizens.

CONCLUSION

Nancy Pelosi and her Democrat party have never accepted the 2016 election outcome because they *felt* that Hillary Clinton should have won. Feelings define the identity politics of the Democrat party. The party refuses to accept President Trump as their president because they hate him, and since their *feelings* are more important than *facts* they behave as if he is not the president. The Democrat party is participating in the countdown to civil war.

In my August 2018 article "Countdown to Civil War," I referred to Daniel Greenfield's brilliant January 2018 speech in South Carolina, "The Second Civil War." In that speech Greenfield argued that politics—not guns—make civil wars, saying, "Guns are how a civil war ends, politics is how it begins." What does this mean?

Greenfield explained:

> Two or more sides disagree on who runs the country. And they can't settle the question through elections because they don't even agree that elections are how you decide who's in charge. That's the basic issue here. Who decides who runs the country? When you hate each other but accept the election results, you have a country. When you stop accepting election results, you have a countdown to a civil war.

Above all else, we are free in America because our Constitution and its laws guarantee it. We simply cannot allow apoplectic leftists, Islamists, and globalists to shatter our Constitution and transform our beloved country into a lawless Third World banana republic of anarchy, violence, coups, and civil wars. Saul Alinsky is wrong—the ends do not justify the means. Feelings are not facts.

President Donald Trump is demanding a return to the Constitution and the rule of law. He is demanding that America honor and accept election outcomes because without acceptance there is only civil war to determine who runs the country. The leftist Democrat party is the hypocritical party of feelings. They only accept election outcomes if their preferred candidate wins. They only accept the outcome of a Senate vote if it is their preferred outcome. Like self-absorbed children, *their* feelings are the only feelings that matter.

Those of us who did not like or vote for Barack Obama accepted the 2008 and 2012 election outcomes. Because we are Americans we accepted Obama's victory regardless of our personal feelings. We did not "resist" and leaders of the opposition party did not participate in coup attempts to overthrow Obama. We waited until 2016 and cast our votes for Donald J. Trump—the duly elected forty-fifth president of the United States of America.

Like Alan Dershowitz's speech before the Senate, Daniel Greenfield's speech focused on the WHAT of government and not the WHO. The rule of law and balance of power must apply regardless of who wins the election. America is at a tipping point—if we allow the angry *feelings* of the Left to supersede the rule of law, the country will tilt further toward anarchy and descend into violent civil war.

Accepting election outcomes is essential to the ordered liberty and structure of our constitutional republic. The will to absolute power discussed by Lawrence Sellin, taught by Herbert Marcuse, and embraced by the Democrat party has a name. Daniel Greenfield calls it *professional government.*

Greenfield's insightful speech exposed the staggering hypocrisy of the Left and its political objective of maintaining a professional government:

> Our system of government is based on the Constitution, but that's not the system that runs this country.
>
> The Left's system is that any part of government that it runs gets total and unlimited power over the country.
>
> If it's in the White House, then the president can do anything. And I mean anything. He can have his own amnesty for illegal aliens. He can fine you for not having health insurance. His power is unlimited.
>
> He's a dictator.
>
> But when Republicans get into the White House, suddenly the president can't do anything. He isn't even allowed to undo the illegal alien amnesty that his predecessor illegally invented.
>
> A Democrat in the White House has "discretion" to completely decide every aspect of immigration policy. A Republican doesn't even have the "discretion" to reverse him.
>
> That's how the game is played. That's how our country is run. . . .
>
> Whether it's Federal or State, Executive, Legislative or Judiciary, the Left

moves power around to run the country. If it controls an institution, then that institution is suddenly the supreme power in the land. . . .

This is what I call a moving dictatorship. . . .

There's no consistent legal standard. Only a political one.

America was founded on getting away from professional government. The British monarchy was a professional government. Like all professional governments, it was hereditary. Professional classes eventually decide to pass down their privileges to their kids.

America was different. We had a volunteer government. That's what the Founding Fathers built. . . .

Freedom can only exist under a volunteer government. Because everyone is in charge. Power belongs to the people. A professional government is going to have to stamp out freedom sooner or later. Freedom under a professional government can only be a fiction. Whenever the people disagree with the professionals, they're going to have to get put down. That's just how it is. No matter how it's disguised, a professional government is tyranny. . . .

President Trump is what volunteer government is all about.

When you're a government professional, you're invested in keeping the system going. But when you're a volunteer, you can do all the things that the experts tell you can't be done. You can look at the mess we're in with fresh eyes and do the common-sense things that President Trump is doing.

And common sense is the enemy of government professionals. It is why Trump is such a threat.

A Republican government professional would be bad enough. But a Republican government volunteer does that thing you're not supposed to do in government . . . think differently.

Professional government is a guild. Like medieval guilds. You can't serve in if you're not a member. If you haven't been indoctrinated into its arcane rituals. If you aren't in the club.

And Trump isn't in the club. He brought in a bunch of people who aren't in the club with him.

Now we're seeing what the pros do when amateurs try to walk in on them. They spy on them, they investigate them and they send them to jail. They use the tools of power to bring them down.

That's not a free country.

It's not a free country when FBI agents who support Hillary take out an "insurance policy" against Trump winning the election. It's not a free country when Obama officials engage in massive unmasking of the opposition. It's not a free country when the media responds to the other guy winning by trying to ban the conservative media that supported him from social media. It's not a free country when all of the above collude together to overturn an election because the guy who wasn't supposed to win, won.

We're in a civil war between conservative volunteer government and leftist professional government. . . .

But civil wars come down to an easy question. Who runs the country?

They've given us their answer and we need to give them our answer.

American Thinker author David Prentice affirmed Daniel Greenfield's dire warning. In his August 9, 2017, article, "Trump's Unintended Consequences: The Unmasking of the Deep State," Prentice explained the Deep State involvement in leftist professional government:

> The Left has weaponized the bureaucracies and agencies it inhabits. Leftists have decided they will become the dominant culture in the CIA, FBI, NSA, IRS, EPA, and the rest of our bureaucracies. They decided it's okay to be totalitarian, it's okay to break the law, it's okay to go after their political opponents with the force of government, it's okay because they are the ones who deserve to win. The Deep State running rampant is fine, as long as they run it. From Valerie Jarrett to Barack Obama to James Clapper and James Comey, they all visibly overstepped their rightful boundaries. . . .
>
> The Deep State did not originate with them, but they [Obama administration] stocked it with their cronies. They stocked it with people of similar left-leaning ideas, with similar left-leaning willingness to misuse power. The Deep State became a weapon of intimidation and a deep abuser of power. . . .
>
> We may not understand the mechanism, but we do know that the Deep State has become the vanguard of the Left's civil war, and it is not fictional. . . . They are self-motivated with a set of goals. Get rid of Trump if they can. Get Trump's base to be embarrassed of him or depressed if they can. Make certain that Trump cannot succeed.

RAHM'S RULE AND THE FOURTH COUP ATTEMPT

Rumblings of a second Democrat impeachment effort against President Trump began immediately after his Senate acquittal on February 5, 2020. All talk of a second impeachment halted abruptly as soon as the coronavirus outbreak in Wuhan, China made the news. I could not send this book to print without warning you about the political disinformation campaign that followed.

Rahm Emanuel, Barack Obama's chief of staff, is remembered for saying, "You never let a serious crisis go to waste. And what I mean by that is it's an opportunity to do things you think you could not do before." Rahm's Rule is a political calculation for exploiting an otherwise apolitical event.

The Russia-collusion coup attempt had failed. The Ukraine quid pro quo coup attempt had failed. The impeachment coup attempt had failed. President Trump's enormously successful America-first policies remained an existential threat to globalism. The coronavirus outbreak presented an extraordinary crisis of opportunity for the increasingly desperate Democrats and their globalist handlers.

A disproportionate and hysterical response to the coronavirus outbreak provided the vehicle for the fourth coup attempt against President Trump. The globalist coup strategy of enhanced public panic followed Rahm's Rule and did something the Democrats could not do before. It created the social chaos necessary to destabilize Trump's roaring economy—his signature America-first achievement.

Dr. Nancy Messonnier, director of the National Center for Immunization and Respiratory Diseases, released the first salvo of fear on February 21, 2020, saying a global pandemic was likely. Messonnier introduced the terrifying idea to the nation without most Americans realizing that Nancy Messonnier's brother is former assistant attorney general Rod Rosenstein, head of the failed Mueller investigation. Next, the World Health Organization (WHO) initiated worldwide hysteria on March 11, 2020, by declaring the coronavirus outbreak a pandemic. So, who is the WHO?

The WHO is a specialized health agency of the globalist United Nations. Director-general of the WHO since 2017, Ethiopian politician Tedros Adhanom Ghebreyesus, severely overstated the fatality rate of the coronavirus, creating a global panic. Fatality rates for coronavirus are actually much lower than fatality rates for the flu. President Trump was correct when he tried to calm the nation saying the WHO's reported fatality rate was much too high. Why the obvious discrepancy?

Tedros, former Ethiopian Minister of Health (2005–2012) and Minister of Foreign Affairs (2012–2016), belongs to the Tigray People's Liberation Front, the most powerful political party within the Marxist Ethiopian People's Revolutionary Democratic Front, that ruled Ethiopia until December 2019.

A shocking March 17, 2020, article in *The Federalist* exposed the symbiotic relationship between Tedros and China:

> China worked tirelessly behind the scenes in lobbying to ensure the election of Tedros. . . . So why did China push so hard for Tedros? The ex-revolutionary's tenure is merely part of the broader Chinese Communist Party (CCP) strategy to take over international organizations to "reshape the international system to accommodate its political and economic interests." . . . As noted by Assistant to the U.S. President, Peter Navarro, the CCP has a "broad strategy to gain control over the 15 specialized agencies of the UN. China already leads four, no other country leads more than one."

> Once ushered in as director-general, Tedros quickly repaid China's support. The first day after his election he expressed support for the Chinese Communist Party's claim over Taiwan. Not long after, he appointed brutal dictator Robert Mugabe, a China ally, as a "goodwill ambassador" in a move described by diplomats as an obvious "payoff." This support was quickly reciprocated. China decided to fund a new $80 million World Health Organization "Center for Disease Control" in ... Ethiopia.

China wants Trump OUT! The Chinese need an administration like Obama/Biden that will negotiate on trade issues to benefit China, not America. Dr. Ezekiel Emanuel, Rahm Emanuel's older brother and former Obama administration health adviser, just happens to be the current special adviser to the director-general of the WHO. So, China's patron Tedros Adhanom Ghebreyesus, the politically corrupt Marxist director-general of the globalist WHO, advised by anti-Trump Dr. Ezekiel Emanuel, declared the coronavirus a pandemic.

The ensuing panic destabilized financial markets around the world. The economic crisis in America is the fourth coup attempt against President Trump. China and the globalist elite are willing to shatter the world economy to defeat President Trump on November 3, 2020. After all, they know it is an artificial catastrophe that can be reversed on November 4, 2020.

The fourth coup attempt is the contrived, strategic, tactical collaboration of the opportunistic Democrats and their globalist bosses. It is a political full court press designed by the enemies of American sovereignty that relies completely on fear. The coronavirus hysteria in America is not about our health—it is about our votes.

Fear is an extremely manipulative tool for social engineers. If the coup engineers can create enough panic to mobilize our frightened inner children, we will regress back to a state of childish powerlessness and compliance where we will willingly surrender our freedoms to be safe. Henry Kissinger famously described the path to a New World Government at the Bilderberg Conference in Evian, France 1991:

> Today, America would be outraged if U.N. troops entered Los Angeles to restore order. Tomorrow they will be grateful! This is especially true if they were told that there was an outside threat from beyond, whether real or promulgated, that threatened our very existence. It is then that all peoples of the world will plead to deliver them from this evil. The one thing every man fears is the unknown. When presented with this scenario, individual rights will be willingly relinquished for the guarantee of their well-being granted to them by the World Government.

The consequential presidential 2020 election is not about the future of one man. It is about the future of the United States of America.

FINAL THOUGHTS

The November 3, 2020, election is a contest between the Deep State's leftist professional government and conservative volunteer government. It is the battle between internationalism and American national sovereignty—the war of the *Leftist/Islamist/Globalist Axis v. President Donald J. Trump.*

Your vote is the privilege and responsibility of American freedom. Your vote has the power to reverse the course of Deep State totalitarian professional government. Your vote can return the United States of America to a constitutional republic of the people, by the people, and for the people.

This is what President Trump means when he says, "They're not after me, they're after you. I'm just in the way."

Donald J. Trump ✓
@realDonaldTrump

THE WHITE HOUSE

WASHINGTON

December 17, 2019

The Honorable Nancy Pelosi
Speaker of the House of Representatives
Washington, D.C. 20515

Dear Madam Speaker:

I write to express my strongest and most powerful protest against the partisan impeachment crusade being pursued by the Democrats in the House of Representatives. This impeachment represents an unprecedented and unconstitutional abuse of power by Democrat Lawmakers, unequaled in nearly two and a half centuries of American legislative history.

The Articles of Impeachment introduced by the House Judiciary Committee are not recognizable under any standard of Constitutional theory, interpretation, or jurisprudence. They include no crimes, no misdemeanors, and no offenses whatsoever. You have cheapened the importance of the very ugly word, impeachment!

By proceeding with your invalid impeachment, you are violating your oaths of office, you are breaking your allegiance to the Constitution, and you are declaring open war on American Democracy. You dare to invoke the Founding Fathers in pursuit of this election-nullification scheme—yet your spiteful actions display unfettered contempt for America's founding and your egregious conduct threatens to destroy that which our Founders pledged their very lives to build. Even worse than offending the Founding Fathers, you are offending Americans of faith by continually saying "I pray for the President," when you know this statement is not true, unless it is meant in a negative sense. It is a terrible thing you are doing, but you will have to live with it, not I!

Your first claim, "Abuse of Power," is a completely disingenuous, meritless, and baseless invention of your imagination. You know that I had a totally innocent conversation with the President of Ukraine. I then had a second conversation that has been misquoted, mischaracterized, and fraudulently misrepresented. Fortunately, there was a transcript of the conversation taken, and you know from the transcript (which was immediately made available) that the paragraph in question was perfect. I said to President Zelensky: "I would like you to do us a favor, though, because our country has been through a lot and Ukraine knows a lot about it." I said do us a favor, not me, and our country, not a campaign. I then mentioned the Attorney General of the United States. Every time I talk with a foreign leader, I put America's interests first, just as I did with President Zelensky.

You are turning a policy disagreement between two branches of government into an impeachable offense—it is no more legitimate than the Executive Branch charging members of Congress with crimes for the lawful exercise of legislative power.

You know full well that Vice President Biden used his office and $1 billion dollars of U.S. aid money to coerce Ukraine into firing the prosecutor who was digging into the company paying his son millions of dollars. You know this because Biden bragged about it on video. Biden openly stated: "I said, 'I'm telling you, you're not getting the billion dollars'...I looked at them and said: 'I'm leaving in six hours. If the prosecutor is not fired, you're not getting the money.' Well, son of a bitch. He got fired." Even Joe Biden admitted just days ago in an interview with NPR that it "looked bad." Now you are trying to impeach me by falsely accusing me of doing what Joe Biden has admitted he actually did.

President Zelensky has repeatedly declared that I did nothing wrong, and that there was No Pressure. He further emphasized that it was a "good phone call," that "I don't feel pressure," and explicitly stressed that "nobody pushed me." The Ukrainian Foreign Minister stated very clearly: "I have never seen a direct link between investigations and security assistance." He also said there was "No Pressure." Senator Ron Johnson of Wisconsin, a supporter of Ukraine who met privately with President Zelensky, has said: "At no time during this meeting...was there any mention by Zelensky or any Ukrainian that they were feeling pressure to do anything in return for the military aid." Many meetings have been held between representatives of Ukraine and our country. Never once did Ukraine complain about pressure being applied—not once! Ambassador Sondland testified that I told him: "No quid pro quo. I want nothing. I want nothing. I want President Zelensky to do the right thing, do what he ran on."

The second claim, so-called "Obstruction of Congress," is preposterous and dangerous. House Democrats are trying to impeach the duly elected President of the United States for asserting Constitutionally based privileges that have been asserted on a bipartisan basis by administrations of both political parties throughout our Nation's history. Under that standard, every American president would have been impeached many times over. As liberal law professor Jonathan Turley warned when addressing Congressional Democrats: "I can't emphasize this enough...if you impeach a president, if you make a high crime and misdemeanor out of going to the courts, it is an abuse of power. It's your abuse of power. You're doing precisely what you're criticizing the President for doing."

Everyone, you included, knows what is really happening. Your chosen candidate lost the election in 2016, in an Electoral College landslide (306-227), and you and your party have never recovered from this defeat. You have developed a full-fledged case of what many in the media call Trump Derangement Syndrome and sadly, you will never get over it! You are unwilling and unable to accept the verdict issued at the ballot box during the great Election of 2016. So you have spent three straight years attempting to overturn the will of the American people and nullify their votes. You view democracy as your enemy!

Speaker Pelosi, you admitted just last week at a public forum that your party's impeachment effort has been going on for "two and a half years," long before you ever heard about a phone call with Ukraine. Nineteen minutes after I took the oath of office, the *Washington Post*

2

published a story headlined, "The Campaign to Impeach President Trump Has Begun." Less than three months after my inauguration, Representative Maxine Waters stated, "I'm going to fight every day until he's impeached." House Democrats introduced the first impeachment resolution against me within months of my inauguration, for what will be regarded as one of our country's best decisions, the firing of James Comey (see Inspector General Reports)—who the world now knows is one of the dirtiest cops our Nation has ever seen. A ranting and raving Congresswoman, Rashida Tlaib, declared just hours after she was sworn into office, "We're gonna go in there and we're gonna impeach the motherf****r." Representative Al Green said in May, "I'm concerned that if we don't impeach this president, he will get re-elected." Again, you and your allies said, and did, all of these things long before you ever heard of President Zelensky or anything related to Ukraine. As you know very well, this impeachment drive has nothing to do with Ukraine, or the totally appropriate conversation I had with its new president. It only has to do with your attempt to undo the election of 2016 and steal the election of 2020!

Congressman Adam Schiff cheated and lied all the way up to the present day, even going so far as to fraudulently make up, out of thin air, my conversation with President Zelensky of Ukraine and read this fantasy language to Congress as though it were said by me. His shameless lies and deceptions, dating all the way back to the Russia Hoax, is one of the main reasons we are here today.

You and your party are desperate to distract from America's extraordinary economy, incredible jobs boom, record stock market, soaring confidence, and flourishing citizens. Your party simply cannot compete with our record: 7 million new jobs; the lowest-ever unemployment for African Americans, Hispanic Americans, and Asian Americans; a rebuilt military; a completely reformed VA with Choice and Accountability for our great veterans; more than 170 new federal judges and two Supreme Court Justices; historic tax and regulation cuts; the elimination of the individual mandate; the first decline in prescription drug prices in half a century; the first new branch of the United States Military since 1947, the Space Force; strong protection of the Second Amendment; criminal justice reform; a defeated ISIS caliphate and the killing of the world's number one terrorist leader, al-Baghdadi; the replacement of the disastrous NAFTA trade deal with the wonderful USMCA (Mexico and Canada); a breakthrough Phase One trade deal with China; massive new trade deals with Japan and South Korea; withdrawal from the terrible Iran Nuclear Deal; cancellation of the unfair and costly Paris Climate Accord; becoming the world's top energy producer; recognition of Israel's capital, opening the American Embassy in Jerusalem, and recognizing Israeli sovereignty over the Golan Heights; a colossal reduction in illegal border crossings, the ending of Catch-and-Release, and the building of the Southern Border Wall—and that is just the beginning, there is so much more. You cannot defend your extreme policies—open borders, mass migration, high crime, crippling taxes, socialized healthcare, destruction of American energy, late-term taxpayer-funded abortion, elimination of the Second Amendment, radical far-left theories of law and justice, and constant partisan obstruction of both common sense and common good.

There is nothing I would rather do than stop referring to your party as the Do-Nothing Democrats. Unfortunately, I don't know that you will ever give me a chance to do so.

3

After three years of unfair and unwarranted investigations, 45 million dollars spent, 18 angry Democrat prosecutors, the entire force of the FBI, headed by leadership now proven to be totally incompetent and corrupt, you have found NOTHING! Few people in high position could have endured or passed this test. You do not know, nor do you care, the great damage and hurt you have inflicted upon wonderful and loving members of my family. You conducted a fake investigation upon the democratically elected President of the United States, and you are doing it yet again.

There are not many people who could have taken the punishment inflicted during this period of time, and yet done so much for the success of America and its citizens. But instead of putting our country first, you have decided to disgrace our country still further. You completely failed with the Mueller report because there was nothing to find, so you decided to take the next hoax that came along, the phone call with Ukraine—even though it was a perfect call. And by the way, when I speak to foreign countries, there are many people, with permission, listening to the call on both sides of the conversation.

You are the ones interfering in America's elections. You are the ones subverting America's Democracy. You are the ones Obstructing Justice. You are the ones bringing pain and suffering to our Republic for your own selfish personal, political, and partisan gain.

Before the Impeachment Hoax, it was the Russian Witch Hunt. Against all evidence, and regardless of the truth, you and your deputies claimed that my campaign colluded with the Russians—a grave, malicious, and slanderous lie, a falsehood like no other. You forced our Nation through turmoil and torment over a wholly fabricated story, illegally purchased from a foreign spy by Hillary Clinton and the DNC in order to assault our democracy. Yet, when the monstrous lie was debunked and this Democrat conspiracy dissolved into dust, you did not apologize. You did not recant. You did not ask to be forgiven. You showed no remorse, no capacity for self-reflection. Instead, you pursued your next libelous and vicious crusade—you engineered an attempt to frame and defame an innocent person. All of this was motivated by personal political calculation. Your Speakership and your party are held hostage by your most deranged and radical representatives of the far left. Each one of your members lives in fear of a socialist primary challenger—this is what is driving impeachment. Look at Congressman Nadler's challenger. Look at yourself and others. Do not take our country down with your party.

If you truly cared about freedom and liberty for our Nation, then you would be devoting your vast investigative resources to exposing the full truth concerning the FBI's horrifying abuses of power before, during, and after the 2016 election—including the use of spies against my campaign, the submission of false evidence to a FISA court, and the concealment of exculpatory evidence in order to frame the innocent. The FBI has great and honorable people, but the leadership was inept and corrupt. I would think that you would personally be appalled by these revelations, because in your press conference the day you announced impeachment, you tied the impeachment effort directly to the completely discredited Russia Hoax, declaring twice that "all roads lead to Putin," when you know that is an abject lie. I have been far tougher on Russia than President Obama ever even thought to be.

4

Any member of Congress who votes in support of impeachment—against every shred of truth, fact, evidence, and legal principle—is showing how deeply they revile the voters and how truly they detest America's Constitutional order. Our Founders feared the tribalization of partisan politics, and you are bringing their worst fears to life.

Worse still, I have been deprived of basic Constitutional Due Process from the beginning of this impeachment scam right up until the present. I have been denied the most fundamental rights afforded by the Constitution, including the right to present evidence, to have my own counsel present, to confront accusers, and to call and cross-examine witnesses, like the so-called whistleblower who started this entire hoax with a false report of the phone call that bears no relationship to the actual phone call that was made. Once I presented the transcribed call, which surprised and shocked the fraudsters (they never thought that such evidence would be presented), the so-called whistleblower, and the second whistleblower, disappeared because they got caught, their report was a fraud, and they were no longer going to be made available to us. In other words, once the phone call was made public, your whole plot blew up, but that didn't stop you from continuing.

More due process was afforded to those accused in the Salem Witch Trials.

You and others on your committees have long said impeachment must be bipartisan—it is not. You said it was very divisive—it certainly is, even far more than you ever thought possible—and it will only get worse!

This is nothing more than an illegal, partisan attempted coup that will, based on recent sentiment, badly fail at the voting booth. You are not just after me, as President, you are after the entire Republican Party. But because of this colossal injustice, our party is more united than it has ever been before. History will judge you harshly as you proceed with this impeachment charade. Your legacy will be that of turning the House of Representatives from a revered legislative body into a Star Chamber of partisan persecution.

Perhaps most insulting of all is your false display of solemnity. You apparently have so little respect for the American People that you expect them to believe that you are approaching this impeachment somberly, reservedly, and reluctantly. No intelligent person believes what you are saying. Since the moment I won the election, the Democrat Party has been possessed by Impeachment Fever. There is no reticence. This is not a somber affair. You are making a mockery of impeachment and you are scarcely concealing your hatred of me, of the Republican Party, and tens of millions of patriotic Americans. The voters are wise, and they are seeing straight through this empty, hollow, and dangerous game you are playing.

I have no doubt the American people will hold you and the Democrats fully responsible in the upcoming 2020 election. They will not soon forgive your perversion of justice and abuse of power.

5

There is far too much that needs to be done to improve the lives of our citizens. It is time for you and the highly partisan Democrats in Congress to immediately cease this impeachment fantasy and get back to work for the American People. While I have no expectation that you will do so, I write this letter to you for the purpose of history and to put my thoughts on a permanent and indelible record.

One hundred years from now, when people look back at this affair, I want them to understand it, and learn from it, so that it can never happen to another President again.

Sincerely yours,

Donald J. Trump
President of the United States of America

cc: United States Senate
        United States House of Representatives

AUTHOR BIO

Linda Goudsmit is the devoted wife of Rob and they are the parents of four children and the grandparents of four. She and Rob owned and operated a girls clothing store in Michigan for forty years until retiring to the beaches of sunny Florida in 2013. A graduate of the University of Michigan in Ann Arbor, Linda has a lifelong commitment to learning and is an avid reader and observer of life.

She is the author of the philosophy book *Dear America: Who's Driving the Bus?* and the children's picture book series *MIMI'S STRATEGY*. It is with pride and humility that Linda is sharing her thoughts, observations, and synthesizing political philosophy in *The Book of Humanitarian Hoaxes: Killing America with 'Kindness'*.

ENDNOTES

URLs that have disappeared from the Internet are retrievable on the Internet Archive Wayback Machine; https://archive.org/web/web.php

How to use Wayback Machine:
https://www.youtube.com/watch?v=HDpPz5om3Wc

HOAX 1: The Humanitarian Hoax of Transgender Training in the Military

1   Tier Three Transgender Training; https://thefederalist.com/2017/07/05/new-army-training-tells-female-soldiers-put-naked-men-showers/

1   PowerPoint; https://thefederalist.com/wp-content/uploads/2017/07/Tier-Three-Training-G-1.pptx

1   accompanying lesson plan; https://thefederalist.com/wp-content/uploads/2017/07/Lesson-Plan-for-Tier-Three-Training-w-legal-review.docx

HOAX 3: The Humanitarian Hoax of Raising the Minimum Wage

7   University of Washington; https://evans.uw.edu/sites/default/files/NBER Working Paper.pdf

8   The Weight of the Poor: A Strategy to End Poverty; https://www.commondreams.org/news/2010/03/24/weight-poor-strategy-end-poverty

HOAX 4: The Humanitarian Hoax of Climate Change

10   six-minute video; https://www.youtube.com/watch?v=LRhkKjquWZw

11   transcript; https://www.epw.senate.gov/public/_cache/files/415b-9cde-e664-4628-8fb5-ae3951197d03/22514hearingwitnesstesti-monymoore.pdf

12   Obama signed; https://obamawhitehouse.archives.gov/blog/2016/09/03/president-obama-united-states-formally-enters-paris-agreement

HOAX 6: The Humanitarian Hoax of Diversity

20   Preston Mitchum; http://www.libertyheadlines.com/georgetown-univ-prof-white-people-racist/?AID=7236

HOAX 9: The Humanitarian Hoax of Sanctuary Cities

30   300 sanctuary jurisdictions; https://cis.org/Map-Sanctuary-Cities-Counties-and-States?gclid=CjwKCAjw3rfOBRBJEiwAam-Gs-D2uPe-uPrWOlMdFDq0LYvwCvixywYOVsMkcW8duyH1bcVH9vGqFE-hoCJiEQAvD_BwE

31   courtroom observer; https://www.wnd.com/2017/06/news-black-out-on-refugee-boys-who-sexually-assaulted-idaho-girl/

31   Mathew Staver; https://www.wnd.com/2017/06/news-black-out-on-refugee-boys-who-sexually-assaulted-idaho-girl/

32    $116 *billion* per year; https://www.irli.org/single-post/2017/09/27/New-FAIR-Study-Illegal-Immigration-Costs-116-billion-Annually

32   Priority Enforcement Program; https://www.numbersusa.com/news/obama-administration-implements-priority-enforcement-program-limits-interior-enforcement

32   8 U.S.C. § 1373; https://www.law.cornell.edu/uscode/text/8/1373

32   letter; https://culberson.house.gov/news/documentsingle.aspx?DocumentID=398522

HOAX 11: The Humanitarian Hoax of Gun Control

38   Gun Deaths in America; https://fivethirtyeight.com/features/gun-deaths/

HOAX 12: The Humanitarian Hoax of Community Organizing

40   The Weight of the Poor: A Strategy to End Poverty; https://www.commondreams.org/news/2010/03/24/weight-poor-strategy-end-poverty

40   Freedom Center; https://www.davidhorowitzfreedomcenter.org/

41   leftist apostate; http://horowitzbiobooks.com/

HOAX 13: The Humanitarian Hoax of Socialism

46   1961 farewell address; https://www.ourdocuments.gov/print_friendly.php?flash=false&page=transcript&doc=90&title=Transcript+of+President+Dwight+D.+Eisenhowers+Farewell+Address+%281961%29

HOAX 14: The Humanitarian Hoax of George Soros

48   deceptively positive names; https://www.discoverthenetworks.org/

49   Popper; https://en.wikipedia.org/wiki/Karl_Popper

49   *The Open Society and Its Enemies*; https://books.google.com/books?id=_M_E5QczOBAC&pg=PA581#v=onepage&q&f=false

50   liberal mainstream media; http://www.mrc.org/special-reports/george-soros-media-mogul

50   Media Research Center; https://www.mrc.org/commentary/soros-spends-over-48-million-funding-media-organizations

50   Soros media empire; https://www.mrc.org/special-reports/george-soros-media-mogul

50   Media outlets; http://www.mrc.org/commentary/soros-spends-over-48-million-funding-media-organizations

50   reflexivity; https://macro-ops.com/understanding-george-soross-theory-of-reflexivity-in-markets/

50   Reflexivity; https://www.investopedia.com/terms/r/reflexivity.asp

HOAX 16: The Humanitarian Hoax of Relativism

56   The Mathematics of the Culture War on America; http://goudsmit.
pundicity.com/20600/the-mathematics-of-the-culture-war-on-america

57   interviewed; https://www.youtube.com/watch?v=xfO1veFs6Ho

58   World Health Organization; https://www.who.int/news-room/fact-
sheets/detail/mental-health-strengthening-our-response

HOAX 17: The Humanitarian Hoax of Net Neutrality

61   UNCENSORED: Time for Real Net Neutrality; https://dailycaller.
com/2017/12/08/roger-stone-time-for-real-net-neutrality/

61   Title II; http://transition.fcc.gov/Reports/1934new.pdf

62   Restoring Internet Freedom Order; https://transition.fcc.gov/
Daily_Releases/Daily_Business/2017/db1128/DOC-347980A1.pdf

63   *Breitbart News*; https://www.breitbart.com/tech/2017/12/14/the-
end-is-nigh-9-crazy-leftist-predictions-for-net-neutrality-repeal/

HOAX 18: The Humanitarian Hoax of Sanctuary States

65   sanctuary state; http://dailysignal.com/2018/01/02/califor-
nia-is-officially-a-sanctuary-state/

66   The law signed by Governor Brown; https://www.fairus.org/legis-
lation/state-local-legislation/california-sanctuary-state-bill-sb-54-sum-
mary-and-history

66   Thomas Homan; http://www.washingtonexaminer.com/
ice-chief-lists-worst-sanctuary-cities-chicago-nyc-san-francisco-philadel-
phia/article/2629466

66   study; http://www.irli.org/single-post/2017/09/27/
New-FAIR-Study-Illegal-Immigration-Costs-116-billion-Annually?g-
clid=EAIaIQobChMIyeftlee-2AIV27XACh1VWAsDEAAYASA-
AEgKoefD_BwE

66   disproportionately; https://fairus.org/sites/default/files/2017-09/
Fiscal-Burden-of-Illegal-Immigration-2017.pdf

67   *Newsweek*; https://www.newsweek.com/trumps-ice-pick-thomas-homan-warns-sanctuary-state-california-hang-tight-amid-768816

HOAX 19: The Humanitarian Hoax of Common Core

69   No Child Left Behind Act; https://en.wikipedia.org/wiki/No_Child_Left_Behind_Act

69   Alfie Kohn; http://www.schoolsmatter.info/2007/05/alfie-kohn-on-nclb-appalling-and.html

70   Race to the Top; https://truthinamericaneducation.com/race-to-the-top/

70   Common Core State Standards Mission Statement; http://www.uwosh.edu/coehs/cmagproject/common_core/documents/CC_Standards_Myths.pdf

70   Global Education First Initiative; http://www.unesco.org/new/en/gefi/about/

70   The 3 Priorities; http://www.unesco.org/new/en/gefi/priorities/

70   Priority 3; https://www.thenewamerican.com/culture/education/item/20038-schooling-for-world-gov-t-unesco-s-global-citizenship-education-forum-kicks-off-2015-agenda

71   Connect All Schools; http://www.connectallschools.org

71   Common Core Ties Libya, Qatar, Saudi Arabia; https://www.washingtontimes.com/news/2015/apr/7/bethany-blankley-parents-must-reject-common-core-i/

71   *World Net Daily*; https://www.wnd.com/2013/01/muslim-brotherhood-group-to-connect-all-u-s-schools/

71   Islam; http://www.socialstudiescms.com/islamic-world

71   Qatar Foundation International; http://www.qfi.org/about-us/frequently-asked-questions/

71   map; http://www.qfi.org/about/#map

71   Al Masdar; http://arabicalmasdar.org/

72   global citizenship; http://www.unesco.org/new/en/gefi/priorities/global-citizenship/

72   globalized curriculum; https://connectallschools.wordpress.com/

72   Agenda 21; https://sustainabledevelopment.un.org/outcomedocu-ments/agenda21

72   United Nations Sustainable Development; https://sustainabledevel-opment.un.org/content/documents/Agenda21.pdf

72   Transforming Our World: The 2030 Agenda for Sustainable Devel-opment; https://sustainabledevelopment.un.org/post2015/transform-ingourworld

72   World Core Curriculum; http://www.unesco.org/education/tlsf/mods/theme_c/popups/mod18t01s03.html

73   UNESCO; https://www.ed.gov/news/speeches/vision-educa-tion-reform-united-states-secretary-arne-duncans-remarks-unit-ed-nations-ed

73   member states; http://humanrightsvoices.org/EYEontheUN/un_101/facts/?p=16

73   Pearson Education; http://fortune.com/2015/01/21/every-body-hates-pearson/

73   educational materials; https://www.pearson.com/corporate/sus-tainability/un-sustainable-development-goals.html

73   Muammar Gaddafi's; https://www.huffingtonpost.com/alan-singer/pearson-education-new-york-testing-_b_1850169.html

73   The Sovereign Fund of Libya; http://education-curriculum-re-form-government-schools.org/2013/03/pearsons-libyan-owner-ship-and-islam-biased-textbooks/

HOAX 20: The Humanitarian Hoax of DACA

75   DACA; https://en.wikipedia.org/wiki/Deferred_Action_for_Childhood_Arrivals

75   DAPA; https://en.wikipedia.org/wiki/Deferred_Action_for_Par-ents_of_Americans

75   *Breitbart* article; https://www.breitbart.com/politics/2017/12/28/anchor-baby-population-in-u-s-exceeds-one-year-of-american-births/

76   *USA Today*; https://www.usatoday.com/story/news/nation/2018/01/18/there-3-5-m-dreamers-and-most-may-face-nightmare/1042134001/

76   Migration Policy Institute; https://www.usatoday.com/story/news/nation/2018/01/18/there-3-5-m-dreamers-and-most-may-face-nightmare/1042134001/

77   illegal aliens; https://www.migrationpolicy.org/programs/us-immigration-policy-program-data-hub/unauthorized-immigrant-population-profiles

77   Michael Cutler; https://www.frontpagemag.com/fpm/269095/daca-trump-and-congress-must-look-they-leap-michael-cutler

77   Immigration Trojan Horse; https://www.frontpagemag.com/fpm/268988/daca-immigration-trojan-horse-michael-cutler

77   revoking DAPA; http://thehill.com/latino/338082-trump-administration-ends-dapa-rule-protecting-undocumented-immigrant-parents

77   ending DACA; https://www.nbcnews.com/politics/immigration/trump-dreamers-daca-immigration-announcement-n798686

HOAX 21: The Humanitarian Hoax of Collectivism

79   Saudi al-Qaeda Muslims; https://www.cia.gov/news-information/speeches-testimony/2002/DCI_18_June_testimony_new.pdf

80   The Mathematics of the Culture War on America; http://goudsmit.pundicity.com/20600/the-mathematics-of-the-culture-war-on-america

80   The Re-education of America; http://goudsmit.pundicity.com/20136/the-re-education-of-america

80   Birdman and the Reality Revolution—Part 1; http://goudsmit.pundicity.com/20469/birdman-and-the-reality-revolution-part-1

81   John Fogerty; https://en.wikipedia.org/wiki/Woodstock

81   Globalism: The Existential Enemy of Sovereignty, Security, and Prosperity; http://goudsmit.pundicity.com/20330/globalism-the-existential-enemy-of-sovereignty

81   *The Liberal Mind: The Psychological Causes of Political Madness*; http://www.libertymind.com/

HOAX 22: The Humanitarian Hoax of 'For Your Own Good'

83   Lobbyists spent; https://www.opensecrets.org/lobby/index.php

83   *Opensecrets.org*; https://www.opensecrets.org/lobby/lobby_con-tribs.php?cycle=2016&type=P

84   House seat; https://en.wikipedia.org/wiki/History_of_lobbying_in_the_United_States

84   Super PACs; https://www.opensecrets.org/pacs/pacfaq.php

85   Difference Between PAC and Super PAC; http://www.differ-encebetween.net/miscellaneous/politics/difference-between-pac-and-super-pac/

85   October 2016; http://dailysignal.com/2016/10/26/this-senator-wants-to-make-career-politicians-obsolete-with-term-limits/

85   Personal Gain Index; https://ballotpedia.org/Changes_in_Net_Worth_of_U.S._Senators_and_Representatives_(Personal_Gain_Index)

85   79 Members of Congress Have Been in Office for at least 20 Years; https://www.zerohedge.com/news/2015-05-18/79-members-congress-have-been-office-least-20-years

86   amendment; https://www.cruz.senate.gov/files/documents/Bills/20170103_TermLimitsBill.pdf

HOAX 23: The Humanitarian Hoax of Multiple Realities

87   *The Liberal Mind: The Psychological Causes of Political Madness*; http://www.libertymind.com/

87   Birdman and the Reality Revolution; https://goudsmit.pundicity.com/20469/birdman-and-the-reality-revolution-part-1

88   The Mathematics of the Culture War on America; http://goudsmit.pundicity.com/20600/the-mathematics-of-the-culture-war-on-america

89   globalist dream; http://goudsmit.pundicity.com/20057/global-ism-persuading-the-individual-to-stop-being

HOAX 24: The Humanitarian Hoax of Globalism

91   asymmetric information; https://www.investopedia.com/terms/a/asymmetricinformation.asp

91   Wikipedia explains; https://en.wikipedia.org/wiki/Information_asymmetry

92   adverse selection; https://www.investopedia.com/terms/a/adverse-selection.asp

92   moral hazard; https://www.investopedia.com/terms/m/moralhazard.asp

92   Connecting the Dots: Islamism . . . Socialism . . . Globalism; http://goudsmit.pundicity.com/20055/connecting-the-dots

HOAX 25: The Humanitarian Hoax of the Federal Reserve System

94   Federal Reserve System; http://www.newswithviews.com/Barnewall/marilyn201.htm

94   The Act; http://www.newswithviews.com/Barnewall/marilyn201.htm

95   fiat currency; http://www.newswithviews.com/Barnewall/marilyn200.htm

95   Federal Reserve Bank; https://www.thebalance.com/who-owns-the-federal-reserve-3305974

95   First Bank of the United States; https://en.wikipedia.org/wiki/First_Bank_of_the_United_States

95   First Congress; https://en.wikipedia.org/wiki/1st_United_States_Congress

95   Second Bank of the United States; https://en.wikipedia.org/wiki/Second_Bank_of_the_United_States

96   Panic of 1837; https://en.wikipedia.org/wiki/Panic_of_1837

96   Jekyll Island; https://www.federalreservehistory.org/essays/jekyll_island_conference

96   Senator Nelson W. Aldrich; https://www.federalreservehistory.org/people/nelson_w_aldrich

96   draft legislation; https://en.wikipedia.org/wiki/Jekyll_Island

96   Jekyll Island; https://www.amazon.com/Creature-Jekyll-Island-Federal-Reserve/dp/091298645X

HOAX 26: The Humanitarian Hoax of the Muslim Brotherhood

100   *An Explanatory Memorandum: On the General Strategic Goal for the Group in North America*; https://www.centerforsecuritypolicy.org/wp-content/uploads/2014/05/Explanatory_Memoradum.pdf

101   Isik Abla; https://www.christianpost.com/news/what-are-the-8-types-of-jihad-former-radical-muslim-explains-179338/

102   Saudi Arabian oil; https://en.wikipedia.org/wiki/History_of_the_oil_industry_in_Saudi_Arabia

103   Muslim Brotherhood arrived in Saudi Arabia; https://gulfnews.com/news/gulf/saudi-arabia/how-the-muslim-brotherhood-betrayed-saudi-arabia-1.2039864

103   George W. Bush; https://georgewbush-whitehouse.archives.gov/news/releases/2001/09/20010917-11.html

104   Rachel Ehrenfeld; http://acdemocracy.org/banning-the-muslim-brotherhood/

104   Cynthia Farahat; https://www.frontpagemag.com/fpm/270080/islamists-ties-terror-lobby-congress-cynthia-farahat

104   Reuters; https://www.reuters.com/article/us-saudi-brotherhood/saudi-arabia-says-revamping-education-to-combat-extremist-ideologies-idUSKBN1GX0XH

105   How can US Leaders NOT Know About Islam?; https://www.understandingthethreat.com/how-us-leaders-dont-know-islam/

HOAX 27: The Humanitarian Hoax of 'Convenient' Google Chrome-book Education

106   smart homes; https://www.smarthomeusa.com/smarthome/

106   Metadata; https://en.wikipedia.org/wiki/Metadata

107   The House That Spied on Me; https://gizmodo.com/the-house-that-spied-on-me-1822429852

107   determine our socioeconomic status; https://www.dailymail.co.uk/sciencetech/article-5346733/Facebook-patent-uses-track-socio-economic-status.html

107   smart speaker can suddenly become the hub of a social network; http://www.gizmodo.com.au/2017/07/surprise-echo-owners-youre-now-part-of-amazons-random-social-network

107   can have one of its key features taken away in a firmware update; https://www.engadget.com/2018/01/22/nokia-disables-pulse-wave-velocity-body-cardio/

107   66.87 percent; https://www.windowslatest.com/2018/07/05/google-chrome-the-preferred-choice-according-to-latest-data/

107   cloud; https://en.wikipedia.org/wiki/Cloud_computing

107   dashboard; https://en.wikipedia.org/wiki/Dashboard_(business)

108   Cassi Caputo; https://web.archive.org/web/20180614164711/ https://www.districtadministration.com/article/benefits-google-chromebooks-and-apps-education

108   YouTube video; https://www.youtube.com/watch?v=8GJU-PZnlVPA&feature=youtu.be&t=14m9s

108   Google's Search Bias Against Conservative News Sites Has Been Quantified; https://pjmedia.com/lifestyle/2017/09/11/report-google-bias-against-leading-conservative-websites-is-real/

109   Influence Watch.org; https://www.influencewatch.org/non-profit/center-for-media-and-democracy/

109   Agenda 21; https://en.wikipedia.org/wiki/Agenda_21

110   Agenda 21; https://sustainabledevelopment.un.org/content/documents/Agenda21.pdf

110   17 Sustainable Development Goals; https://en.wikipedia.org/wiki/Sustainable_Development_Goals

HOAX 28: The Humanitarian Hoax of Illegal Immigrant Family Separation at the U.S. Border

113   The Truth about Separating Kids; https://www.nationalreview.com/2018/05/illegal-immigration-enforcement-separating-kids-at-border/#slide-1

114   *Flores v. Loretta Lynch*; https://www.conservativedailynews.com/2018/06/flores-v-loretta-lynch-the-9th-circuit-decision-that-created-the-illegal-alien-family-separation-mess/

114   *Conservative Daily News*; https://www.conservativedailynews.com/2018/06/flores-v-loretta-lynch-the-9th-circuit-decision-that-created-the-illegal-alien-family-separation-mess/

114   Carolyn Glick; https://www.jpost.com/Opinion/Column-One-The-peril-of-politicized-antisemitism-560599

115   Who's Responsible for Separating Alien Kids from Their Parents? Many People, but Not Trump; https://www.dailysignal.com/2018/06/21/whos-responsible-for-separating-alien-kids-from-their-parents-many-people-but-not-trump/?mkt_tok=eyJpIjoiWkRobE1qVmxPVGMzTTJFeiIsInQiOiJvVjlUdlBIUGNseXJwbllSWTNTUWV1WmZUbkJ3dGUwQkJSUjVIUDJGN2dNdlY1ME1zWEJcL2c1TVErTmp

115   says; https://www.dhs.gov/news/2018/02/15/unaccompanied-alien-children-and-family-units-are-flooding-border-because-catch-and

HOAX 29: The Humanitarian Hoax of Political Correctness

119   The Squeaky Wheel Gets the Grease; https://goudsmit.pundicity.com/22541/the-squeaky-wheel-gets-the-grease

HOAX 30: The Humanitarian Hoax of Pearson Education

122   2017 share; https://www.washingtontimes.com/news/2015/
apr/7/bethany-blankley-parents-must-reject-common-core-i/

122   One World Education; https://www.washingtontimes.com/
news/2015/apr/7/bethany-blankley-parents-must-reject-com-
mon-core-i/

122   United Nations Agenda 2030; https://www.thenewamerican.
com/tech/environment/item/22267-un-agenda-2030-a-recipe-for-glob-
al-socialism

123   *An Explanatory Memorandum: On the General Strategic Goal for
the Group in North America*; https://www.centerforsecuritypolicy.org/
wp-content/uploads/2014/05/Explanatory_Memoradum.pdf

123   took over; http://www.regents.nysed.gov/common/regents/files/
documents/meetings/2012Meetings/March2012/312hed5.pdf

123   Alan Singer; https://www.huffpost.com/entry/pearson-educa-
tion-new-york-testing-_b_1850169?guce_referrer=aHR0cDovL2dvd-
WRzbWl0LnBlbmRpY2l0eS5jb20vMjI2ODgvdGhlLWh1bWFuaXRh-
cmlhbi1ob2F4LW9mLXBlYXJzb24tZWR1Y2F0aW9u&guce_referrer_
sig=AQAAAMpvcIoW_zaTPYTaPBN4rODrJs8Ej1AP82WMs

124   The Angry Election of 2016; https://www.toddstarnes.com/
campus/new-high-school-textbook-describes-trump-as-mental-
ly-ill-supporters-as-racist/?fbclid=IwAR1SFK6AIgi6IQmgdqJ9uGNot-
1MiZ-OIQg6yu862cHkNzfhMEPMFkgayo1U

124   Pearson sold; https://www.reuters.com/article/pear-
son-disposal-k12/pearson-sells-k12-us-textbook-unit-for-250-mln-
idUSL5N20D10N

124   own words; https://www.globallegalchronicle.com/nexus-capi-
tal-managements-250-million-acquisition-of-pearsons-u-s-k12-course-
ware-business/

125   EMPEA; https://www.empea.org/our-story/

126   *EdTech*; http://www.edtechupdate.com/chromebook/pearson/?open-article-id=3403697&article-title=do-school-districts-need-their-own-data-centers-anymore-&blog-domain=blogspot.com&blog-title=educational-technology-guyhttps://www.powerschool.com/solutions/

126   PowerSchool; https://www.powerschool.com/solutions/

126   Pearson announced; https://www.prnewswire.com/news-releases/pearson-realize-selected-as-google-for-education-premier-partner-300782149.html

HOAX 31: The Humanitarian Hoax of Five-Times-a-Day Islam

130   *Slavery, Terrorism, and Islam: The Historical Roots and Contemporary Threat*; https://rebaneruminations.typepad.com/files/drpeterhammond.pdf

131   Dearborn, Michigan; http://zipatlas.com/us/mi/zip-code-comparison/percentage-arab-population.htm

131   Minneapolis, Minnesota; https://www.americanthinker.com/articles/2019/06/somalis_have_changed_minneapolis.html

131   *An Explanatory Memorandum: On the General Strategic Goal for the Group in North America*; https://www.centerforsecuritypolicy.org/wp-content/uploads/2014/05/Explanatory_Memoradum.pdf

HOAX 32: The Humanitarian Hoax of Black-Only College Graduation Ceremonies

134   article; https://www.thecollegefix.com/more-than-75-universities-now-host-blacks-only-graduation-ceremonies/

134   National Association of Scholars; https://www.nas.org/blogs/article/separate_but_equal_again_neo_segregation_at_yale

135   Harvard University; https://theundefeated.com/whhw/dont-hate-on-black-graduation-ceremony-at-harvard-university/

136   Richard Carranza; https://nypost.com/2019/05/20/richard-carranza-held-doe-white-supremacy-culture-training/

137   implicit bias; https://www.city-journal.org/richard-carranza-im-plicit-bias

137   toxic whiteness; https://nypost.com/2019/05/18/nyc-schools-chancellor-richard-carranza-has-made-whiteness-toxic-doe-insid-ers-claim/

137   Nation of Islam's; https://en.wikipedia.org/wiki/Malcolm_X

137   letter; http://okra.stanford.edu/transcription/document_images/undecided/630731-000.pdf

137   supported by his leftist boss; https://www.city-journal.org/html/richard-carranza-16136.html

HOAX 33: The Humanitarian Hoax of 'Neutral' Google Searches

140   Carole Cadwalladr; https://www.bbc.co.uk/events/e26gfx/play/p07brdlb

140   Facebook Cambridge Analytica; https://en.wikipedia.org/wiki/Facebook%E2%80%93Cambridge_Analytica_data_scandal

140   Google spokesperson; https://www.theguardian.com/technology/2016/dec/05/google-alters-search-autocomplete-re-move-are-jews-evil-suggestion

141   The Political Purpose of Anti-Semitism; http://goudsmit.pundic-ity.com/20344/the-political-purpose-of-anti-semitism

141   Connecting the Dots: Islamism . . . Socialism . . . Globalism; http://goudsmit.pundicity.com/20055/connecting-the-dots

142   YouTube video; https://www.youtube.com/watch?v=KyCYyoGusqs

142   Neil Patel; https://neilpatel.com/blog/how-google-search-en-gine-really-works/

142   The PageRank Citation Ranking: Bringing Order to the Web; http://ilpubs.stanford.edu:8090/422/1/1999-66.pdf

143   16 Biggest Advertisers Ally to Censor 'Hate Speech' on Social Media; https://www.frontpagemag.com/point/274059/16-biggest-ad-vertisers-ally-censor-hate-speech-daniel-greenfield

HOAX 34: The Humanitarian Hoax of Planned Parenthood

145   Planned Parenthood; https://en.wikipedia.org/wiki/Planned_Parenthood

145   Katharine McCormick; https://en.wikipedia.org/wiki/Katharine_McCormick

146   *Roe v. Wade*; https://en.wikipedia.org/wiki/Roe_v._Wade

146   balancing test; https://en.wikipedia.org/wiki/Balancing_test

146   trimesters of pregnancy; https://en.wikipedia.org/wiki/Trimester_(pregnancy)#Physiology

146   Reproductive Health Act, S.240; https://legislation.nysenate.gov/pdf/bills/2019/S240

146   section 4164 of New York's Public Health Law; https://newyork.public.law/laws/n.y._public_health_law_section_4164

147   SIECUS; https://siecus.org/about-siecus/our-history/

147   Guidelines for Comprehensive Education: Kindergarten-12th Grade; http://www2.gsu.edu/~wwwche/Sex ed class/guidelines.pdf

147   education business; https://www.plannedparenthood.org/learn/for-educators/what-sex-education

147   Sex ed is a vehicle for social change; https://siecus.org/sex-ed-is-a-vehicle-for-social-change/

148   Comprehensive Sexuality Education; https://advocatesforyouth.org/issues/sex-education-definitions-and-select-programs/

148   Wikipedia; https://en.wikipedia.org/wiki/Planned_Parenthood

148   Dr. Duke Pesta on the Shocking K-12 Common Core Sexual Education Standards; https://drrichswier.com/2014/06/22/dr-duke-pesta-shocking-k-12-common-core-sexual-education-standards/

149   National Sexuality Education Standards: Core Content and Skills, K-12; http://answer.rutgers.edu/file/national-sexuality-education-standards.pdf

150   *Conspirators' Hierarchy: The Story of The Committee of 300*; http://educate-yourself.org/cn/johncolemancommof300order-14mar05.shtml

150   Tavistock Institute; https://educate-yourself.org/nwo/nwotavis-tockbestkeptsecret.shtml

HOAX 35: The Humanitarian Hoax of Ballot Harvesting

153   How Ballot-Harvesting Became the New Way to Steal an Election; https://thefederalist.com/2018/12/14/ballot-harvesting-became-new-way-steal-election/

153   250,000 harvested ballots; https://www.sfchronicle.com/politics/article/California-s-late-votes-broke-big-for-13432727.php

153   *PJ Media*; https://pjmedia.com/blog/obamaholder-doj-sues-flori-da-over-voter-roll-clean-up

154   won a huge case; https://www.judicialwatch.org/press-releases/california-begins-massive-voter-roll-clean-up-notifies-up-to-1-5-million-inactive-voters-as-part-of-judicial-watch-lawsuit-settlement/

154   voter registration lists; https://www.eac.gov/news/2017/03/10/fact-sheet-voter-registration-list-maintenance-fact-sheet-me-dia-factsheet/

154   *Breitbart* article; https://www.breitbart.com/poli-tics/2019/06/19/new-york-law-gives-illegals-ability-to-vote-after-obtain-ing-drivers-license/

HOAX 36: The Humanitarian Hoax of the United Nations

157   United Nations; https://en.wikipedia.org/wiki/History_of_the_United_Nations

158   fifty-one sovereign nations; https://www.un.org/en/sections/member-states/growth-united-nations-membership-1945-present/index.html

158   Security Council; https://en.m.wikipedia.org/wiki/List_of_mem-bers_of_the_United_Nations_Security_Council

158   regions; https://en.m.wikipedia.org/wiki/List_of_members_of_the_United_Nations_Security_Council

159 United Nations System; https://en.wikipedia.org/wiki/United_Nations_System

159 *Directory*; https://www.unsystem.org/directory

160 UN Paris Agreement; https://en.wikipedia.org/wiki/Paris_Agreement

160 Climate Change; https://www.un.org/sustainabledevelopment/climate-change/

160 UN Global Compact for Safe, Orderly, and Regular Migration; https://www.un.org/pga/72/wp-content/uploads/sites/51/2018/07/migration.pdf

160 UN Global Education Initiative; https://en.unesco.org/gem-report/about

160 propagandized textbooks; http://goudsmit.pundicity.com/22688/the-humanitarian-hoax-of-pearson-education

160 Google's Chromebooks; http://goudsmit.pundicity.com/21275/the-humanitarian-hoax-of-convenient-google

160 Google searches; http://goudsmit.pundicity.com/22837/the-humanitarian-hoax-of-neutral-google-searches

160 17 Sustainable Development Goals; https://www.gbes.com/blog/united-nations-sustainable-development-goals/

161 Freedom House; http://www.humanrightsvoices.org/EYEon-theUN/un_101/facts/?p=16

161 anti-hate-speech campaign; https://www.un.org/sg/en/content/sg/speeches/2019-06-18/un-strategy-and-plan-of-action-hate-speech-remarks

161 defensible borders; https://www.gatestoneinstitute.org/14391/un-global-compact-next

HOAX 37: The Humanitarian Hoax of Leftism

165 the mixture is yellow; https://www.youtube.com/watch?time_continue=3&v=IWe_N_hHKqs&feature=emb_logo

166 lying in the service of Islam; http://goudsmit.pundicity.com/20056/jihad-violence-by-any-other-name-is-still-jihad

167 The Life of Washington; https://apnews.com/9f3037c7ec-9d48a286059ac8f9975afe

167 Salute to America; https://heavy.com/news/2019/07/trump-4th-of-july-salute-to-america/

167 Revolutionary Communist Party; https://www.blabber.buzz/conservative-news/609048-update-communists-throw-burning-us-flag-on-secret-service-officer-in-front-of-white-house-two-officers-taken-to-hospital-with-minor-injuries?utm_source=c-alrt&utm_medium=c-alrt-email&utm_term=c-alrt-Yahoo

168 medieval return to feudalism; http://goudsmit.pundicity.com/20055/connecting-the-dots

HOAX 38: The Humanitarian Hoax of Tolerism

170 *An Explanatory Memorandum: On the General Strategic Goal for the Group in North America*; https://www.centerforsecuritypolicy.org/wp-content/uploads/2014/05/Explanatory_Memoradum.pdf

HOAX 39: The Humanitarian Hoax of the 2020 Democrat Party Platform

174 The Democratic National Committee; http://www.democraticnationalcommittee.org/about.html

174 Territory; https://www.answers.com/Q/What_characteristics_do_all_countries_have_in_common

175 stunning interview; https://www.youtube.com/watch?v=tnwtX-ufqr3A&feature=youtu.be

175 Allen West; https://www.westernjournal.com/ct/lt-col-allen-west-says-pelosi-just-committed-high-crime-misdemeanor/?utm_source=Email&utm_medium=WJBreaking&utm_campaign=ct-breaking&utm_content=western-journal

175 Population; https://www.census.gov/topics/population.html

175   United States; https://en.wikipedia.org/wiki/Demography_of_the_United_States

176   Barack Obama; https://humanevents.com/2019/07/06/trumps-citizenship-question-isnt-controversial-obama-deleting-it-shouldve-been/

176   2010 Census; https://www.washingtontimes.com/blog/watercooler/2010/jan/11/no-question-birthplace-asked-census/

176   10 Questions in 10 Minutes; https://www.census.gov/2010census/about/interactive-form.php

176   Demography; https://en.wikipedia.org/wiki/Demography

177   data; https://www.wnd.com/2015/11/staggering-number-of-muslim-refugees-under-obama/

177   43,000; https://www.washingtonexaminer.com/99-muslim-43-000-somali-refugees-settled-in-us-under-obama

177   *World Net Daily*; https://www.wnd.com/2016/04/disturbing-reality-muslim-sex-grooming-gangs/

177   Grooming Gangs and Sharia; https://www.americanthinker.com/articles/2013/12/grooming_gangs_and_sharia.html

178   Islamic doctrine; https://www.thereligionofpeace.com/pages/quran/slavery.aspx

178   The Danger in Islamic Prayer; https://www.americanthinker.com/articles/2015/12/the_danger_in_islamic_prayer.html

178   Culture; https://historyplex.com/characteristics-of-culture

179   Culture is not innate. It is learned; https://historyplex.com/characteristics-of-culture

179   Parents and Educators Against Common Core; https://www.facebook.com/groups/PEACCS/

181   United States of America; https://en.wikipedia.org/wiki/Federal_government_of_the_United_States

HOAX 40: The Humanitarian Hoax of Department of Homeland 'Security'

184   DHS website; https://www.dhs.gov/operational-and-support-components

185   New Beginning; https://www.nbcnews.com/id/31102929/ns/politics-white_house/t/full-text-obamas-speech-cairo/#.XSulZC2ZNdA

186   Islamic Movement in U.S. Preparing for Battle; https://www.understandingthethreat.com/islamic-movement-in-u-s-preparing-for-battle/

186   Fox News; https://dailycaller.com/2019/07/04/tsa-airport-security-loophole/

187   According to the DOJ; https://freebeacon.com/national-security/iran-caught-smuggling-nuke-materials-out-of-u-s/

187   security theater; https://dailycaller.com/2019/07/04/tsa-airport-security-loophole/

188   One World Education; https://www.washingtontimes.com/news/2015/apr/7/bethany-blankley-parents-must-reject-common-core-i/

188   UN Agenda 2030; https://www.thenewamerican.com/tech/environment/item/22267-un-agenda-2030-a-recipe-for-global-socialism

188   Common Core's; https://www.theatlantic.com/education/archive/2015/10/the-common-core-sat/412960/

189   The Saudi Fifth Column on Our Nation's Campuses; https://www.meforum.org/campus-watch/8843/the-saudi-fifth-column-on-our-nation-campuses

189   reprinted; https://lubpak.net/archives/76216

189   Wahhabi Lobby; https://lubpak.net/archives/76216

189   Qatari influence; https://clarionproject.org/qatar-on-our-campuses/?utm_source=Clarion+Project+Newsletter&utm_campaign=8d5df415d8-EMAIL_CAMPAIGN_2019_03_17_12_03_COPY_02&utm_medium=email&utm_term=0_60abb35148-8d5df415d8-6715677&mc_cid=8d5df415d8&mc_eid=5334181005

189   American universities; https://dailycaller.com/2018/12/16/qatar-georgetown-texas-university/

190   Qatar Paid for Congressional Democrats' Doha Trip; https://www.investigativeproject.org/7959/qatar-paid-for-congressional-democrats-doha-trip

190   *An Explanatory Memorandum: On the General Strategic Goal for the Group in North America*; https://www.centerforsecuritypolicy.org/wp-content/uploads/2014/05/Explanatory_Memoradum.pdf

HOAX 41: The Humanitarian Hoax of the 2019–2020 Equality Act

191   H.R. 5: Equality Act; https://www.congress.gov/bill/116th-congress/house-bill/5/text

191   1964 Civil Rights Act; https://civil.laws.com/civil-rights-act-of-1964

192   Chromosomal sex determination; https://www.ncbi.nlm.nih.gov/books/NBK9967/

192   gonads; https://medical-dictionary.thefreedictionary.com/Gonads

193   Wikipedia; https://en.wikipedia.org/wiki/Gender_identity

194   Congressional Record on January 10, 1963; https://cns7prod.s3.amazonaws.com/attachments/communist_goals.pdf

197   Connally Reservation; https://opil.ouplaw.com/view/10.1093/law:epil/9780199231690/law-9780199231690-e23

198   Proposed Repeal of Connally Reservation—A Matter for Concern; https://scholarship.law.marquette.edu/cgi/viewcontent.cgi?article=2871&context=mulr

199   Franklin Graham; https://www.lifesitenews.com/news/franklin-graham-equality-act-will-lead-to-christian-persecution-as-never-before

199   U.S. Conference of Catholic Bishops; http://www.usccb.org/news/2019/19-092.cfm

199   *Dark Agenda: The War to Destroy Christian America*; https://horowitzfreedomcenterstore.org/collections/books/products/dark-agenda

200   Hey, Hey, Ho, Ho, Western Civ Has Got to Go; https://amgreatness.com/2019/06/10/hey-hey-ho-ho-western-civ-has-got-to-go/

HOAX 42: The Humanitarian Hoax of Islamic Zakat

202   New Beginning; https://obamawhitehouse.archives.gov/the-press-office/remarks-president-cairo-university-6-04-09

202   Five Pillars of Islam; https://en.wikipedia.org/wiki/Five_Pillars_of_Islam

203   *An Explanatory Memorandum: On the General Strategic Goal for the Group in North America*; https://www.centerforsecuritypolicy.org/wp-content/uploads/2014/05/Explanatory_Memoradum.pdf

203   Holy Land Foundation for Relief and Development; https://www.discoverthenetworks.org/organizations/holy-land-foundation-for-relief-and-development-hlf/

203   government streamlined its presentation; https://www.investigativeproject.org/860/hlf-redux-streamlined-with-more-punch

203   November 25, 2008; https://archives.fbi.gov/archives/news/stories/2008/november/hlf112508

204   May 2009; https://archives.fbi.gov/archives/dallas/press-releases/2009/dl052709.htm

204   biggest Islamic "charity"; https://www.nationalreview.com/2007/08/coming-clean-about-cair-scott-w-johnson/

204   Justice Department; https://www.justice.gov/opa/pr/federal-judge-hands-downs-sentences-holy-land-foundation-case

204   Coming Clean About CAIR; https://www.nationalreview.com/2007/08/coming-clean-about-cair-scott-w-johnson/

205   exposes CAIR; https://www.understandingthethreat.com/cair-is-hamas-2/

205   Refugees Sending Suitcases of Welfare Cash Home to Somalis; https://www.wnd.com/2016/05/REFUGEES-SENDING-SUITCASES-OF-WELFARE-CASH-HOME-TO-SOMALIA/

205   hawala system; http://www.globalsecuritystudies.com/Faith Hawala FINAL.pdf

206   Kerns recounted; https://www.wnd.com/2016/05/REFUGEES-SENDING-SUITCASES-OF-WEL-FARE-CASH-HOME-TO-SOMALIA/

207   U.S. Citizenship and Immigration Services; https://www.uscis.gov/legal-resources/terrorism-related-inadmissibility-grounds-trig

207   TRIG; https://www.uscis.gov/legal-resources/terrorism-re-lated-inadmissability-grounds/terrorism-related-inadmissibili-ty-grounds-trig

207   USCIS; https://www.uscis.gov/legal-resources/terrorism-re-lated-inadmissability-grounds/terrorism-related-inadmissibili-ty-grounds-trig-situational-exemptions

207   Senate hearing; https://www.youtube.com/watch?v=74htrpscB2Q

208   Al-Shabaab terrorists; https://aclj.org/persecuted-church/al-shabaab-jihadists-strike-somalia-with-their-deadliest-terror-at-tack-to-date

208   genocide against Christians; https://www.theodysseyonline.com/christian-persecution-somalia

HOAX 43: The Humanitarian Hoax of 'Assisted' Suicide

210   Dr. Jack Kevorkian; https://en.wikipedia.org/wiki/Jack_Kevorkian

211   growing list of individuals; http://www.whatreallyhappened.com/WRHARTICLES/THE CLINTON BODY COUNT.pdf

211   Barry Seal; https://en.wikipedia.org/wiki/Barry_Seal

212   FBI Special Agent David Raynor; https://newspunch.com/fbi-clinton-fast-furious-dead/

212   Fast and Furious; https://nypost.com/2016/05/21/the-scandal-in-washington-no-one-is-talking-about/

212   CNS News; https://www.cnsnews.com/news/article/hillary-clin-ton-no-evidence-doj-sought-required-license-send-guns-mexico-fast-and

212   criminally complicit; https://newspunch.com/fbi-clinton-fast-furious-dead/

213   lawsuit; https://theconservativetreehouse.com/2019/07/15/lawsuit-claims-julian-assange-confirmed-dnc-emails-received-from-seth-rich-not-a-russian-hack/

213   Klaus Eberwein; https://www.libertyheadlines.com/clinton-foundation-witness-found-dead/?AID=7236

213   Eberwein; https://www.zerohedge.com/news/2017-07-16/haiti-official-who-exposed-clinton-foundation-found-dead

213   *Atlanta Black Star*; https://atlantablackstar.com/2018/01/24/really-happened-clinton-foundation-haiti/

213   Arkancide; https://www.conservapedia.com/Clinton_body_count

214   Is Jeff Epstein Also Running a Ponzi Scheme; https://www.businessinsider.com/is-convicted-sex-offender-jeff-epstein-running-a-ponzi-scheme-2009-7

214   Doug Band; https://en.wikipedia.org/wiki/Doug_Band

214   investigation; https://www.grassley.senate.gov/sites/default/files/judiciary/upload/Response Letter to Chairman Grassley Ltr on State Email -SGE 4-8-15 Sign....pdf

214   *The Atlantic*; https://www.theatlantic.com/politics/archive/2016/10/the-man-at-the-center-of-bill-clinton-inc/505661/

215   *Virgin Island News*; http://claudettevferron.com/virgin-islands-news-crime-and-corruption-updates/

HOAX 44: The Humanitarian Hoax of White Supremacy

218   284,000 manufacturing jobs; https://www.cnsnews.com/news/article/terence-p-jeffrey/2018-saw-largest-increase-manufacturing-jobs-21-years

220   According to Alinsky; https://www.frontpagemag.com/fpm/269085/party-saul-alinsky-its-war-trump-john-perazzo

HOAX 46: The Humanitarian Hoax of Climate Change II: Debunking the Bunk

227   The Riddle of Climate Change; http://goudsmit.pundicity.com/22378/the-riddle-of-climate-change

227   hypocritical purchase; https://pjmedia.com/trending/obamas-accused-of-hypocrisy-on-climate-change-for-buying-waterfront-property-in-marthas-vineyard/

228   Climategate; https://www.conservapedia.com/index.php?title=-Climategate

228   reported warming trend in New Zealand;   https://www.conservapedia.com/index.php?title=Climategate

228   fraudulent; https://www.conservapedia.com/index.php?title=-Climategate

228   Speech Gives Climate Goals Center Stage; https://www.nytimes.com/2013/01/22/us/politics/climate-change-prominent-in-obamas-inaugural-address.html

229   enacted by Barack Obama; https://obamawhitehouse.archives.gov/blog/2016/09/03/president-obama-united-states-formally-enters-paris-agreement

229   without Senate ratification; https://www.washingtontimes.com/news/2016/aug/29/obama-will-bypass-senate-ratify-paris-climate-acco/

229   Doomsday articles; https://nypost.com/2018/10/08/terrifying-climate-change-warning-12-years-until-were-doomed/

229   climate sensitivity; https://archive.is/4cqKU

230   United Nations Agenda 2030; https://sustainabledevelopment.un.org/post2015/transformingourworld

231   Patrick Moore; https://www.breitbart.com/radio/2019/03/07/greenpeace-founder-global-warming-hoax-pushed-corrupt-scientists-hooked-government-grants/

231   U.S. Senate Environment and Public Works Committee, Subcommittee on Oversight; https://www.epw.senate.gov/public/_cache/files/415b9cde-e664-4628-8fb5-ae3951197d03/22514hearingwitnesstestimonymoore.pdf

231   reported on an interview; https://www.breitbart.com/radio/2019/03/07/greenpeace-founder-global-warming-hoax-pushed-corrupt-scientists-hooked-government-grants/

232   Democrat Senator Edward Markey; https://www.frontpage-mag.com/fpm/273001/senate-democrats-introduce-bill-push-radi-cal-sara-dogan

HOAX 48: The Humanitarian Hoax of Zero Population Growth

239   *An Essay on the Principle of Population*; http://www.eco-nomicsdiscussion.net/articles/malthusian-theory-of-population-ex-plained-with-its-criticism/1521

HOAX 49: The Humanitarian Hoax of Impeachment

245   Trump's Real Crime? 'He's Serious About Draining the Swamp'; https://www.worldtribune.com/trumps-real-crime-hes-serious-about-draining-the-swamp/

245   CrowdStrike; https://sharespost.com/crowdstrike_stock/

245   *Bloomberg News*; https://www.bloomberg.com/news/arti-cles/2017-05-17/crowdstrike-raises-100-million-as-cybersecuri-ty-makes-headlines

245   Warburg Pincus; https://www.holdingschannel.com/top/stocks-held-by-warburg-pincus-llc/?page=1&type=&confirm=1

245   Atlantic Council; https://www.worldtribune.com/check-out-the-globalist-think-tank-behind-latest-anti-trump-coup/

245   Clinton Foundation; https://www.clintonfoundation.org/contrib-utors?category=%2410%2C000%2C001+to+%2425%2C000%2C000

245   *The Markets Work*; https://themarketswork.com/2018/03/11/victor-pinchuk-the-clintons-endless-connections/

245   partnership; https://burisma-group.com/eng/news/the-atlan-tic-council-of-the-united-states-and-burisma-group-sign-coopera-tive-agreement/

HOAX 50: The Humanitarian Hoax of Eternal Childhood

249   *Dear America: Who's Driving the Bus*?; https://www.amazon.com/gp/product/B004YDUUZE?ref=dbs_p2d_P_R_popup_yes_pony_T1

EPILOGUE

254   How Should the Senate Deal with an Unconstitutional Impeachment by the House?; https://deref-mail.com/mail/client/NDwo9HOen0I/dereferrer/?redirectUrl=https%3A%2F%2Fwww.gatestoneinstitute.org%2F15269%2Fsenate-unconstitutional-impeachment#_blank

254   Impeachers Looking for New Crimes; https://deref-mail.com/mail/client/uGO9Qiu3jDc/dereferrer/?redirectUrl=https%3A%2F%2Fwww.gatestoneinstitute.org%2F15069%2Fimpeachers-new-crimes#_blank

255   shown live on videotape; https://www.realclearpolitics.com/video/2019/09/27/flashback_2018_joe_biden_brags_at_cfr_meeting_about_withholding_aid_to_ukraine_to_force_firing_of_prosecutor.html

256   Ukrainian MP Claims $7.4 Billion Obama-Linked Laundering, Puts Biden Group Take at $16.5 Million; https://www.zerohedge.com/geopolitical/ukrainian-indictment-reveals-hunter-biden-group-made-165-million-mp

257   Financial Disclosure Report #10016142; http://clerk.house.gov/public_disc/financial-pdfs/2016/10016142.pdf

257   2013 promotional videos; https://www.youtube.com/watch?time_continue=1&v=g1KfU5ifhqE&feature=emb_logo

257   EXPOSED: Pelosi Jr. Worked in Ukraine with Accused Fraudster Facing Prison; https://nationalfile.com/exposed-pelosi-jr-worked-in-ukraine-with-accused-fraudster-facing-prison/

257   president's letter; https://www.whitehouse.gov/wp-content/uploads/2019/12/Letter-from-President-Trump-final.pdf

258   Dershowitz: Pelosi Doesn't Have the Impeachment Power She Believes; https://deref-mail.com/mail/client/w3Mn-pmsK_jc/dereferrer/?redirectUrl=https%3A%2F%2Fdailycaller.com%2F2019%2F12%2F20%2Ftakala-dershowitz-pelosi%2F#_blank

258   Trump Isn't Impeached Until the House Tells the Senate; https://www.bloomberg.com/opinion/articles/2019-12-19/trump-impeach-ment-delay-could-be-serious-problem-for-democrats

259   October 8, 2019, letter; https://www.whitehouse.gov/wp-content/uploads/2019/10/PAC-Letter-10.08.2019.pdf

260   Meet Pelosi's 7 Impeachment Managers; https://thehill.com/homenews/house/478886-meet-pelosis-7-impeachment-managers

260   Alan Dershowitz; https://www.youtube.com/watch?v=uqmhfyH-09jM&feature=youtu.be

260   speech; https://www.rev.com/blog/transcripts/alan-dershow-itz-defense-argument-transcript-trump-impeachment-trial-january-27

261   Evening News Spin: 100% Negative on Trump Defense, 95% Positive Dems; https://www.newsbusters.org/blogs/nb/nicholas-fon-dacaro/2020/01/29/evening-news-spin-100-negative-trump-defense-95-positive-dems

262   TV's Trump News: Three-fourths Impeachment and 93% Nega-tive; https://www.newsbusters.org/blogs/nb/rich-noyes/2020/01/13/tvs-trump-news-three-fourths-impeachment-and-93-negative

263   *Webfx*; https://www.webfx.com/blog/internet/the-6-companies-that-own-almost-all-media-infographic/

263   Complaint From So-Called 'Whistleblower' Is Riddled With Gossip, Blatant Falsehoods; https://thefederalist.com/2019/09/26/complaint-from-so-called-whistleblower-is-riddled-with-gossip-blatant-falsehoods/

265   complaint; https://www.les-crises.fr/breaking-news-prosecutor-shokin-files-a-complaint-against-joe-biden-for-interference-in-ukraine-s-legal-proceedings/

265   UkraineGate; https://ukrainegate.info/part-2-not-so-dormant-in-vestigations/

265   *fact* witnesses; https://republicans-intelligence.house.gov/upload-edfiles/rm_letter_to_chm_re_witness_request.pdf

267   Schumer: Any acquittal of Trump 'has no value'; https://www.youtube.com/watch?v=_nHXt7qwjdM

267   Brian Williams; https://txarmyvet.blogspot.com/2020/02/dem-senator-mazie-hirono-i-dont-care.html

267   ICIG Whistleblower Form Recently Modified to Permit Complaint 'Heard from Others'. . .; https://theconservativetreehouse.com/2019/09/27/icig-whistleblower-form-recently-modified-to-permit-complaint-heard-from-others/

267   complaint form; https://www.dni.gov/files/ICIG/Documents/Hotline/Urgent Concern Disclosure Form.pdf

267   Did the Inspector General's Office Help the 'Whistleblower' Try to Frame Trump?; https://thefederalist.com/2019/09/30/did-the-inspector-generals-office-help-the-whistleblower-try-to-frame-trump/#.XZHzB1kL4Cg.twitter

268   Intelligence Community Whistleblower Protection Act [ICWPA] of 1998; https://uscode.house.gov/statutes/pl/105/272.pdf

268   Intel Community Secretly Gutted Requirement of First-Hand Whistleblower Knowledge; https://thefederalist.com/2019/09/27/intel-community-secretly-gutted-requirement-of-first-hand-whistleblower-knowledge/

269   It's Time to Question Michael Atkinson on FISA Abuses; https://amgreatness.com/2020/01/27/its-time-to-question-michael-atkinson-on-fisa-abuses/

269   tied; https://amgreatness.com/2020/01/09/intelligence-communitys-inspector-general-is-the-link-between-fisagate-and-impeachment/

270   Intelligence Community's Inspector General is the Link Between FISAgate and Impeachment; https://amgreatness.com/2020/01/27/its-time-to-question-michael-atkinson-on-fisa-abuses/

270   complaint; https://intelligence.house.gov/uploaded-files/20190812_-_whistleblower_complaint_unclass.pdf

270   wrote; https://www.cotton.senate.gov/?p=press_release&id=1232

270   this week; https://www.foxnews.com/media/nunes-slams-intel-community-ig-says-hes-either-in-on-whistleblower-complaint-inconsistencies-or-incompetent

270   letter; https://www.scribd.com/document/428134118/House-GOP-letter-to-ICIG#download&from_embed

270   Intel Community IG Stonewalling Congress on Backdated Whistleblower Rule Changes; https://thefederalist.com/2019/10/07/intel-community-ig-stonewalling-congress-on-backdated-whistleblower-rule-changes/

270   August 12, 2019; https://intelligence.house.gov/uploaded-files/20190812_-_whistleblower_complaint_unclass.pdf

271   Whistleblower Protection Act of 1989; https://www.usda.gov/oig/webdocs/whistle1989.pdf

271   PJ Media; https://pjmedia.com/trending/revealed-rand-pauls-question-that-chief-justice-roberts-refused-to-read/

272   Schiff, House Democrats Conceal Testimony of 18th Witness from Trump Team; https://www.thegatewaypundit.com/2020/01/schiff-house-democrats-conceal-testimony-of-18th-witness-from-trump-team/

273   State of the Union Address; https://www.whitehouse.gov/briefings-statements/remarks-president-trump-state-union-address-3/

275   Herbert Marcuse and the Democrats' Impeachment; https://www.americanthinker.com/articles/2019/12/herbert_marcuse_and_the_democrats_impeachment.html

275   Why Americans Are Not Taught History; http://public.callutheran.edu/~mccamb/hitchens.htm

276   Countdown to Civil War; https://goudsmit.pundicity.com/21553/countdown-to-civil-war

276   The Second Civil War; https://sultanknish.blogspot.com/2018/01/this-civil-war-my-south-carolina-tea.html

279   Trump's Unintended Consequences: The Unmasking of the Deep State; https://www.americanthinker.com/articles/2017/08/trumps_unintended_consequences_the_unmasking_of_the_deep_state.html

280   likely; https://www.usatoday.com/story/news/world/2020/02/21/coronavirus-who-contain-outbreak-iran-deaths-south-korea-cases/4829278002/

280   severely overstated; https://www.thegatewaypundit.com/2020/03/exclusive-evidence-shows-director-general-of-world-health-organization-severely-overstated-the-fatality-rate-of-the-coronavirus-leading-to-the-greatest-global-panic-in-history/

281   *The Federalist*; https://thefederalist.com/2020/03/17/u-s-funds-world-health-organization-that-boot-licks-china-with-deadly-results/